ROMAN SATIRE

BLACKWELL INTRODUCTIONS TO THE CLASSICAL WORLD

This series will provide concise introductions to classical culture in the broadest sense. Written by the most distinguished scholars in the field, these books survey key authors, periods and topics for students and scholars alike.

Published

Roman Satire
Daniel M. Hooley

Ancient History
Charles W. Hedrick, Jr.

Homer
Barry B. Powell

Classical Literature
Richard Rutherford

Ancient Rhetoric and Oratory
Thomas Habinek

In Preparation

Classical Mythology
Jon Solomon

Ancient Comedy
Eric Csapo

Ancient Fiction
Gareth Schmeling

Augustan Poetry
Richard Thomas

Sophocles
William Allan

Euripides
Scott Scullion

Greek Tragedy
Nancy Rabinowitz

Catullus
Julia Haig Gaisser

Cicero
Robert Cape

Roman Historiography
Andreas Mehl

Ovid
Katharina Volk

Greek Historiography
Thomas Scanlon

ROMAN SATIRE

Daniel M. Hooley

Blackwell
Publishing

BLACKWELL PUBLISHING
350 Main Street, Malden, MA 02148-5020, USA
9600 Garsington Road, Oxford OX4 2DQ, UK
550 Swanston Street, Carlton, Victoria 3053, Australia

The right of Daniel M. Hooley to be identified as the Author of this Work has been asserted in accordance with the UK Copyright, Designs, and Patents Act 1988.

First published 2007 by Blackwell Publishing Ltd

1 2007

Library of Congress Cataloging-in-Publication Data

Hooley, Daniel M.
    Roman satire / Daniel M. Hooley.
      p.cm.— (Blackwell introductions to the classical world)
    Includes bibliographical references and index.
    ISBN-13: 978-1-4051-0688-7 (hardback : alk. paper)
    ISBN-10: 1-4051-0688-3 (hardback : alk. paper)
    ISBN-13: 978-1-4051-0689-4 (pbk. : alk. paper)
    ISBN-10: 1-4051-0689-1 (pbk. : alk. paper) 1. Satire, Latin—History and
    criticism. I. Title. II. Series.

    PA6056.H66 2006
    877.0109—dc22
                                    2006014203

A catalogue record for this title is available from the British Library.

Set in 10.5pt/13pt Galliard
by SPi Publisher Services, Pondicherry, India
Printed and bound in Singapore
by C.O.S. Printers Pte Ltd

The publisher's policy is to use permanent paper from mills that operate a sustainable forestry policy, and which has been manufactured from pulp processed using acid-free and elementary chlorine-free practices. Furthermore, the publisher ensures that the text paper and cover board used have met acceptable environmental accreditation standards.

For further information on
Blackwell Publishing, visit our website:
www.blackwellpublishing.com

Contents

Preface

As is the case of other volumes in this series, this book is meant to be introductory. Consequently, I've not sought to develop or deepen specialists' understanding of the many poems that come into consideration here; nor have I attempted to set out major controversies or positions held by those specialists; nor have I made reference in the course of my presentation to non-Anglophone criticism, since the intended audience, intelligent English-reading students, can do pretty well beginning with what a limited selection of English-writing critics in readily available sources have said. Needless to say, there is a great deal more out there in the European languages, and in English, for the curious and philologically adept – a good portion of it extremely important.

That's enough by way of apology; what this book doesn't do will be immediately evident to every reader. What was wanted, I thought as I wrote, was a friendly book that went some distance toward bringing a somewhat difficult and distant Roman literature into nearer familiarity. Satire has the perennial problem of being locked into its contemporary world; it is "topical," its references and contexts local, even while good satire, like good literature in general, breaks free of its situational gravity so as to appeal to readers of other times and places, as the abiding popularity of Juvenal testifies to. But ask even a well-read acquaintance her thoughts on Horace's first book of satires, or better, Lucilius' first book, and you're likely to get a blank stare – or a proposal to run down to the pub for a beer and change of subject. While a drink with friends is nearly always a good idea, the change of subject, I contend in this book, is not. For, although a little tricky for moderns to get a handle on at first, Roman satire is in fact remarkably compelling poetry. Even now. And the more so when seen as a singular flowering of a broader satiric impulse (commonly found in pub and coffee-shop discourse) that we all, frankly, love. My job, then, has been to make us better acquainted with what, particularly, Horace and Persius and Juvenal were up to, what their literary backgrounds were, what makes them especially worth spending time with, and what they and other classical satirists did for later European literature.

Toward those ends I've structured the book with endpiece chapters that sketch out, respectively, background and the post-classical afterlife of Roman satire. Neither chapter, especially the latter, is intended to be more than a partial summary, but both will I hope provide at least *essential* guidance. The major verse satirists, Horace, Persius, and Juvenal, have a chapter each his own. The methodology of presentation is generally consistent (more or less detailed summaries of most poems, with attendant general commentary), but Horace's first book, because so important for the whole Roman satiric enterprise in its details and structure, gets more lavish treatment, poem by poem. Further reading sections at the end of each chapter will lead back to the sources of many of the better ideas of this book and get the curious started on the road to fuller discussions elsewhere.

Even if I knew a whole lot more than I do, I wouldn't think it a good idea to oversimplify a volume like this, to talk down to clever readers. A book won't be interesting (to anyone) if it doesn't challenge people to engage its subject ambitiously, to work a bit, thinking, questioning, quibbling with arguments and interpretations. Readers will have to pay attention, and I imagine most will not agree with at least several things I say here: that's all to the good. Horace's word for satire is *sermo*, talk, discussion; satire talks at us and fully expects to be talked back to. The same holds for critics of satire and their readers. This book is best conceived, then, not as an introduction to a "subject," but as an invitation to a dialogic relationship with a literature that gets richer and more fascinating the more time one spends with it. Satire is fun, often naughty, at times surprising, difficult, offensive, delightful, earnest, cynical, deceptive, moral, amoral, almost always challenging. Sorting out *what* it's doing *when* requires close regard, a certain persistence, and a good brain to work with.

Helping me sort out my own thoughts have been generous and kind colleagues with the very best brains. Kirk Freudenburg and John Henderson read through the manuscript in its entirety and commented extensively; their responses, laced with judicious corrections, are treasure-troves of ideas. Many of those ideas I've silently incorporated; a few others of particular note I document in the footnotes with a mysterious "per litteras," yet others I've just tucked away for use elsewhere. All writers should have such readers. In addition, my near neighbor in satire Cathy Keane has, in savvy conversation and biblio-graphical advice, been a great help, as have in sundry ways my colleagues and friends: Michael Barnes, John Foley, Jim McGlew, Anatole Mori, Charles Saylor, David Schenker, Dennis Trout, and Barbara Wallach. Al Bertrand, Sophie Gibson, Ben Thatcher, Angela Cohen, and Marga-ret Aherne at Blackwell, saintly in their patience, have been perceptive, thoughtful, in all respects superb. I owe them all, colleagues and editors, great thanks and immunity from responsibility for any foolishness contained herein.

I am grateful for permission to quote from W. H. Auden, "In Memory of W. B. Yeats," copyright 1940 and renewed 1968 by W. H. Auden, from *Collected Poems* by W. H. Auden. Used by permis-sion of Random House, Inc., and Faber and Faber, Inc.

My son Matthew is one of those clever students of literature for whom this book was written. I've already learned enormously from his own writing on American and Native American literatures – even in ways that bear on this study. In gratitude and love, I dedicate this book to him.

Timeline: Roman Satire and Its Influence

(Dates in some cases are approximate)

BCE

700–540	Greek iambic poetry, Archilochus through Hipponax
440–405	Greek Old Comedy, Eupolis, Cratinus, Aristophanes
320–250	Greek New Comedy, Menander
315–245	Bion of Borysthenes in Athens
305(?)–240	Callimachus, poet and librarian of the Ptolemaic court at Alexandria
300–250(?)	Menippus of Gadara
239–169	Quintus Ennius
168/7(?)–102	Gaius Lucilius
116–27	M. Terentius Varro, 150 books of "Menippean" satires
84–54(?)	Catullus
65	Horace (Quintus Horatius Flaccus) born
42	Battle of Philippi, M. Antonius and Octavian defeat Brutus
35	Horace's First Book of *Satires* (*Sermones*) published
31	Battle of Actium, Octavian defeats M. Antonius
30–29	Book 2 of Horace's *Satires* and his book of *Epodes* published
27	Octavian designated "Augustus"
23	Books 1–3 of Horace's *Odes* published
20	Book 1 of Horace's *Epistles* published
18–13(?)	Book 2 of Horace's *Epistles* published

15(?)	Phaedrus, freedman of Augustus, born
13	Book 4 of Horace's *Odes* published
8	Horace's death

CE

14	Death of Augustus
14–37	Reign of Tiberius
34	Persius (Aules Persius Flaccus) born
37–41	Reign of Gaius (Caligula)
41–54	Reign of Claudius
54	Accession of Nero, deification of Claudius
62	Death of Persius
65–6	Suicides of Seneca and Petronius
67(?)	Birth of Juvenal
68	Suicide of Nero
69	Year of four emperors
69–81	Reigns of Vespasian and Titus
81–96	Reign of Domitian
86–96	Martial in Rome, composes *Epigrams* Books 1–10
98	Accession of Trajan
100–130	Juvenal's *Satires*
117	Death of Trajan, accession of Hadrian
180	Lucian, *Dialogues of the Dead, Icaromenippus*
361	Julian "the Apostate," *The Caesars*
410–430	Martianus Capella (*fl.*), *Marriage of Philology and Mercury*
467–532	Fulgentius, *Mythologies*
524	Boethius executed, *Consolation of Philosophy*
1387–1400	Chaucer, *Wife of Bath's Tale*
1460–1529	John Skelton
1509	Erasmus, *The Praise of Folly*
1532	Rabelais, *Gargantua* and *Pantagruel*
1558–1625	Thomas Lodge
1572–1631	John Donne
1572–1637	Ben Jonson
1574–1656	Joseph Hall
1575–1634	John Marston
1599	Bishops' ban against the publication of satires
1601	Ben Jonson, *Poetaster*
1605	Isaac Casaubon, *De Satyrica Graecorum et Satira Romanorum*

1631–1700	John Dryden
1660s	Nicolas Boileau-Despréaux, imitations of Horace's *Satires*
1667–1745	Jonathan Swift
1675	John Wilmot, Earl of Rochester, *Allusion to Horace*
1688–1744	Alexander Pope
1693	John Dryden, *Discourse on Satire*
1709–1784	Samuel Johnson
1726	Jonathan Swift, *Gulliver's Travels*
1728	Alexander Pope, *Dunciad*
1731–1764	Charles Churchill
1732	Pope begins *Imitations of Horace*
1749	Samuel Johnson, *The Vanity of Human Wishes*

Introduction

A World of Satire(s)

We all have an intuitive sense of what satire is. Satire of our politicians, our habits, our preoccupations, our waistlines – just about everything we are and do – appears in every day's newspaper; it is ubiquitous on television. Most of us think of it in a vague sort of way as something funnily critical, or critically funny – the stress varies. And that description will do for a beginning, since that broad understanding of satire goes right back to its beginnings, beginnings that come far earlier than the Roman Satire that is the subject of this book. The urge to satirize antedates written literature; indeed it is locked foundationally in the gestures of early ritual. It is incorporated, with a twist, in the trickster figures of folklore and story, China's Monkey King, West Africans' Eshu and Legba, Native Americans' Coyote and Nanabozho, among thousands of others. And it appears in the earliest literature we have; you can find traces of it in Homer and Hesiod, and it adopts an exclusive voice of its own in ancient literary invective, blame poetry. At one of the highest moments of Greek intellectual achievement, the satirical impulse virtually dominates the Old Comedy of Aristophanes, which, along with tragedy, was the major cultural institution of its day. Aristophanes used satire to criticize Athens' long war with the Peloponnesian alliance, to criticize intellectual showboats (especially Socrates), to criticize the major dramatists and politicians of his time. Ancient "comedy" is in fact a misleading designator; this "comedy" means satire.

Conceived in these terms, satire is simply one of the fundamental modes of human expression. It is always with us, and has left its traces in artistic, and artless, expression throughout human history. It is always interesting to us because it is always about us, our habits, our manners, our leaders, our enemies, our sins, our absurdities. Humankind will stop satirizing only when it stops existing – which, a satirist would point out, could be at any moment now. A comprehensive book about this satire might be very interesting (or very boring) if it could map out both the varieties of satiric expression and the ways in which satire is wired into human consciousness. But it would be impossibly huge. Scholars and critics have therefore had to focus (it is what scholars like to do anyway) – focus on particular periods or kinds of satire. That may sound characteristically unenterprising to an intelligent general reader, but in some instances, focus has its merits. In the present case, it can fairly be said that the Romans did something unique enough with the satiric spirit as to justify a special look – for they made a literary genre out of it, one that was to leave its imprint on literary history up to the present moment.

We can start with a list of names: Horace, Persius, Juvenal – these are the canonical Roman verse satirists most of us know about. We can grow the list a little fuller to include the names of the lost and fragmentary, thus: Ennius, Lucilius, Pacuvius Turnus. Or make another, adding in writers of Menippean satire, fable, and satiric epigram: Varro, Seneca, Petronius, Martial, Gellius. Or another, with some Greek names (for Greek, in that curious assimilation of cultures, *becomes* Roman) to season the mix with comedy, invective, and later mixtures of prose and verse: Aristophanes, Eupolis, Cratinus, Archilochus, Hipponax, Bion, Callimachus, Posidippus, Lucian, Julian, Boethius – stopping where? For satire certainly doesn't end (whether it did or did not begin) with the Romans. If you know anything about these variously collocated names, you see something of the problem that satire has had in its literary-historical life: satire is a generic child of other genres, precisely a mixture of lineages, with a lifelong identity problem. To say so is a commonplace, but it really is true. Scholars from Quintilian onward have speculated about origins, about registers of discourse, generic affinities, typical subjects and targets. Handbooks and guides resort to broad definition, like mine above, and bland sets of attributes to do the descriptive job. Here, for instance, is one:

> it may be loosely defined as a piece of verse, or prose mingled with verse, intended both to entertain and to improve society by exposing to derision and hatred the follies, vices, and crimes of men. Among its

salient characteristics are spontaneity (real or apparent), topicality, ironic wit, coarse humour, colloquial language, frequent intrusions of the author's personality or *persona*, and incessant variations of tone and style.[1]

These features are meant to translate through history and hence describe a quality we call the satiric, but in their generality and imprecision fail to define sufficiently what might constitute the formal thing we call "genre." Within ostensible ranges of characteristic elements scholars have further pursued questions of satire's transparency to life, its *personae*, the reliability of its voice(s), its relation to authority, its complicities – without resolving any of them.

Of course, there *is* a way out: to rely on the kind of formal definition the ancients themselves espoused. Thus Roman verse satires are hexameter poems composed in a certain conversational register that *generally* turn on some kind of criticism. If we leave out the fragmentary and lost authors, this leaves us with the first of the lists above: Horace, Persius, and Juvenal. This is how much of the subsequent European literary tradition, satire's reception-history, understood it, and that is still a powerfully normative force. In fact it is with these three hexameter poets that we shall be spending most of our time in this book. At the same time, we recognize that the problem of generic categorization is still with us. Horace, Persius, and Juvenal clearly had uncertainties about the generic identity of their own poems, as did Lucilius their major forebear; if one considers what some of the others listed above wrote, things get really confused.[2] An indicator of this radical uncertainty is the fact that satire, like all identity-challenged children, is almost pathologically self-conscious. No genre is more programmatically burdened, none more busily and inconclusively talkative about itself, its limits and place in the scheme of things. The situation has been just too tempting for any number of scholars keen to join the identity hunt; hence, satirists' programmatic musings, their recalling the "right," definitive ancestors, answered by a veritable rush of scholarship focusing precisely on this self-reflective aspect of the genre, giving it all the appearance at times of the compound creature opening Horace's *Ars Poetica* in ever more earnest pursuit of its tail.

One is tempted to avoid the fuss. Just get on with the business of thinking as best we can about what these, as it happens, great writers composed for themselves and their readers. But the generic-identity issue entails legitimate concerns. First, it is intrinsically good to know where and how this literary enterprise got going; what literary influences contributed to the formulation of these poems and how these influences might map out for us what our satires intend. Hence, those Greek names above. Further, it is good to know how the satire game unfolds, where it generates new, related work both in the classical Roman tradition proper and in subsequent literary history. Hence, those extra names in the third list, Varro, Seneca, Petronius, Martial, Boethius, et al. – it goes on; the epigrammatists and later Menippeans play a role that moderates a transformation of satire as genre into satire as cultural modality or modalities. Hence more names: Erasmus, More, Rabelais, Rochester, Dryden, Boileau, Pope, Gay, Swift, Johnson, Churchill, Sterne, Byron, Waugh, Orwell, Huxley, Monty Python's Flying Circus, Lenny Bruce, Richard Pryor – a representative few.

Making a Name for Itself

These are issues of placement and comprehension in (ostensibly) objective terms. But there is another, less objective, implication of satire's conspicuous quest to make a name for itself, having to do with *how* we see this literature. The first way has been a leitmotif of the way *this* book has been talking in its first few paragraphs: satire is, was, a latecomer to the generic party, unsure of itself, clearly parasitical on others of nobler parentage (epic, didactic, invective, comedy, philosophy), a lesser genre speaking in a lesser voice. Minor, in short. And that has certainly been the prevailing impression of satirists from ancient times right down to the present. The classical hierarchy of literary genres – seen for instance in Quintilian, the Roman rhetorician and educator whose major work, the *Institutiones Oratoriae*, comprised a rhetorical and literary history – ranks satire right near the bottom, uncomfortably close to mime and the kinds of invective we see, prettied up a bit, in Horace's *Epodes*. Its subjects and topics, too, are drawn from ordinary life, from the dining hall (pretentious vulgarity of), bustling street, even the schoolhouse; no gorgeously decorated celebrations of Olympian triumphs, no epic or tragic grandeur of language or emotion (but for parodic enactments of), no philosophical density or sublimity. Horace, in *Satire* 1.4, declares bluntly that satire is not proper poetry. But this is a satirist writing, and besides, to some ears the oral-freestyling of HipHop is not proper poetry either, which doesn't keep it from touching a lot of people where they live and becoming a significant cultural medium packing no small message. Satire, too, seeks to make a name for itself because it is a lowborn genre on the make, hoping for a *little* street cred.

There is a paradox in this, for satire was from its Ennian/Lucilian beginnings a literary expression of the privileged, secure, leisured, and educated. The equestrian Lucilius with his affiliations to the Scipionic aristocracy sets this tone; Horace, the genre's most revolutionary practitioner, writes satire as a means of access to the most celestial literary circle of his day; Persius, an old-blood aristocrat, never shakes the stamp of his class; the massively well-read Juvenal writes through the mentality of the aggrieved, shabby gentry. Verse satire's sister genre, Menippean satire, has the scholarly Varro, the posh Seneca, and the decadent courtier Petronius as its major classical practitioners. Moreover, the texture of the writing itself, despite satire's reputation for plain speaking, betrays highbrow literary consciousness. Lucilius was an amateur scholar who wrote learnedly about linguistics, even in his satires. Varro was the very paradigm of the professional scholar; Petronius (called *arbiter elegantiae*) was the model of the decadent man of letters. Seneca was a significant philosopher and tragedian. Horace, Persius, and Juvenal consciously allude to other canonical work on a massive scale. Satire, despite appearances, was really no game for marginal outsiders or cultural naïfs.

So a second reading of satire making a name for itself might consider the paradox of privileged insiders writing satire. Could there possibly be any objective moral force in its criticisms? Or how must what it says be conditioned by the position and interest of its writers?[3] And then there is the ambition implicit in satire's canny, self-deprecating literary sophistication, a quality that may be tied to satire's historical place. Ennius (239–169 BCE), "father" of Roman literature, composed *Saturae* that were largely miscellaneous collections of poetry on a variety of subjects, in a variety of moods.[4] He is generally held not to be a proper satirist because his verse, what we have of its satiric remains, does not seem to have contained much of the element of aggressive criticism that subsequent scholarship has deemed essential to the genre. But the fragments are so scant as to make it really impossible to exclude stringent criticism from his range. Further, Ennius was, crucially, a Hellenizing Roman writer, soaked in Greek, who knew his Posidippus, Callimachus, and popular Hellenistic philosophy, and already *these* Greeks were dismantling, reconfiguring classical genres in new experiment. Ennius' own experiment with occasional, polymetric, personal verse led to Lucilius' further experimentation and development of "satire" in thirty books, beginning with metric variety but soon settling down to what became the dactylic hexameter that formally defined later verse satire. Ennius and Lucilius both write with an awareness of historical moment; theirs is *the* time when Rome transforms itself from provincial polis to national and even world power. Ennius' *Annales* tell the story, and as Ennius has it, it is precisely a story: the tale of Rome's development rendered in high, Homeric style; the chronicle, like Rome, is important, and Ennius knew it. That fact doesn't necessarily make his *Saturae* important too, but their novelty and experiment, combined with Ennius' sense of living in a pivotal time, suggest the image of the engaged intellectual emerging from his scriptorium and having his say about being Roman on this particular day. That is clearly the image that Lucilius picks up, and he has his say on virtually every aspect of private and public life, at some volume. There is no inferiority complex in any of this; quite the contrary.

The notion of literary experiment is in itself important. While modeled after Hellenistic Greek innovation, the new satire clearly intends something else. Hellenistic Greek intellectuals imagined their way out of classic scripts: Homer and that daunting Fifth Century. They created works on smaller scales, made up new kinds of epic heroes, domesticated comedy. Both Ennius and Lucilius imagined still differently: their problem was to address what they saw coming and what they were living through, a dramatically, sometimes frighteningly changing world, a very big story. Now, one can write epic and/or tragic poems about that, and Ennius did so. Epic and tragedy cope with unsettled circumstances by effecting narrative structure and closure; events of history can be thematized and placed in relation, logics of causality constructed, large questions raised and resolved, ideologies propagated. One might also set about cobbling together a less secure discourse out of sundry inherited elements, one inherently unresolved or unresolving and whose approach to circumstances calls into question the authority of its own formulations. A new discourse that somehow answers the felt need of the moment. If the *Annales* are the big story of Rome coming on, the satires of both Ennius and Lucilius constitute other stories about being Roman and what that might mean, played out on a more human scale. Already, in its first beginnings, satire was neither the artful construction of epic/tragedy nor a simple window into Roman social life (one of the abiding myths we've inherited from people who should have known better); Ennius' satires, the bits we have, are composed of fable, dialogue, and direct, indirect, and ventriloquized speech: "he do the Police in different voices," as T. S. Eliot put it in his *Waste Land* draft. From the beginning, satire did its job in different voices – refracted impressions, observations, perspectives, opinions, confessions. Personal voices from the vortex. Sometimes these voices are comfortingly homely, sometimes urgent or vehement; always they are in play within a conspicuously "present" social context. What this gives us is precisely an invention designed for a purpose, not just *sermo*, as the Romans came to call it, plain conversation written up; nor is it just personal, occasional, topical, or trivial; the moment and conditions of its inception tell us that.

Yet a persistent impression the major verse satirists, Horace and Persius and Juvenal, give – it has been said – is of (just) pointing out the follies of humanity in the larger swim of Roman civil life. A consequence of that impression has been an exceptional consistency and, in some senses, superficiality of critical treatment. While specialists have treated satire with due seriousness and on occasion have brought remarkable insight to bear on particular authors and poems, the larger themes of synthetic treatments of the genre as a whole have tended to be of the question-begging sort: origins, generic identity, developments through its various canonical practitioners. A begged question tangles premises and conclusions; satire is thus and such because we assume thus and such in looking at its beginnings. It is a nasty circle that hasn't led us to the implicit "why." Why did men of learning and position find their way to this particular mode of expression; what role did it play in that important but brief two and a half centuries of Roman history (130 BCE through 140 CE)? Conceding a secondary rank to satire, criticism has essentially left the poems to speak for themselves as (merely) literary artifacts with a portable "moral" burden. And indeed there was a long period of time when satire was widely read in both Latin and translation as moral didactic by the educated classes. As people found other reasons for reading literature, the Roman satirists slipped into the cryogenic preservation systems of the classical curriculum. Until, that is, the salutary critical attentions of feminism and culture criticism began to stir things up. Foucault, Bakhtin, Lacan, variously influential, along with broader new historicist and politically engaged criticism, have led scholars to functionalities of satire on a number of levels, bringing it, thus, back to a more central role in twenty-first-century reception of Roman culture. What role might that be? If satire is not to be seen (still) as (only) didactic, or simply as a collection of "classic poems," or as verbal artifacts now to be read as specimens of a flawed, regressive morality, but rather as the literary trace of a certain, ambitious human response to specific pressures at a particular time (with some consequences for us), we have to raise briefly a few more possible conceptions, ways of seeing satire.

One might, for instance, think of it as a particular kind of generic space, a place where certain unruly sides of ourselves come out to play – those aspects of our animal humanness that get excluded from or bottled up in other genres (nobody pisses in epic). Shit, vomit, pus, gas, semen (not much blood, an epic fluid), the smells of brothel sex, grotesqueries of human disfigurement – the shaming, unpleasant, embarrassing, laughable and contemptible in people, and yet, how we really in some respects are. So, Roman Literature Noir; the underside, the back streets and alleys of the world power's world capital. Satire says things not allowed in polite discourse, transgresses, steps over the limit, provokes. There is fun in this, satire contends, and liberation too. As we shall explore in Chapter 5 (pp. 155–6), Bakhtinians have played with the idea that satire (or one of its versions, Menippean) is a species of carnival, that variously institutionalized social exercise wherein the enslaved, suppressed, and marginalized of us have our moment of exuberant license before the clamps come down again. My sense is that all of satire is up to more than this, but there *is* release and relief in satire's opening up to view and expression the body, in both its literal and (often deeply) metaphorical senses;[5] hence the common medical notions of satire as relieving bile – and so, in part, the proliferation of bile, piss, pus, etc. Satire centerstages the disfigured body: flawed, maimed, contorted, decaying. Let the body be seen in literature and its symbology ramifies, morphs. Decadent and decayed, it takes in everything from psychic implosion to the disintegrating "bodies" of polity, culture, and society. "Things fall apart," and satire is there to map their regresses – to cheer or deplore, but above all to show us how it happens.

Or one might think of satire as the (first?) place where the poet's "I" gets to run with the possibilities of literary discourse. The 1950s ushered in a sea-change in satire criticism wherein the idea of a poet's potentially fictive persona displaced conventional notions of satire's naive reportage. Rather than a moralizing record of the corruptions of Rome, satire came to be the genre where the poet could manipulate his textual image as a self-consciously foregrounded character or caricature in his own work. We learned not to trust satire's *personae*, those configurations of voice and perspective that were seen to be unreliable: partial, self-interested, sometimes bigoted. Recognizing this meant that the reader could take the whole of any particular satire as a literary construction made to purpose; it also meant that readers could take the whole as "literary" *tout court* so that, consequently, any aspect of real life that satire might incorporate could become (just) literary setting, estranged from social or other semantic fields and twisted into fictional shape for the poem's sake. Though their day is past, the New Critics and formalists in general did wonderful things with the satires, exploring the possibilities of rhetorical color implicit in their mixing in authorial unreliability or fictionalized narrator with ostensibly moralizing discourse. More current criticism, while recognizing satire's sexed-up speaker, has sought to bring more of the poet and his world back into discussion, exposing the limitations of satire's exposure of poetry's rhetoric, identifying features of Roman reality that can't be neatly transposed into the netherworld of "just literature." Just possibly satire already knew all this before the partial eyes of our criticisms got to it. Satire challenges the ordinary reader to fess up too. How much of our participation in the poem's rhetorical reciprocity is *fashioned*, how much of our moralizing, or otherwise responding, selves, if we go along with satire's moralizing, is a made up, better front for a more complex, darker, less certain reality? What self do we push up there to meet the poet's constructed self? And if the author's and reader's selves are concocted for the occasion, can either, satire asks, be anything else? Satire is not the only Graeco-Roman genre where this sort of thing goes on, but it may have spotted first of all those qualities of literature we lately call postmodern.[6]

Satire is at once the most and least mundane of literary kinds. Its themes are basic and repetitive, its literary register is far from sublime, low to middle, in fact, with street talk and colloquialism in healthy doses, it does not even try to move us or make us laugh *very* hard, it shuns the political spotlight, it is always about little things, even when they are big (fish). But all that quotidian mundanity makes satire paradigmatically the genre where displacement and indirection provoke larger questions. Emily Gowers, for instance, has shown us how all that food in satire means so much more than the stuff we, or they, eat: food is cultural ritual.[7] Whether that food is rough greens or egregiously large turbot, it is, in satire, precisely a spectacle of values put on display. Kirk Freudenburg puts it nicely: "Every Roman knows that food isn't just stuff you eat to stay alive. It's elaborate showmanship, outlandishly produced to please and seduce and gratify and move ahead in the world."[8] So too are drink and sex and prayer and money-grubbing and the other ordinary things satire likes to talk about. Satire does not (just) say "these are the ordinary compulsions and addictions that, unduly, occupy our lives" but "let us consider how they mean to us and what they say about us." One could, for instance, write satires of football mania, European and American style, that would have serious and very different things to say about the social constellations of the respective fans. The football analogy is fair enough, since satire goes further than just presenting itself to the odd reader who happens along. Not framed as a romanticized, fantasized, or epicized imaginative act, satire plumps down right there in front of us, not pretending to be of another time or place. It is street theater, consciously theatrical in its self-references,[9] that buttonholes us as we walk by and literally requires our participation. The show can't go on unless we're part of it. Aristotle writes of the appeals of tragedy – pity and fear, cartharsis of emotion – and we might generalize those appeals to epic as well; comedy and lyric please us in different ways; satire calls us out, confronting us with some impression of our world and requiring us to place ourselves within the complex triangulation of poet-speaker, satirized target, audiences (there are perhaps several in question). Just where we place ourselves is always tricky, entailing a decision that is not entirely voluntary, and satire makes us think about that fact too. Satire, crucially, *criticizes*. At times facilely, cheaply, even deviously, especially in the fact that the criticism is open-ended, asking you to agree. Do you? How *can* you? In the end, satire's mundane scenarios and stock criticisms lead to tough and serious questions. It makes us commit, and, once we have, catches us out.

Satire's criticism has a final complication. It targets in obvious ways people and practices it disapproves of, or seems to; as we've noted, it asks us into the process of targeting and so compromises our distance from the textual performance; but satire explicitly targets itself as well. That is most conspicuously seen in its famous programmatic passages where each satirist positions himself in relation to his predecessors, always formulating some compound of "I am doing this better than they" and "I am to some degree compromised, less than the others." Horace dances around these poles openly with Lucilius in his *Satires*

1.4, 1.10, and 2.1; in his prologue and first satire, Persius outlines his own compromised position relative to Lucilius and Horace, but in so doing delineates an almost abrasive independence from tradition; Juvenal's first satire marks, most of all, its distance from satire's beginnings and the expressive possibilities characteristic of those beginnings; its most explicit bearing is Lucilius, so to designate as it were the beginning and end of the tradition: what Lucilius could do, Juvenal avers, he could not, yet the satire, cut and trimmed for his belated day, will in the end be every bit as prepossessing, or more so, most would say. To be sure, this, along with the numerous metapoetic (self-) references, never so thick on the ground in ancient literature as here, is generic self-consciousness, born in part out of a need to find a place for this kind of writing within the literary cosmos of its day. But it also establishes (again, for the first time?) a textual space where poetry performs its own criticism. Satire's reiterated geneses, born again in Horace, Persius, and Juvenal, are inherently critical acts, reading-down forebears as they refashion something else in explicitly critical terms; criticism and creation fused. It further sets up a paradigm within which "what one creates" and "how one reads" are obverse facets of the same thing. Satire's own poetry tells us that (this) literature *is* its reception; Lucilius can only be what his satiric readers, Horace, Persius, and Juvenal, say him to be, and that saying is part and parcel of their different formulations of their different sorts of satire. In all this are implications for *our* reading of satire: satiric poems invite us into a conceptual space where textuality turns all ways: to the real worlds of its topicality and ours, to itself, commenting on its own comment, to its auditors, dialogically anticipating – needing – response.

That response is all yours. This book won't script it for you. Read (satire) on.

Further Reading

Valuable general works on Roman satire include M. Coffey, *Roman Satire*, 2nd edition (London, 1989), a clearly written, reliable introduction; J. P. Sullivan, ed., *Critical Essays on Roman Literature: Satire* (London, 1963) still has valuable things to say in its essays by various hands; C. A. Van Rooy, *Studies in Classical Satire and Related Literary Theory* (Leiden, 1970) remains invaluable. You will also find very good things in C. Witke, *Latin Satire* (Leiden, 1970), N. Rudd, *Themes in Roman Satire* (London, 1986), and, for some seminally important work, W. S. Anderson, *Essays on Roman Satire* (Princeton, 1982). More recently, K. Freudenburg's *Satires of Rome* (Cambridge, 2001) is an incisive, comprehensive modern study of the three major Roman satirists. Freudenburg has also edited *The Cambridge Companion to Roman Satire* (Cambridge, 2005); the many times its essays turn up in this book are an index of the *Companion*'s importance. See too the several individual studies, profoundly influential, by J. Henderson, gathered in his *Writing Down Rome: Satire, Comedy, and Other Offences in Latin Poetry* (Oxford, 1999); Henderson's is the most exhilarating and challenging writing on satire you will find. Other very good books of recent vintage, though not intended as introductions, include C. Keane, *Figuring Genre in Roman Satire* (Oxford, 2006) and C. Schlegel, *Satire and the Threat of Speech* (Madison, 2005). On a much smaller scale, but packed with good introductory information, is S. Braund's *Roman Verse Satire, Greece and Rome*: New Surveys in the Classics, 23 (Oxford, 1992). C. J. Classen's "Satire – the Elusive Genre," *Symbolae Osloenses* 63 (1988): 95–121 is a thoughtful introduction to generic issues.

On satire, broadly construed and theorized, see F. Bogel, *The Difference Satire Makes: Rhetoric and Reading from Jonson to Byron* (Ithaca, 2001); B. A. Connery and K. Combe, eds., *Theorizing Satire* (New York, 1995); R. C. Elliott, *The Power of Satire: Magic, Ritual, Art* (Princeton, 1960); N. Frye, *Anatomy of Criticism* (Princeton, 1957); D. Griffin, *Satire: A Critical Reintroduction* (Lexington, 1994); G. Highet, *The Anatomy of Satire* (Princeton, 1962); M. A. Rose, *Parody: Ancient, Modern, and Post-Modern* (Cambridge, 1993); L. Hutcheon, *A Theory of Parody* (London, 1985) and *Irony's Edge: The Theory and Politics of Irony* (London, 1994); and G. A. Test, *Satire: Spirit and Art* (Tampa, 1991).

1

Beginnings (?)

Every general or introductory book on classical satire you can find in
the library contains a section trying to explain how satire got its name.
That story, as all those books will say, is no longer very controversial,
though in the sixteenth and seventeenth centuries people got worked
up into quite a lather over whether the Latin word *satura* derived from
satyrs or from *satur*, a Latin adjective roughly meaning "full."[1] There
was good reason for the preoccupation: knowing its "original" sense
could be a key to the dispositions of the genre's earliest practitioners: is
this a poetry "intended" in its first instances to be naughty, irreverent,
satyr-like, or is it a term reflecting the diversity of elements collected
within its "fullness"? The fourth century (CE) grammarian Diomedes
doesn't himself know the truth of the matter, but he does seem to have
derived his opinions from sources as far back as Varro (116–27 BCE),
and he has set out what have become definitive options:

> *Satura* is the name of a verse composition amongst the Romans.
> At present certainly it is defamatory and composed to carp at human
> vices in the manner of the Old (Greek) Comedy: this type of *satura* was
> written by Lucilius, Horace, and Persius. Previously however *satura* was
> the name of a composition in verse consisting of miscellaneous poems,
> such as Pacuvius and Ennius wrote. ... Now *satura* is so called either
> from the Satyrs, because in this type of poem (i.e. *satura*) laughable and
> shameful things are related in the same way even as those recited and
> performed by the Satyrs, or it is called *satura* from a platter which was
> laden full with a large variety of first fruits, and used to be offered to the
> gods in the cult of the ancients; and from the abundance and fullness
> of the dish it was called *satura* ... or from a kind of stuffing which was
> crammed full with many ingredients and called *satura* according to the

testimony of Varro. . . . Others however think it derives its name from a law, *satura*, which includes many provisions at once in a single bill, for it is evident that the verse composition *satura* also comprises many poems at once . . . [2]

By the time Diomedes was writing, opinion had settled on the first of these options, since the critically abrasive side of satire had become its most identifiable characteristic. But it appears that Diomedes' source Varro thought otherwise, and in fact the Latin word, because of its short second vowel, cannot legitimately derive from *satyros* with its long u-sound.[3] By default, then, the source-meaning of the word suggests fullness (thus related to *satis*, "enough," the occasion of frequent self-conscious puns in Roman satires), with the further idea of a composite mixture of things. Certainly interesting things can be teased out of this originary definition: there is correspondence here to Juvenal's figure for his own poems as a *farrago*, mixed feed for cattle (*Sat.* 1.86); the idea of a miscellaneous collection paradigmatically seen in Ennius and Lucilius; the easy figural assimilation of culturally loaded themes of food – feasting, overeating, entertaining, what one does to get ahead, the perils of the patronage system, the culture of the *triclinium* (dining room) as index of Roman identity. But there is a significant sense, too, in which this "original" sense of satire is no help at all, rather like the "goat-song" etymology of tragedy. There is, after all, nothing in it that prescribes what ought to be stuffed into these miscellaneous collections of verse, nothing suggesting tone, approach, register, attitude. To take another example, Livy (7.2.4–10) tells us that *satura* was once the name of an early, native form of Roman drama; but here too, apart from a vague connection to dialogue within some satires and to the occasional presence of Greek Old Comedy as a model for satire's social criticism, this early source tells us little about what satire came to be, and as crucially, how it came to be. For that we have to look at its extant practitioners.

Ennius

Quintus Ennius (239–169), whose very few remaining fragments of satire make him the vaguely remembered grandfather of the genre, seems to authorize the paradigm of satire as medley.[4] One of the few things generally known about his four, or six, books (we are unsure of the number) is that they combined poems written in different meters on a number of themes and topics. There are fables, dialogues, debate, anecdotes, satiric portraits of parasites and botherers, references to food – in short much of the farrago that would appear in later satire. So few fragments of the *Satires* survive that it is impossible to make a comprehensive judgment of the poetry as a whole, or of the *Saturae* as satire in anything like the later Roman or modern senses. But the satires do offer intriguing glimpses into a remarkable and dare we say novel poetic chemistry. Perhaps the first thing to keep in mind about Ennius is that he takes himself seriously as a writer, as one of the fragments of the Satires tells us:

> Your health, poet Ennius, you who pass to mortal men
> a cup of flaming verses drawn from your very marrow.[5]

The "flaming verses" have to be a reference to his patriotic history, *Annales,* or his tragedies, for the remaining fragments of the *Saturae* don't have much firepower, but this little couplet reminds us that this is the poet who in the early verses of his great annalistic epic imagines Homer himself appearing to the poet in a dream vision. It is the egoism of that gesture that mainly strikes us today, but for Ennius it was at least as much a conscious metapoetic act, linking his own ambition (and achievement) to a distinctly pre-Roman tradition. And elements of that tradition surely influence the formation of satire as a genre. Horace names, for instance, writers of Greek Old Comedy, Eupolis, Cratinus, and Aristophanes, as foundational (*Sat.* 1.4.1–7):

> Consider the poets Eupolis and Cratinus and Aristophanes
> and the others who composed Old Comedy,
> if anyone ever deserved to be written up, because he was no-good,
> or a thief, or adulterer or cutthroat, or otherwise
> notorious, they used to satirize them liberally.
> Lucilius depends altogether on these, and follows them,
> with only the meter changed.

And Persius affirms comedy's still current affinity of spirit (*Sat.* 1.123–125):

> Whenever you are stirred up by daring Cratinus
> or you become devoted to tetchy Eupolis or great old Aristophanes,
> look also here, if perchance you'd hear something cooked down and sharp.

This Old Comedy, while very different from satire in verse-form and many of its qualities in intent and performance conditions, was nonetheless frank in its critical appraisal of individuals and society. The satirists seize on its license to say what it wants to and its unwillingness to mince words. Satire also takes in, like a generic sponge, features of other Greek writing: invective, philosophical diatribe, and epistle. Ennius' affinities for Greek literature of a number of kinds make him, symbolically, a pivotal figure. He wrote tragedies, history, comedies, gastronomic poetry, encomiastic poetry, and a rationalizing prose work on mythology, as well as a few books of miscellaneous verse called *Saturae*. If we think of him, as Horace arguably does, as satire's *auctor* (*Sat.* 1.10.66), we are reminded that his literary scope is emblematic of the genre that would name itself after one of his works. We think back through Ennius, wondering what made up (composed) Ennius making up those *Saturae* – through him to all those other poetic kinds and especially, since they will become important to developing satire, to comedy, popular philosophy, even to Greek invective. Ennius is usually not seen to be prominently influenced by the invective poets, Archilochus, Hipponax, Semonides, and Anacreon, generally from the seventh and sixth centuries BCE, or by writers of Hellenistic iambic such as Alcaeus, Callimachus, Sotades, and Menippus. But he did write some of his *Saturae* in iambic meter, perhaps intending to invoke both comedy and iambic invective.[6] And sometimes his tone sounds a little like proper invective: *malo hercle magno suo convivat sine modo!* ("Let him be one of the guzzlers without limit, and, by god, may he be utterly damned for it!").[7] Van Rooy summarizes Ennius' blending of comic and lyric iambic: "It is probably not without significance that the poet who was so fond of personal utterance . . . should have made considerable use of the iambic meter which, being the natural medium for dialogue, had been made by Archilochus the literary medium for free, colloquial, personal utterance. Nor is it without significance that both these poets should have reflected their individual personality in their poetry."[8] But Ennius is no Roman Archilochus; what is striking is the transformation of Archilochian influence; transformative because it seeks to make something else: not quite comedy, not quite invective, not quite diatribe. The artistry of this particularly delicate balancing act is Ennius' first contribution to the genre.

There is another sense, too, in which the larger conditions of the invective tradition touch Ennius, initially, and satire in general later.

David Mankin fits invective into a broader category of blame poetry, which includes satire and comedy as well, and centers its criticisms around the idea of *philotes*: "[t]he *iambus* was meant to remind the audience of what might be a threat to the very shared customs, morals, and so on which brought them together and united them as an audience. Whether as fellow citizens or as drinking companions, the members of the audience would consider themselves *philoi* ("friends") and what they shared as *philotes* ("friendship"), a term which has the same complex range of meaning in Greek as *amicitia* has in Latin."[9] *Amicitia* was that network of alliance and patronage, more political than personal, which underpinned Rome's version of republican government and social disposition. When Horace wrote his epodes or *Iambi* (30s BCE), roughly contemporaneously with his *Satires*, he may have been thinking, Mankin contends, of the profound crisis in Roman *amicitia* brought about by decades of social disruption and civil war: "Horace turned to a type of poetry whose function had been the affirmation of 'friendship' in its community . . . he may have hoped that his *iambi* would somehow 'blame' his friends and fellow citizens into at least asking themselves *quo ruitis* ["what are you (madly) rushing to?"] ([*Ep.*] 7.1)."[10] That appraisal may be optimistic, though a full five of the seventeen epodes focus thematically on recent civil disruption and Mankin is right in pointing to a larger contingency in the writing of iambic verse in general.

Thus, a crucial overlap with satire. Neither genre is blame poetry *tout court*; both fashion a vocabulary of blame out of a larger fabric, intertextual and social, within which the blaming "means" more than sending a wretched victim of abuse off to the gallows tree. So when Persius invokes Hipponax in his prologue by employing the latter's characteristic meter, the scazon or limping iambic, he means to suggest more than verbal abuse.[11] In fact, Persius' prologue scarcely abuses at all in a personal sense; rather it attacks the entire social system responsible for generating bad verse, corrupt patronage and cultural values. Both iambic and satire are "about" human, social relations, and while specific targeting may be local, consequences of that targeting are never so. Yet overlap does not mean identity. We could say that iambic is the preferred verse form for satire in Greek; hexametric for satire in Latin; or we could say that iambic tends toward personal abuse while (Roman) satire tends toward criticism of stock figures and broader social mores. These are fair generalizations, but even in making them we see how mixed and interlocked these things are.

Ennius will, then, sometimes sound, in his *Saturae*, a little like an iambic poet, sometimes like a satirist, for instance like one of Horace's longwinded (satirized) stoics:

> Why, when you come along carefree,
> spick and span, your cheeks unstuffed, your arm bared, ready,
> tripping a-tip-toe waiting all taut like a wolf –
> when next you are lapping up another's goods,
> in what mind, do you think, is your host?[12]

And sometimes he will sound like neither. And while we can arguably claim that Ennius's *Saturae* include more than later satire comes to do, it would be merely arbitrary to argue that they are not satire for that reason. That larger Ennian grasp, in point of fact, itself designates one of satire's crucially defining features, its transformative incorporation of other generic influences.

There is another such defining feature, already mentioned above. Ennius writes his *Saturae* in pivotal and parlous times, when Greek cultural bearings and the realities of Roman political and military power were sweeping whole peoples into their train. Ennius lived every Greek teacher's fantasy, which is to say he was "important" (one of his first Greek students was Cato). Born a non-citizen in old Calabria in the year 239 BCE, Ennius' arrival in Rome brought him into contact and even friendship with Rome's leading citizens: Marcus Fulvius Nobilior, his son Quintus Fulvius, and the Scipionic clan. Those major players were riding and driving Rome's rise in the Mediterranean basin in the decisive days of the second Punic war. Ennius' adult life corresponds to the period (220–168 BCE) selected by the historian Polybius to mark Rome's triumph in the Mediterranean. Ennius would die barely a year before the defeat of the Macedonian Perseus at Pydna. In Rome's relatively rapid metamorphosis from polis to world-power, literature as well as *Realpolitik* is involved; or rather, literature might be seen as an element of, or closely involved with, that *Realpolitik*. Ennius' very association with Scipio Africanus made what he wrote worthy of attention. The fact that Cato, initially a patron, came reportedly to resent Ennius and his (Hellenizing) influence is a tribute to the sway a Greek pedagogue and man of letters might have. Ennius' experiments with Romanized Greek genres, virtually inventing a literature for Rome, initially define, as well as help shape, Romans' sense of self in and for the wider world. A passage from

Ennius' *Annales*, passed down to us from Gellius whose quotation is responsible for the fragment's survival, has been frequently cited to make this very point. The passage has to do with the relation of one Geminus Servilius with a trusted friend of lesser rank; Gellius refers to Lucius Aelius Stilo who contends that the friend is a self-portrait of Ennius:

> So saying he (Servilius) called to one with whom he shared willingly and cheerfully and right often his table, his talks, and his affairs, when, tired out, he had spent long hours of the day in managing the greatest affairs, by counsel given in the wide mart and sacred senate-house; one to whom care-free he would often speak out boldly matters great and small, and joke the while, and blurt out words good and bad to say, if so he wished at all, and store them in loyal keeping . . .[13]

There is more than a touch of saccharine idealizing in this picture, but the image of the writer (if this is an Ennian self-portrait) as the intimate confidante of the powerful, not directly involved in issues of state but counselor and friend of those who are, is programmatically important. As Frances Muecke points out, it is taken up by later satirists, Lucilius and Horace, who find in this personal intimacy with public men a "place" for satire.[14] It allows the satirist to play off his own servility and the modesty of his discourse against the sense of importance it may derive from being close to the beating heart of Rome. It represents the private side of the voice of authority, and no matter how public and ordinary its scenes are in Ennius and will become in others, it bears with it something of this insider's perspective, secret knowledge, the implicit power of secrets unrevealed. Satire is not the plain man's commentary on the big world out there. Like the politician claiming to speak for ordinary folk, it is a compounded voice, darker and duplicitous. Ennius' image tells us too that the satirist is not an apolitical creature. Rather he writes from within a rather tightly pre-scribed political position: both Ennius and Lucilius are partisans of the Scipios; Horace positions himself within Augustus' coterie; Persius and Juvenal define themselves in opposition to different manifestations of imperial power, perforce ambiguously and elusively and (as they alert us) not without care to their own interests. Whatever its pretense to disinterested observation of society, Roman satire is always born of a highly developed awareness of the satirist's political position. Ennius tells us this from the beginning.

Lucilius

But it is Lucilius (168/7–102 BCE), aristocratic friend of P. Cornelius Scipio Aemilianus, who is the widely acknowledged father of satire; Horace calls him the "inventor" of the genre (*Sat.* 1.10.48).[15] All three major "hexameter" satirists, Horace, Persius, and Juvenal, refer to Lucilius as the authorizing inaugurator of their craft. Certainly, Lucilius' decision to compose his satires in hexameters was generically determinative; his earliest books, owing to a quirk in transmission, are numbered 26–30, the first four of which books were composed in a number of meters, but 30 and the later books, numbered 1–21, are all hexameters, the meter that succeeding satirists would adopt.[16] We can see in this circumstance the origins of an evolving generic autobiography or composition of theme and variations: Lucilius invents a genre to be developed and altered in Horace, Persius, Juvenal (and others lost), so that we have by Juvenal's death a rather neat, entirely Roman generic package; *satura quidem tota nostra est*, "at least *this* genre's all ours," wrote the Roman Quintilian in simplifying summation. The various Greek influences, or prefigurations, initially drawn together by Ennius are elided. In this spirit, the later grammarian Diomedes marginalized Ennius and his nephew Pacuvius: "Previously however *satura* was the name of a composition in verse consisting of miscellaneous poems, such as Pacuvius and Ennius wrote . . ."[17] Diomedes thus distinguishes satire from grab-bags like Posidippus' epigrammatic collection, the *Soros* ("Pile"). But Quintilian's formulation of a popular impression, *tota nostra est*, is not disinterested description. It is a statement, too, of Roman identity, a declaration that the words of the satirist, whatever their source or influence, become naturalized, born of and about Rome. This fashioning of verses reflecting Roman identity is not much different from Ennius' practice, but it is Lucilius whose gathering of diverse elements and qualities is founded most deeply and aggressively on recording a certain kind of *Romanitas* in a moment of national identity crisis. That *Romanitas*, as we shall now see via a grammarian's non-thematic filtration system, is less about what is said or subjects covered than a certain posture.

(Short-order) Cook's tour

The grammarian is one Nonius, of the fourth century CE. In composing his *De Compendiosa Doctrina*, he found Lucilius a good source for words and usages, odd and otherwise, that he wanted to discuss. Consequently, after the full texts of Lucilius were lost, the fragments Nonius quoted as illustration became posterity's chief source of the sketchy outlines of "our" Lucilius. A number of other post-Lucilian authors made several further contributions, and much thought has been put into placing them all in their contexts and in reconstructing the organization of the books and poems within them. But it is all very uncertain, and today no one can read through Lucilius as a literary text simply because there is not enough continuity among the fragments to make a lot of sense of them. Still, Nonius' grammatical dragnet and others' variously interested anglings have pulled up interesting tidbits for the satirical table.

Books 26–30: Preprogramming satire

Lucilius programs satire's notoriously self-reflexive programmatic verse (see pages 4–11). He tells us up front that he is writing for only the middling-clever (632–634[18]), thus welcoming the general run of us, but excluding too: no scholars, no culture snobs ("I don't want [scholarly] *Persius* to read me" [635]). But he *must* write ("I've *got* to speak out" [696]). This too will be paradigmatic; Persius will twist fragment 696 into the grotesque imagery of a satirical fig tree bursting from the writer's spleen, but Lucilius' imperative, that satire will out, remains constant through Juvenal. Lucilius will do more programming later, but we note that from this first beginning satire maps its place in the generic geography, a decisive gesture. Ensuing fragments survey the thematic field: wives, mostly bad, bothersome agents, especially if they are not quite Roman, drink, boon companions, food – scenes at table are everywhere in Lucilius, and they become ubiquitous in later satire. Eating is perfect for satire; utterly trivial yet the place where class, social codes, and personal habits come under scrutiny. Lucilian satire first recognizes that it is precisely over the banal and necessary process of filling one's belly that issues of "taste" (*sapio*), discrimination, distinction, propriety, the limits of meagerness and excess become primary. Satire's favorite bad pun is *satis*, a moralizing "what's enough." Paradoxically, satire fills itself beyond *satis*faction until the writer or reader, too late, cries *satis*, "enough," naming the genre even while trying to escape it: you can't escape satire. Feasting defines a world where little and big things matter: big fish, stuffed dormice, stuffed boars, stuffed diners, coarse food too, tough veg to show the fastidious what's what, some vinegary wine, but more faux Margaux than Mogen David. An occasional healthy snack to juxtapose the rarified fare of desperately climbing gourmands. All of it culturally coded; food is about how society works. Food for thought, too; Lucilius introduces philosophy in these books, mostly the Hellenistic concoctions of the Cynics, Stoics, Epicureans: recipes for living. Satire first gets its moralizing mission here, and its first stress on the "real" as opposed to the fictive subjects of tragedy and epic: "something important – the people's health and prosperity – this is Lucilius' greeting imparted to verses such as he can write, and all this with heartiness and earnestness" (791–792). Ideas like food get digested and sometimes go bad, and the body becomes the site for moral diagnosis ("we see him who is sick in mind showing the mark of it on his body" [678] . . . "before he felt the rascal's pulse and tested his heart" [680]); mind, "soul," and society are entailed in the body's palpitations and ulcers.[19]

What else in these chartering first books? Literature: poetry, historiography, comedy, tragedy, none of it treated in appreciative terms. That attitude is more than satiric mean-spiritedness, for satire invokes other literature as much as any dimension of human living. Certainly part of the interest is self-interest, making a place for itself in the cosmos of Graeco-Roman literature. We have seen and will see considerably more evidence of precisely this generic self-fashioning in later satirists, and it is easy to discern in this the kind of parlor game self-conscious literary artists and critics like to play. But there is a deeper and more important sense that literature taps deep into fundamental currents of life and human values, and it too is about taste. Persius' searing critique of his contemporary literary scene opens his book of satires, and to see that poem as (just) "about literature" is to miss the point. Here again we might see in satire a first, in satire's reading of literature as cultural artifact, drawn from and invested in the political life of Rome. Then there is sex, of the chummy, misogynist sort – the libertas, free speech, of the privileged male with sexual choices, the power to take his satisfactions. What matters most to Lucilius is the body on offer ("Here you will find a firm, full body / and breasts standing out on a marble-white chest" [923–924]) and convenience (in the brothel, "[I want] women who will ask for less and also make their offers with much more propriety / and without reproach" [927–928]). He happily goes both ways, not unusually for his class and day, but there's never a question of who's on top – at least figuratively.

There is invective in these books, and friendship too, and law (805–813). This last association will become intrinsic, for satire has its brushes with the law. The satirist sometimes-pretendingly fears libel laws, fears retribution; yet he is a law unto himself: he accuses, he passes judgement, he punishes ("Lucilius flayed the city, cracked down on its Lupuses and Muciuses; Horace twisted the conscience of his smiling friend" [Persius *Sat.* 1.114–117]).

Books 1–21: Program, map, menu

Horses, fish, Latin grammar, Homer, superstition, misers, sex(-ism), rhetoric, travel, autobiography, luxury and poverty, country living, defecation, law, friendship, literary criticism, gods, enemies, polemic, politics, gladiators, wanton women, gangrene, food, more food, drink and drunkenness, one good belch, and much else in these books. Even within such a farrago, the reader can discern themes and recurrent obsessions. These books thus become, even more decisively than do the first five, the chartering conceptual map of the genre. All subsequent verse satire is to some degree traceable to Books 1–21 of Lucilius. Almost as if he were aware of that situation, Lucilius opens with program. If Persius' scholiast is correct, the first line of the first satire of the later satirist quotes the first line of Lucilius's "first": *O curas hominum! O quantum est in rebus inane!* ("Oh, the cares of humankind, oh, the triviality of things!"). Satire's focus is immediately, and permanently, bifocal: that *inane* is meant to gloss *curas hominum* as well as *rebus* [the world], so that human responses to pressures from without come under as much scrutiny as any absurdity "out there." Yet *rebus* doesn't just mean "things" or the stuff of material existence, but the world as seen and conceived by people; it entails society, what we broadly call culture, and the movements of human history. Crucially, therefore, satire is less about particular things or situations than about *how* we are connected, plugged into the Zeitgeist.

Sometimes that plugging-in channels nastiness; Lucilius glosses the art with an image: "the letter, r[rrrrr], which the teased dog speaks more clearly than a man does" (3–4). Satire, voice of the provoked outsider, growls. Later, Lucilius will tell us, using an anatomical figure to locate satire's disdain that will be much imitated, that it snorts as well: "I found fault with the severe law of Calpurnius Piso, and snorted my anger through the nostrils at the tip of my nose" (607–608). It can also tell an amusing tale, punctuated with growls and snorts.

Fragments 5 and following come from his Second Satire devoted to an imaginary debate among the gods (*Concilium Deorum*) considering the admission of an enemy of Scipio, one Lucius Cornelius Lentulus Lupus. This satirical treatment will map out parts of Juvenal's Fourth Satire and Seneca's satirical treatment of Claudius in his *Apocolocyntosis* ("Pumpkinification"). In Book 2, Lucilius goes after another enemy, Quintus Mucius Scaevola, without mincing words: Scaevola is a "corrupt man, and scot-free thief" (57), who is hot with boy-lust (63), and knows how to "penetrate into a hairy bag" (61). It is in this accusatory context that Lucilius drops a suggestive word: *non dico "vincat licet"; et vagus exul et erret exlex* ("I do *not* say 'let him win the case,' no, let him be an exiled vagabond and an outlawed wanderer" [64–65]). *Exlex* captures not only the victim's but also satire's ambiguous relation with law, both (fearful of) being subject to it and somehow beyond it, acting as legal agency unto itself. Like the duly sentenced Scaevola, the satirist travels, and Book 3 is all about Lucilius' trip to Sicily. Not a Cook's Tour at all, for its focus is less on the seen than the focalized perceptions of the seer: gladiator contests, animal births, fetching hostesses, eating, drinking, belching. Horace would imitate this satire in his first book (1.5), describing his own journey with Maecenas, Vergil, and others on a diplomatic mission to Brundisium, an imitation that, in its considered and complex responses to the Lucilian model, goes far in establishing Horace's own program and poetic identity.

Incerta (and uncentered to boot)

The fragments unassigned to particular books offer some of the longer and more interesting selections from Lucilius' writing. Here we find his intriguingly dismissive description of his satire as "makeshift verse" (*schedium fac<io>* [1131]) – an evasive gesture that Horace will pick up and develop in his first book of satires. The Forum (the City, Wall Street) – paradigmatic setting of satire – appears with sufficient trimmings here (1145–1151):

> But now from morning to night, holidays or not,
> the whole commons and senators too,
> all bustle about the forum and never leave;
> all give themselves over to one and the same enthusiasm and artifices,
> to swindle with impunity, to fight cunningly, to contend

through ingratiation, to act the fine fellow,
to set traps as if everyone were enemies of everyone.

Counterpoint to such cynicism stands just a few fragments away, an old-fashioned version of Roman virtue (1196–1208):

Virtue is to be able to pay a fair price for things
in the world we live and work in;
virtue is knowing what every situation holds for one;
virtue is knowing what is correct, useful, and honorable for one,
what things are good, what bad, what without use, wicked, and dishonorable;
virtue is knowing the proper end and limit of acquiring;
virtue is being able to pay out the full price from our stores;
virtue is giving what in truth is due to honour,
being an enemy and hostile to bad men and their ways,
a defender of good men and their ways,
to value greatly the latter, wish them well, and live a friend to them;
beyond all this, to prize our country's interests first,
our parents' next, and lastly our own.

It should now not surprise us to see in proximity to this kind of idealizing, ethical set-piece, which would become a *topos* in later satire, a fair number of salaciously coarse fragments: "the whores of Pyrgi," "the nightly-poked slut," "the rump, my dear Hortensius, that provides the jerks born for the purpose" (1178–1180), "she stains you, but he bedungs you," "I wet the bed and soiled the bedclothes" (1182–1183). Or crude invective and the tumors, pimples, and blisters of the vile body. Satire thrives on this counterpoint; its readers deflected from instance to instance in a world whose values remain unsettled, perpetually in play. Which is why the image of the *soros*, the pile, the farrago, the proper limits and, precisely, definition of all these, is so decisively indicative of satire. To know what is "enough," *satis*, is to know where the beginning and end are, where the center, the center of values, is. Lucilian satire is uncentered writing, its matter the predilections and interests of a particular aristocratic Roman whose personal and political values are both specific to his time and largely unformulated.

Lucilius' books are thus so surprisingly inclusive that the reader/critic's job is less to describe what is included than to mark what is excluded. Big ideas, obviously, run outside satire's ambit. The themes of tragedy and epic, of high-minded, celebratory lyric, of encomium, of propagandistic historiography aren't much found in Lucilian or later satire. Lucilius made an initial decision about that and it stuck. Yet Lucilius' social position, privileged and powerful, his remarkable access to Scipio and other members of the political elite, and his involvement in political polemic ensure that his chosen satiric register and discourse is not an outsider's counter-genre, the protesting voice of the unempowered. Rather Lucilius created another means of looking into not the real stuff of Roman life, but the sensibility of the contemporary Roman engaged in that real stuff. It's all about how a Roman gent like Lucilius takes it in, how he processes the encounters and events of quotidian existence. He has ideas about drink, dinners, words, sex, bodies – his own and others'. In some corner of his mind he is concerned about mortality and morality, about questions posed by the philosophers he has read, but he knows too that what he might write about (his version of) mundane things seen in this particular Roman way, can/should stir things up in the minds of like- and unlike-minded contemporaries and might just possibly be worth putting down in books – the better to remember with. Lucilian satire is not, precisely not, a "history" of current events; its very anti-canonical posture is an indication that it is to be taken as both a version of "things out there" (Lucilius' view, elitist, etc., etc.) and a discourse whose status is "to be questioned." Eschewing the credibility of the big, canonical genres, Lucilius tries out a look at the under-and-other sides of living in a Rome growing into a new place in the world and out of its old assumptions, while asking his readers to believe it or not. Lucilian satire is the first (Roman or other) genre to instate dubiety as chartering dictum. In the radically uncertain and rapidly changing state of Roman things, Lucilius' satire is a "certain" voice whose very normative impulse is subverted the moment it comes into satire. Lucilius may thus say, without risking triviality, "Here (amid seismic changes in the world polity) are my ideas about ... fish." This is the most challenging conceptual paradox of satire.

Further Reading

The most available texts for Ennius and Lucilius are the Loeb editions, edited by E. H. Warmington, *Remains of Old Latin* (Cambridge, MA, 1967), in four volumes. For satire's beginnings, C. A. Van Rooy, *Studies in Classical Satire and Related Literary Theory* (Leiden, 1965) is essential. And now see

F. Muecke's hospitable introduction, "Rome's First 'Satirists': Themes and Genre in Ennius and Lucilius," in K. Freudenburg, *The Cambridge Companion to Roman Satire* (Cambridge, 2005), 33–47 as well as S. Goldberg's good chapter "Enter Satire" in his recent *Constructing Literature in the Roman Republic* (Cambridge, 2005). A. S. Gratwick in "The Satires of Ennius and Lucilius" in E. J. Kenney and W. V. Clausen, eds., *The Cambridge History of Classical Literature*, vol. 2 (Cambridge, 1982), 156–71, lays out the Hellenistic background of Ennius' *Saturae*. Others of note include M. Coffey, *Roman Satire* (London, 1989), 11–23; J. H. Waszink, "Problems Concerning the *Satura* of Ennius," in O. Skutsch, ed., *Ennius, Fondation Hardt, Entretiens sur l'Antiquité classique* XVII: 99–137 (Geneva, 1972); N. Rudd, *Themes in Roman Satire* (London, 1986); and A. Richlin's *Garden of Priapus: Sexuality and Aggression in Roman Humor* (rev. edn., New York, 1992), 164–74. On Lucilius and his social context, see E. Gruen's *Culture and National Identity in Republican Rome* (Ithaca, 1992), 272–317. W. Raschke has written extensively and informatively on Lucilius: "*Arma pro amico* – Lucilian Satire at the Crisis of the Roman Republic," *Hermes* 115 (1987): 299–318, "The Virtue of Lucilius," *Latomus* 49 (1990): 352–369, and "The Chronology of the Early Books of Lucilius," *Journal of Roman Studies* 69 (1979): 78–89. On style (though you will need your Latin) see H. Petersmann, "The Language of Early Roman Satire: Its Function and Characteristics," in J. N. Adams and R. G. Mayer, eds., *Aspects of the Language of Latin Poetry* (Oxford, 1999), 289–310.

2

Horace

If Lucilius was the first significant writer of satires, it took Horace to make Satire. Lucilius would have represented merely a divergent, Roman strain of invective, and thus rather a sideshow in classical literary history, were it not for Horace's elaborately self-conscious investment in the genre. Horace gave us the very thing, an invented literary kind, precisely as he consciously designed it. And he gave Rome the tools for thinking about satire as well as the occasion to talk about it by staging his great rivalry with Lucilius: as a way of foregrounding theory, literary theory, satiric theory, Horace picked a fight with the past master. It wasn't a real literary fight, for Lucilius was dead and in no position to knock back. Horace fakes the counter-punches by imagining, having us imagine, Lucilius' fans (*fautores*, 1.10.2–3) criticize his criticisms. But each counterpunch is designed to set up a further counter until Horace is left standing, champ – until, weary of it all, he takes a fall at the botched satiric feast of *Sat.* 2.8. There are a few things to remember about all this, things to keep an eye on as we go on. (1) Satire, Horatian satire, is a conscious invention, rather than another instantiation of an evolving genre. Horace is not "writing satires" in his two books, but inventing and constructing a new literary enterprise. The surprising fact that he struggles to even name them – he doesn't use the word *satura* until his second book – stands as testimony to the experimental nature of the project. (2) If Horace represents the way satire went, Lucilius would forever be the way it might have gone. And this polarity too Horace created. Horace wants his readers to remember, and miss, Lucilius. (3) Horace was taking a big chance. While writing his earliest satires he was at best just "admitted" into the select circle of poets sponsored by Octavian's friend Maecenas; he might have been well-advised to write these works with a degree of discretion, even caution. Yet he made a fuss, not by jumping in with the crowd trying to write the Great Roman Epic, but by making a silk purse out of a sow's ear, bringing trendy Hellenistic aesthetics to crusty old Lucilian satire. If he'd failed, he'd really have failed – written off by the posh dandy Maecenas as just another loony poetaster, and sent packing. He didn't fail.

Just the Facts Please

Horace (65–8 BCE) was born into a modestly prosperous Venusian family. His father was, according to Horace (1.6), a freedman, but it is likely he was never a slave in the traditional sense; rather a captured fighter in the so-called Social War between Rome and its Italian allies (*socii*) in the 90s and 80s BCE, and made a freedman citizen thereafter.[1] In any case, he became prosperous enough as an auctioneer's agent (*coactor*) to move to Rome and send his son to the best tutors there and ultimately to the university city of Athens, where Horace was to meet the young Brutus, shortly after the assassination of Julius Caesar. Brutus recruited Horace to his side in the civil war that ensued and offered him an officer's commission (military tribune). This is a pivotal and telling moment, for Horace was no soldier and, it is likely, no passionate believer in Brutus' republicanism. Like most of us he might have stayed out of that fray, but he knew he was clever, could cope, and this was a *chance* for a young man born into a class that could not expect advancement beyond the financial independence his father could leave him – the *cursus honorum* was for another sort. But if he could just ride the war out, he could claim immediate and automatic equestrian status, an honorary membership in the club. Horace claims to have played the coward's role in that hard war at Philippi (*Odes* 2.7), though that may be a fiction imitating Archilochus,[2] coincidentally self-vindicating: "I was no very prepossessing enemy." And despite Brutus' side losing, Horace did in fact ride it out: general pardon, then a job as *scriba* at the treasury, which offered a nice salary and leisure to write poems. Nothing is known about Horace's real literary apprenticeship, his juvenilia, early experiments, but were these extant, they would likely be impressive; he is in fact one of those few "natural born" poets whose first published works are nearly as mature and finished as his last.

The earliest poems remaining to us are his satires and *Iambi* (Epodes), virtually all masterpieces of their kind. Book 1 of the *Satires* was published in 35 BCE, Book 2 and those iambics saw the light of day in 30 or 29. His first three books of *Odes* came out in 23, Book 1 of the *Epistles* in 20, the second book shortly after the *Carmen Saeculare* (17), most likely, and finally his fourth book of *Odes* in or around 13. Soon after writing his earliest poems, he was introduced by the already prominent poet Vergil to Maecenas roundabout 38, and admission into his astral circle of sponsored poets nine months (sc. to conceive and deliver a lifetime partnership) later ensured the poet's lifelong security. By the end, Horace was close to virtually everyone who mattered in the Augustan regime, including Augustus himself. His last years must have been valetudinarian since his final book of *Odes* is conspicuously autumnal and in his remaining five years he published no more. He died a youngish 57, yet his poetry is of a fullness and finality that seems to require no more.

The roles of serendipity, luck, and what must have been considerable personal charm go just so far in explaining the turns of this poet's life; equally determinative are Horace's calculation, his playing for position, taking the right chances, not taking the wrong, above all crafting his own story. That is where the *Satires* come in. Horace's *Satires* are the first pages of his life-script – and more: they write out a new poetry touching on politics, patronage, and friendship. But there is an essential inwardness to these poems, an access to personality, and a way of communicating what it means and how it feels to be Roman. The most striking feature of this quality is the presence of a consistent and oddly compelling voice. Horace had learned from Ennius and Lucilius that it was possible to make poems in a conversational manner about any number of things, many of them mundane. He had learned from Lucilius that, surprisingly, dactylic hexameter was a pliant enough meter to represent plain speech, *sermo cotidianus*, "everyday talk," and he had also learned from Lucilius that satire could capture something of the self on the page. That self is of course a constructed one; these poems are not confessional and certainly not reliable autobiography. But from the very first words – *qui fit, Maecenas, ut nemo, quam sibi sortem / seu ratio dederit seu fors obiecerit, illa / contentus vivat … ?* ("How does it happen, Maecenas, that no one of us manages to live content with his lot … ?") – we hear the sound of a voice, unmistakable, and not remotely like Ennius or Lucilius or any of his contemporaries.

Listen to it. The first line is full of spondees (feet composed of two long syllables), thus slow, halting, deliberative as if the thought were forming there on the page, then slipping into the natural cadences of the dactyls (a long followed by two shorts) in the second line, pace of words and thought quickening; *qui fit* is utterly casual; the address and hence dedication to his patron, Maecenas, is so economical and without laudatory apparatus as to seem supremely confident or guileless, both valences probably intended. And just as the tone and language are unprepossessing, so is the subject matter, announced with astonishing offhandedness. So spontaneous does it seem that one takes the impression that s/he is *overhearing* an understated monologue in verse. The closest analogue might be Shakespeare's blank verse; the tenor and rhythms of natural speech, rendered in poetry; again, unmistakable. Horace too designates personal bearings. Maecenas is the man he wants to please, yet instead of flattering he includes him in the poem's perspective: let *us* see how people thrash around in their discontents. But Horace knows full well that Maecenas knows that Horace has been one of those thrashers, hopeful of a better lot. The *Satires* is the first great work in his new position as one of Maecenas' poets; they are also the record of his progress, showing us just how he talks his way in.[3]

Diatribe

Horace starts as a stock outsider, literally positioned "outside," in imitation of the streetcorner diatribes of the Cynic philosophers, most notably Bion of Borysthenes, known to us through dicta from pupils and later imitators; Horace refers to his own satires as *Bioneis sermonibus* (*Epistles* 2.2.60). Diatribe, Greek διατριβή, is essentially a developed ethical theme that came to incorporate a number of the features we associate with satire: preachiness, type characters, exemplary fables and anecdotes. It is interesting and important that the first three satires, taking on the manner of the diatribist, are a block, fairly consistent in character and tenor. They are meant to be read/seen together; they lock in an image Horace wants to project: for the nonce, a versifying Bion. The three diatribe poems are followed, then, by an "autobiographical" set of three, 1.4–1.6, poems whose personal focus differs from what we see in the first three. They become the means of letting us into his ideas about and plans for this genre of satire. They are also pivotal in (not?) documenting Horace's acceptance in the patronage circle of Maecenas. The next three poems range outward again into the world, whose conflicts and trials are considered through the fictional modes of anecdote and story; this time, though, Horace presents himself as venturing out from a secure home and the company of people that matter. Finally, a closing tenth poem reprises programmatic ideas broached first in 1.4, while very neatly wrapping up salient ideas found in all the satires from 1.1 onward and stamping a flourishing seal on his own rise to prominence. It is an extremely coherent book,[4] and that coherence is an explicit statement about just what Horatian satire would be: a "naturally" evolving *sequence* of poems, thematically interrelated, drawing numerous strands of story and idea into an artistic whole greater than its component parts. It is the kind of thing contemporary Roman poets, elegists and writers of bucolic and georgic, did in making their poetry books, but no one had done it with such design and coherence in satire, whose poetry was supposed to be occasional, (almost) spontaneous outbursts by an aggrieved witness of wrong or folly. So take this as a starting assumption: Horace is always writing more than satires; each poem in his book is an element of a consciously contrived artistic totality *and* personal history. Any particular satire is never its entire story.

He begins, then, in the manner of Bion. **Satire 1.1** is a sermon on the theme of *mempsimoiria*, discontent with one's lot in life. In good diatribe style, examples are instanced, soldier, merchant, lawyer, farmer, each preferring the life of another; but if, Horace writes, a god should swoop down offering to grant the change, no one would go through with it (1–22). As the poem continues, Horace roams into the related theme of greed or acquisitiveness – it's *that* people can't let go of – eventually to link the two in line 108: "I return now to my starting point, how nobody, because of greed, is happy with himself ... " How much better off we'd all be if we accepted our lots and moderated our desires:

Let there, then, be a limit to your grabbing, and when you've piled up more,
Fear poverty the less; and start to limit your labors
When you've got what you were looking for ... (92–94)

Quotable aphorisms, *sententiae*, anecdotes from mythology and the animal world of fable duly turn up as does that stock butt of critical attention, the miser: canonical elements of Cynic diatribe. So this is what Horace has on offer: a cleverly constructed and elegant rendering of the streetcorner commonplaces of the diatribe in rather refreshingly crafted verse. Or perhaps not. Let us first consider the *appeal* of such a poem. Would anyone, much less the posh Maecenas whose accumulated wealth was legendary, be really interested in a sermon on the dangers of accumulation and discontent and greed? Granted, the message per se is not in any sense unhealthy for any of us to hear; it is good at times to be charmingly chastened. Critics sometimes speak of how Horace draws his readers into the diatribe, seeming initially to target others but then subtly turning attention to endemic weaknesses most of us share (think of the lottery when the stakes get high). Still, this is no Sermon on the Mount; its persuasive power is limited. What, then, *is* its appeal?

To read the poem properly we have to understand how Greek and Roman poets used convention and commonplace. Romans didn't, as we generally do, conceive of poetry as simply the object of aesthetic appreciation, something to be assimilated directly, largely in emotional terms. They thought of it, rather, in terms of "kinds" of verse modalities, genres, configurations or groupings of customary elements – particular meters, conventional characters or figures, certain understandings about what could be expected of such figures, common assumptions about the degree of seriousness expected of poems within given genres. A given poem was never considered a naïve expression of a poet's feelings; rather it was always contextualized or conditioned by what readers could expect once they recognized its literary kind. Yet within that range of expectations a poet had enormous liberty to consider and express ideas "through" generic structures; in fact those structures became the means whereby poets said things. Writers of bucolic or pastoral developed complex themes of emotional reach and power in the stock setting of countryside and illiterate shepherds; writers of georgic composed, in Vergil's case, gorgeous poems on (all but) farm chores. Only in genres like epic or love lyric do the subject matter and the emotional and cognitive impact of the poetry jibe naturally in terms we moderns tend to recognize. In other cases, satire among them, poets use the ordinary, predictable, commonplace, even trivial as a means of saying something else, certainly more. If we come to Horace's satires expecting to be captivated by the narrative thrill of the poem, we'll soon put down the book. But it all becomes very interesting once we understand how a Roman would read it: presented with an opening exercise in Bionian mode, he would ask "why this discourse?" and "what's the game our friend Horace is up to?" And while the diatribe model offers enough similarity to the much more varied and unpredictable verse of Lucilius to register the fact that this is still (not quite Lucilian) satire, the Bionian face Horace shows his readers here serves to mark difference, even a kind of satiric insurrection. Assumptions about any direct mapping of critical attention, poet to a specified real target out here in society, are put immediately to rest. Satire isn't going to do all that anymore. Rather, it's going to be a kind of everyman's rumination on the parlous state of things – with implications.

Those implications are in part generic theorizing. This is a favorite theme of modern critics who point out the apparent connection between the idea in 62, *nil satis est* ("nothing is enough"), with attendant moralizing about limiting desire and acquisitive labors, and root meanings of *satura*: a plate piled high, overstuffed. If satire in its root sense is all about overstuffing poems, or books of poems, with this and that, Horace would innovate by reading the pun negatively: (new) satire is about defining limits, finding satisfaction with *satis*, enough (117–119):

> Thus how rare it is to find someone who can say he's lived a happy life,
> who content with his given span, departs life as
> a satisfied guest (*conviva satur*); "that's enough" (*iam satis est*)[5]

It is hard not to feel the truth of this argument; the pun, *satur/satis*, is so obvious. And as Freudenburg points out, Horace's last words, *verbum non amplius addam* ("I'll not add another word"), demonstrate that "he, the poet who writes the poem and 'defines' its beginning and end, has found the very thing that the pile-obsessed fools inside the poem were so notoriously unable to find; that basic 'enough' of nature,"[6] and, as he goes on to say, of poetry. This is all as "programmatic" as a poem can be without coming out and being explicit about it, as he will in 1.4. This decision to preview his program is doubtless part of the program: this first satire, Horace so much as says, is already written for a selected audience: literate, learned enough to know something about the literary values of restraint and control that came to Rome from the Greek poet and literary scholar Callimachus (c. 305–240 BCE) through neoterics, "new poets," like Catullus (83–53 BCE) and others, well-connected (for there is self-interest and promotion in all this too), intellectually curious. The appeal of this metapoetic aspect of the satire can only have extended to this small group of readers, readers able to discern the subtle challenge in this apparently (only apparently) loose collection of moralizing commonplaces. Hence, that opening address to Maecenas, shorthand for so much.

The first satire's targets – discontented farmer, soldier, lawyer, merchant, perpetually greedy miser – are of course stock figures "out there in the world." Easy for a reader to dismiss or avoid implication, until Horace breaks the illusion of quiet rumination with Maecenas and addresses the reader: "Why laugh? Switch out the name and this story's on you" (69–70). The reader has been tricked; thinking he was eavesdropping on a quiet little tirade, he suddenly finds himself drawn into the fabric of the poem: "*you* heap up sacks of money, agape over them even as you sleep … " (70–71). Maybe *you* can say you have no such moneybags (that's somebody else), and go back to enjoying the satire, but for a moment Horace had you worried. He might have had Maecenas, who possessed the stuff in piles, a little worried too. With the lightest of touches Horace has shown he can be just a little serious – that greed really is a problem (isn't it?). Horace's successor in satire, Persius, characterized Horace along these lines: "sly Flaccus, slipping inside, toys with the very vitals of his laughing friend, ferreting out every fault" (Persius, *Sat.* 1.116–117). Horace himself in rather a famous passage writes (23–27),

as to the rest, lest I run through this thing like someone telling a series of jokes –
but what's wrong with telling the truth with a laugh?
Like encouraging teachers who give cookies to schoolkids
so they learn their elements?
But, joking aside, let's examine these things seriously …

Horace is not quite diatribist here, much less pedantic Stoic, nor quite court jester, Shakespearian fool, or parasite, but rather some original version of genial truth-teller with a twist. If one takes the lines above as seriously indicative of his intent, s/he might notice a few things: there is some "truth" here under discussion; Horace is assuming a role as a teacher of sorts; he wants to be a well-liked teacher; he adopts a condescending attitude toward his students (schoolkids = Maecenas & readers), yet keeps his temerity within acceptable social bounds, the limits in fact prescribed by the joke. The (serious) diatribe presumes a speaker from outside the social circle of his targets; even, or especially, when that outsider is of a lower class, a certain authority accrues to his words, the authority of the penniless prophet, disinterested soothsayer. This is Horace's "original" position, tagging him the moment he adopts the language of diatribe. The joke, on the other hand, is a discourse of insiders; it only works, or works best, within shared social perspectives; the joke is on someone else. To tell the truth with a joke, as Horace proposes to do, is an almost paradoxical project. The truth must, in the end, be one acceptable to appreciators of the joke, and what kind of truth is that? What kind of truth-teller can Horace be?

The manner is the man. Horace too is between social stations as he writes this satire, freedman's son to protégé of Maecenas. Like the malcontents he describes in his first twenty-two lines, Horace has longed for a change in his life, one not coincidentally involved with accumulating a comfortable pile. Horace's joke is on Horace too, and he designed it that way. In the long section, from 23 to 107, detailing ways in which people go too far in their greedy heaping up (and moralizing about moderation), Horace thus sets up a multiple focus:

What good does it do secretly, fearfully, to bury in the ground
a huge weight of silver and gold? (41–42)

Tell me what difference it makes to one living within nature's limits
whether he plows a hundred or a thousand acres? (49–51)

But a goodly portion of people, deceived by greed, say
'nothing is enough, because you're valued according to what you have.' (61–62)

In brief, there should be a limit to your acquisition ... (92)

There is a right measure of things, certain limits,
this or that side of which you won't find the proper course. (106–107)

These are all attractive little saws. Harmlessly edifying enough if one reads them for their general ethical guidance. Readers might, on the other hand, get the idea that easy condescension toward this message might be a little dangerous: Horace is well aware that he is writing to an affluent audience, his first audience in his first poem, and they in turn are aware that Horace is up to something tricky in his experiment in satire. "Switch out the name and the story's on you." Just how much of the story is on Horace's wealthy betters would be, for the alert, an open question. But the story's on Horace too, as we have seen, and this long passage frequently reiterating the same theme, hammering home the thought that one ought to be content with *satis*, enough, has to be at least in large part Horace's own *apologia pro vita sua*, a description of the limits of his own ambition.

For Horace took a political chance in claiming to write satire as an outsider-become-insider, to jokingly truth-tell: it was a dangerous game. This opening poem is, therefore, full of assurances that he won't go too far, there is a proper limit after all. He won't, he tells us specifically, go as far as the Stoics go in their inflexible dogmatizing: *iam satis est* ... (120–121):

> now that's enough; so that you don't think I've plundered the desk
> of the blear-eyed [Stoic] Crispinus, I'll not add another word.

Nor will he go as far as Lucilius in attacking the enemies of his friends. He reiterates all this, as we'll see, in 1.4. History has read all this moderation critically; John Dryden in the seventeenth century (see Chapter 5) called Horace "a Temporizing Poet, a well Manner'd Court Slave, and a Man who is often afraid of Laughing in the right place."[7] Yet this verdict is more than unfair. It is easy to appreciate, as did Dryden, the free-wheeling *libertas*, the unafraid aggressiveness of Lucilius, similarly the rock-hard principle of the Stoic preacher. For what is more appealing than simple answers to big questions, especially when the actions and motives of others are in question? Horace sets his satire "between" *libertas* and the preacher's ethics, and that is a far trickier, in the end far more ambitious, place to work. Horace's experiment with satire then, his first poem tells us, is to try on this "middling" persona and craft a satire that works subtly from within. What will emerge is neither bravado from a safe place (Lucilius) nor formulaic certainty about right and wrong (Crispinus et al.), but rather a kind of exploration – that will not go too far, Horace repeatedly tells us: there is a limit, there really, really is (why, the reader has to ask, all that overkill of the same message, 104 lines of it). A limit to what? To accumulated wealth, certainly, but also to affront and challenge of the status quo, to sheer volume of words (decorously slender these satires – all but the ones featuring gassy Stoics, *Sat.* 2.3 and 2.7), to personal ambition, to asking hard questions, to making his auditors uncomfortable, to making them work and even think a little ...

Or so he keeps saying. Ironically, Horace in claiming in this first satire not to go too far disguises his plan to go farther into the unknown territory of the social and political dynamics of Rome's ruling classes than anyone had gone before. *Verbum non amplius addam* is his close to Satire 1.1, "I won't add another word." Then, on *into* the fabric of Roman society, the minds and hearts of his auditors, in 1.2, 1.3 . . . – and many more words.

Satire 1.2 also has its beginnings in diatribe, this time originating in a Roman model, Lucretius 4.1058–1287, his diatribe on love, one of the two great "satiric" swatches in the great didactic poem on Epicurean philosophy (the other on the fear of dying, 3.830ff.). But compounding that model are a number of lines we can locate in the Lucilian corpus that plainly underlie the poem as well (see pp. 21–2). Horace's satire initially picks up the ostensible theme of 1.1; there is a mean between extremes. Like 1.1, *Sat.* 1.2 is structured by a short twenty-some line introduction followed by a long section that veers into related but different territory; in this case, that territory is not money but sex. The poem is Horace's extended meditation on the most satisfying sexual arrangements for one of his ilk. The extremes in this Aristotelian construction of sexual choice – prostitutes or matrons – bring with them difficulties of all sorts, embarrassment, expense, peril, delusion. The preferred mean (available freedwomen, whose unproblematic status tends to slip away in Horace's self-ironizing treatment) is said, ostensibly, to offer carefree satisfaction: "available sex, for I want accessible and easy love" (119). Michael Coffey's verdict is succinct: "[the satire's] ethics are base, but it is at least free from hypocrisy."[8]

The poem as a whole is not easy to pin down. Plentiful Lucilian inspiration makes what Horace says here suspect enough: is this really an account of the man Horace's views on sex? Or is it a loose imitation of Lucilian perspectives, jiggered to fit a later day? Or is it, in adapting Lucilius, a study in Horatian self-portraiture: the poet in this early satire crafting the image of the easy Epicureanism that will follow him throughout his poetry, a comfortable, not too scrupulous, moderately indulgent literary man? Or is it a "satire" of some*thing* (and if so, what?)? As often with Horace, none of the options sufficiently account for the subtlety of the satire, but the reader could begin by looking at the most evident quality of the poem, its frankness, a candor that taps into the social problematics always at the margins of Horace's poetry. On the face of it, Horace's dirty talk about sex in this poem designates Lucilian *libertas*, "freedom" of speech, the satirist's impunity to say what he wants. There is a scarcely disguised political dimension as well: *libertas* is not "freedom" in the idealized modern sense – though even now the word is nearly always vested in political interest and partiality. For Romans, *libertas* was openly a function of privilege and power in a world where all were not equal. In this poem about male sexual gratification and who is placed in its service, *libertas* is then an expression of the inequities built into Rome as a political and social place, and Horace evidently sides with those on top.[9] But while Lucilius and Horace both speak from, or from near, circles of social and political authority, enjoying thereby the *libertas* to exercise the expressive prerogatives of their somewhat different social positions, there is for Horace the curious complication of the diatribe model he is playing with in these opening poems, which *theoretically* transcends, in its reach of maxim and ethical exhortation, local social stratification.[10] Limned behind the political authority of this familiar of the powerful is the perennially licensed *and insubordinate* truth-teller, the informing *Geist* for which comes from the underclass of streetcorner philosophers. The satirist's voice has about it from the start, thus, even in the authority that underwrites its freedom to speak its power, a self-consciously shifting valence that anticipates or patterns further lability. To speak with clout Horace mimes Bionic diatribe, hints at the imperatives of popular ethics, and echoes Lucilian brazenness as well as invokes traditional assumptions about who counts in Roman society. These are not all, on the face of it, natural bedfellows.

Further complication arises from the interface of the satirist's discourse world and the reader's perspective as "outsider." Remember, Horace begins writing his diatribe satires as an outsider to the privileged circle he will come to join; he is aware of boundaries, distinctions, limits, plays with them, and in this case conceives of his poetry as a medium of certain shared (insider) values, even while being written and in some senses read from without. We should not be surprised, then, to see indications of his writing to an outsider-reader, as designated receptor of the poem *qua* poem. This satiric discourse will be seen both as mapped onto the social world it describes and as marked literary language directed to a certain audience. That readerly audience may well be the "same" in most respects as that described within the satire, may share assumptions about the satire's subjects, about sex, women, status, and pleasure, but is different, too, in its (potential) cognizance of satire as an artificial literary medium. Horace's poem, as we've seen, builds that awareness in, making his own satire of and about other satire. Builds in, that is to say, a dynamic of literary reception that at once asserts authorial/authoritative perspective and a reader's potential restiveness, a counter-authority, which is, in minimal terms, simply an awareness larger than that enframed by the rhetorical world of the satire.

This dynamic of potentially contesting views, a shifting or instability of perspective, operates throughout the poem, even the satire's jokes, as, early on in the poem, Horace's retelling of the infamous Cato Censor anecdote (31–36):

When the young man emerged from the brothel,
"good work!" was the inspired verdict of Cato:
"for whenever foul lust swells their veins,
it's a good thing for the young to come on down here
rather than drill at other men's wives." "I'd rather not be praised for *that*,"
says Cupiennius, fancier of cunts robed in white (*cunni ... albi*).

One could say this is just an *outré* example of the poem's frequently noticed moderation theme, avoiding extremes; lust directed in legitimate directions; Cato in a worldly wise vein designed to disarm readerly second thought. But second thought is structured into the passage. The apocryphal story of Cato, apparently from a collection of *apophthegmata*, had been circulated and then dropped by Horace into this satire precisely because of the irony it encapsulates: that of stern moralist cheering on the promiscuous young man, paragon of virtue encouraging "foul lust" (*taetra libido*).[11] We may call this merely a literary turn; the irony justifies, explains, the anecdotal exemplum; but that would disarm the paradox: virtue that implicates vice, that finds an alter ego in low (*taetra* – Cato/Horace's word) sexual gratification. Cato and the promiscuous young aristocrat (*notus homo*) are obverse facets of the same coin, the *ethos* of the male, freeborn Roman. Cato and the boys about town take their pleasure in those over whom they have long-standing and unquestioned institutional power: prostitutes in this case; women in general in the larger scheme, or slaves, of both sexes. Even married aristocratic women – the crude description focalized through Cupiennius, *cunni albi*, enfigures them precisely as sexual conveniences. John Henderson's engaging take on the satire as gendered discourse reads the poem this way, how Roman man sees and uses woman-as-sex:

In 1.2 [Horace] turns his all-seeing eye from money to sex ... Something else the "I" of *men* can have: basic "*property*" ... He finds "us" unbalanced and excessive, using up our resources unwisely on the wrong females. He looks to what you might (not) like to call "the mentality of the amorous male." As he ticks off silly-billies for making such a mess over sex – clowns to the left and jokers to the right – ,

expensive mistresses and dangerous adulteries, all *that* (*You* know ...),
H and his readers can enjoy looking over "the field." *Without* feeling
im-plicated.[12]

The gendering of Horace's language in this poem designates perspective, so much so that it is hard not to read it as just Horace's univocal
version of male-speak, his particular *parole* in the greater *langue* of
anti-feminist role-making and metaphorizing.[13] Yet satire as gendered
writing, as a certain kind of very explicit patriarchal discourse, of
generically empowered male voice, telling things as they are from a
certain perspective, may (intentionally or not) expose that discourse
when the politics of reading and writing are likewise made explicit.
And comic irony, that literary turn, is obtrusive and not without
importance. Cato's "solution" is really viable only in the conceptual
world of the joke. Here, male satisfaction, that gendered desideratum,
slips into that discursive space where reality is suspended, where Cato
can become sensualist, and the whorehouse a club for civic-minded
young men. The world of the joke is, of course, a modal transposition
where not only are reality's norms and limits suspended, expectations
inverted, and so forth, but where wit itself takes on a tendentious cast.
Jokes create temporary communities of insiders, and in so doing
release resentments, desires, aggressions. They are instinct with partiality and ideology. In the case of Horace's Cato joke, the partiality and
ideology are manifest; but their literary framing as joke generates a
fracture in the literary texture of the satire. The joke thus not only
echoes other instances of *parti pris* in the poem, it lifts all that baggage
into a discursive register where it is to be seen as both *only* and *more
than* a joke. Cupiennius, then, who is conspicuously placed as auditor
of the joke, figures for the reader who also listens in, reacts "appro-
priately" – "not me, I don't want *that* kind of praise." And we know
why. Horace makes it clear where Cupiennius stands in relation to the
joke, but the reader, perhaps (one hopes) not sharing Cupiennius'
moral compass, or perhaps sharing it but not comfortable when the
disposition becomes explicit, is left to sort out his or her place, inside
or outside the joke's rhetorical world-view. And that leaves a fissure in
the joke's (and attendant ideology's) closure. Despite all the nasty
certainties of cultural assumption implicit in it, the joke's essence is a
play of excess, transience, and, finally, interrogation; not "common
sense" or the (Horatian, Roman, "our"[?]) considered view. After it
passes, we are left with no authorized sense of right and wrong, wise

and foolish, or viable "middle" ground. Whatever real solution Horace may have dreamed up, it is not here in some Aristotelian mean, and his joke tells us so. The reader (outsider-insider) is quite explicitly drawn into all this, smiles his or even her way into that Cato-story's appealing "unexpectedness" (*para prosdokian*), thus into the poem's poised undecidability. As the reader walks straight into Horace's satiric, ironic word-web, just who is spider in the *middle* (the middle way that has become the antithesis of safe mediocrity) of all that, and who is fly, all entangled in sticky satire's trap, remains a question.[14]

Satire 1.3, while still recognizably a diatribe satire, seems initially very different from 1.2 and, in many respects, from 1.1. It is considerably tamer in subject manner than the poem preceding and its tenor more subdued and domestic than either of the other two. But as we'll see, it draws significantly on its predecessors and brings Horace's experiment with diatribe-satire to a provisional formulation. The addressee in this satire, we learn late in the poem, is Maecenas, and much of the poem seems to turn on features of the friendship between Horace and his patron, both in a personal sense and in the uniquely Roman sense of *amicitia*. Again we have a short opening section, this time featuring Tigellius, recently deceased in 1.2, as an example of someone whose life and habits were a mass of contradictions: *nil aequale homini fuit illi* "nothing steady in the man" (9). That's a lead-in to a moralizing "it's easy to criticize others but not oneself" (19–24), which in turn shifts into an extended riff on the hyperseverity of judgments we pass on one another, a plea for tolerance and regard to the bright side of our friends (25–95). He touches on the genesis and proper character of justice (96–124), and concludes the poem with a slam on the Stoics for their notoriously severe and inflexible "justice" in respect of the peccadilloes of people like Horace – and his friends.

That friendship focus is important for Horace. It inaugurates a preoccupation that will occupy the *Satires* and *Epistles* predominantly, Horace's poetry of friendship. The first book of satires alone will see it recur in 1.4, 1.5, 1.6, 1.9, and 1.10. These poems, and all the others, explore not only dimensions of mutual affection and trust, but also the politics of *amicitia*, the competitive infrastructure of patronage, the cutthroat, exclusionary world of class, prestige, and power. Friendship for Horace is also, more than a wide-ranging preoccupation, a goal; friendship with the well-connected is the aspired-for career destination of a young man of non-aristocratic breeding. Yet more than the *arriviste*'s snobbery, this friendship of Horace's entails intimacy and genuine affection, the dream home that Horace, against all odds, was somehow able to find his way to. *Sat.* 1.3, then, while, crucially, closing his book-initiating exercise in diatribe, is Horace's first adumbration of the social dynamics of the circle of Maecenas. The manner of the satire suits: the diatribe that had begun as paradigmatic outsider's speech in 1.1 has now acquired the intimate registers of insider's talk. The only vestige of diatribe in this poem is its harping on a theme ("let's be tolerant of one another's quirks"); there is closure and transition in this. From this point onward Horace's satire will be able to presume connection and affiliation to the highest circles of Roman power, however humble and self-ironizing the persona that the poet projects. The obvious satiric nature of diatribe now will yield to a different satire, Horace's very own – that is to say, a projection from a world that has *become* his very own.

We see this almost immediately. After the first, generalizing 24 lines ("some people are masses of contradictions, but let us be careful about so easily criticizing 'them' "), Horace lets us *in*:

> When you look at your own flaws through sore, medicated eyes
> why do you look into friends' quirks
> eagle-eyed, snake-eyed?
> The problem is that they look your way too.
> He's a little irritable, a little bedraggled for high society.
> You could laugh at him for his rustic haircut
> or the unstylish drift of his toga
> or for his loose shoes. But he's a good fellow.
> You won't find a better. And he's your friend.
> A huge talent under that uncouth form. (25–34)

The blear eyes are Horace's; he's daubing them with ointment heavily in *Sat.* 1.5, a chronic condition. Here he ascribes them to the provisionally anonymous interlocutor, perhaps the reader – both turn out in the end to be Maecenas who is finally identified in line 64. Maecenas is meant to recognize the reversal and have fun with it: who's the one with sore eyes? Just as he's meant to recognize the "Horace" projected in lines 29 and following: the irritable, sloppy, unstylish, talented Horace we see so often in the rest of his corpus. It is the same Horace "seen" by Damasippus and Davus, Stoic slaves who lecture the poet mercilessly in *Sat.* 2.3 and 2.7. The diatribic *exempla* here are in short not the stock litany, but from the real and intimate world of Maecenas' society. That tweaks the force of the general exhortation: how much can this be about how we "all" need to be more forgiving when crucial points of recognition are interpersonal winks and nods? This is actually a serious programmatic question that will be taken up in the poem immediately following, the so-called "first" of the programmatic satires, 1.4. *Sat.* 1.3 is a canny prolegomenon to that treatment.

The satire also resumes ideas from the earlier two in its sequence. The experiment with writing between Lucilian *libertas* and the preacher's diatribe, from a perspective precariously, (even) insidiously within the fabric of the satirized world, continues here even more explicitly. There is too the play of perspectives so integral to the mechanics of *Sat.* 1.2: "the problem is that they look your way too ..." And in that initial gambit about bleared eyes, the theme of how and what you see takes over the poem: *illuc praevertamur* ("let's focus here") in line 38 draws us into the authorized view of the poem as it instances the ways in which lovers overlook one another's blemishes; shouldn't friends do the same (38–42)?

> ... defects of a beloved escape the notice
> of the lover, blind to them, or perhaps they actually
> please him, as Hagna's wart did Balbinus.
> I'd like it if we made the same oversights in friendship
> and virtue could give an honorable name to such error.

The euphemism goes on; parents do the same with their children, softening blemishes with friendly nicknames (44–48):

> ... **strabonem**
> appellat **paetum** pater, et **pullum**, male parvus
> sicui filius est, ut abortivus fuit olim
> Sisyphus; hunc **varum** distortis cruribus, illum
> balbutit **scaurum** pravis fultum male talis.

> (The father calls his squinting son "cast-eye"
> or "chick" if he's stunted as Sisyphus once was;
> this one, "little knock-knee" if his legs are
> grossly bent; this one "wobbly"
> if he teeters on his wrecked ankles.)

But these instances of affectionate understatement are not just any old nicknames; they are in fact noble Roman cognomina: Strabo, Paetus,

Varus, Pullus, Scaurus. Once again, Horace's sly glance to *his* audience: this is how *we* see our families and friends. The next lines (49ff.) generalize on the theme, but soon Horace returns to the society that matters: "say someone's rather too straightforward, as sometimes / I am to you, Maecenas, perhaps interrupting / one's reading or thinking" (63–65). And it may be that, as some have said, Horace is instancing himself when he itemizes some of the more venial sins a companion may commit: "having drunk a bit too much, he's pissed the couch / or knocked a rare, old bowl from the table, or maybe / in his hungry zeal he's grabbed a chicken put on my side of the serving plate / – should I think him a less charming friend? / Or what would I do if he swiped a little something, / let slip a confidence, or reneged on a pledge?" (90–95).

Finally, in its last 48 lines, Horace broadens the satire to a mock disquisition on the nature and origin of justice, targeting the Stoics who claimed that Nature and Reason prescribed absolute standards of right and wrong, and duly severe punishments. "Let us rather / apply a standard (*regula*) that sorts punishments to the degree of offence" (117–118) – so much saner than the absurd absolutism of Chrysippus and (the lesser spokesman) Crispinus (124–143), right? It *is* all very sane: the forgiving discourse among friends projected across society. But is it satire? Doesn't satire go after human fault and frailty? Paradoxically, the only sharply targeted object of satire in this poem is the Stoic propensity for harsh rebuke. Clearly the Stoics, then, are standing in for a traditional vision of satire, how satire usually sees the world, aggressively, sharply, censoriously; in his only censorious moment in the poem, Horace targets these very Stoics and, by extension, Lucilius and "satire as it has been." It is a marvelously clever reversal that identifies Horace as part of an exclusive social circle, disarms any suspicion that this new satirist will be on the lookout for targets among his friends, declares a perspective on the world that is, precisely, a shared and authorized one, and subtly announces a new modality for satire, a satiric discourse "about the world" in terms radically different from those laid down by Lucilius – and he does this without even mentioning his great predecessor's name. Finally, and most subtly, he embeds a hint that his new satire may not be *entirely* toothless sycophancy; for he has not, conspicuously not, been fair or nice to those Stoics. Nor *should* traditional satire be fair or nice. Horace can do Lucilian satire, then, and perhaps will, in his own way and time. But that's the story of 1.4.

Re-Programming

Satire 1.4 is the first of the so-called programmatic satires. That means it seems to lay out a literary program, a theory of what Horatian satire is or wants to be. Other such poems are *Sat.* 1.10 and 2.1; all are related. Program poems are a common feature of Latin poetry, tracing its influence back to the Greek poet Callimachus (see p. 34) who paradigmatically laid out the principles according to which his own verse was to differ from "classical" Greek poetry. It should not surprise us, then, to see program here in satire, though we might wonder why Horace does not do the conventional thing and put his program up front, at the beginning of his book, or why he feels it necessary to continue the metapoetic talk through two other substantial poems and parts of several others. But we have already seen that Horace "talks" about his theory of satire in *Sat.* 1.1 through 1.3, and 1.4 (while it may have been written even earlier than 1.1 or 1.3) emerges out of the diatribe satires as a natural programmatic consolidation. Programmatic talk is in fact pervasive in Horace, a fact that reflects the self-consciousness of the genre, as we've already mentioned, but since there is more of it in Horace than in either Persius or Juvenal, we know something more than generic insecurity is involved. Reprogramming satire is not just something that Horace "has to do" in making his mark on the genre, but something he pushes, thematizing it, in his two books of satires: how to do satire is centrally part of what Horace's satire is about. The preoccupation marks out these poems from his books of *Epistles*, often lumped together with the satires in critical discussion. The *Epistles* are more desultory, more chatty, even more philosophical, hexameter poems, but they lack this explicit self-description *qua* "satire," constructed before our eyes, overlaid with plans and jottings, thoughts and second thoughts, on "how this particular poetry should be." Horace never lets go of this in any of his satires, but he foregrounds it conspicuously in 1.4, 1.10, and 2.1. Discussion of *Sat.* 1.4 will be developed at somewhat greater length that the rest, since it broaches central ideas that the others will modify.

Horace begins 1.4 almost in midstream, as if he had been talking about this subject all along: (paraphrasing) "The old comic poets, Eupolis, Cratinus, Aristophanes, went right after crooks and thieves, adulterers and killers; now, Lucilius does the same, wholly dependent on them, just the meter changed" (1–7). Horace seems to be explaining himself, defending his satire against the charge that it has been too aggressive; so he claims the authority of Old Comedy and of his major predecessor Lucilius. But Lucilius wasn't perfect, he goes on to say in 8–16: "clever and witty he was, but clumsy in composing his hexameters, and he did rattle on, like a muddy stream you'd want to clean up a bit." At this point Horace signals his difference from Lucilius on aesthetic grounds, declaring for Hellenistic principles deriving from Callimachus: he draws in fact the critical image of the muddy river from Callimachus' *Hymn to Apollo*.[15] Shifting back to the theme of attack in satire, he claims that human folly cries out for poetic redress and that most of us for that reason resent poets, but asserts (lest we fret about that redress) that he is no real poet, for his plain *sermo* has not the fire and pitch of real poetry. Nor does he go out of his way to affront anyone (70–78), or attack friends behind their backs (79–103). But any sense of right and wrong, the basis of his modest criticism, he learned from his good and simple father (104–143).

Horace puts on offer here something new; we'll call him the "new satirist" – the new satirist talking about *his* art. Horace here, bold even in offering to public view his mask of modesty, is setting out to create a new discourse world at the margins of what he would have called traditional satire. Horace or his speaker opens the poem by instancing "the poets Eupolis, Cratinus, and Aristophanes" for the sole reason (apparently) of invoking their satiric authority, that is, their representation of that iambographic tradition of satire – the connection represented in Diomedes: *carmen maledicum* ... ("abusive poetry written in the manner of Old Comedy to attack the vices of humankind").

Horace writes at line 3–5:

> If anyone seemed to deserve to be called a scoundrel or thief,
> an adulterer or assassin, or otherwise notorious
> they used to go right out and brand him.

That Old Comedy fairly represents this traditional conception of the satiric is true. Yet this is only a partial reading of the character of Old Comedy, which is concerned with the project of attacking vice only along the way to more central concerns. Thus comedy's and satire's being defensibly part of the tradition of personal and social criticism along with invective, diatribe, epigram, (some) didactic and more is no argument for generic identity or function, especially in a literary world where there is such heightened awareness of the canonicity and hierarchy of genres; Horace makes his knowing this clear in lines to follow. The question raised is for us: how are we to place this enacting, generic triangulation? Lucilius comes next (6–7):

> Lucilius depends entirely on them, following them
> with but altered rhythms and meters.

Again, Lucilius does plausibly follow in the comic invective *tradition*, but Horace has it *hinc omnis pendet* – *entirely* derives from them, and this is clearly not true in one obvious sense: Lucilius did not write Old Comedy with but changed meter. The misstatement flags an issue, an awkward hitch in the logic of argument. But it is not just a case of one genre (problematically) leading (or not) to another, sharing pedigrees or elements. Horace's invocation of Eupolis, Cratinus, Aristophanes, and Lucilius locates crucial relationships, and the common assumption has been to see them as continuous – sharing somehow the *Geist* of satire's job, a job he wants to take on in his own way. This is of course a customary way of thinking of satire, as a "modality" of expression in contradistinction to a specified genre – the former being how satire is often conceived today. It is possible, however, to see Horace's lumping together of four individual poets as performing an alienating rather than proximating function. Lucilius is not quite the same as the writers of Old Comedy. Placing them together can effectively mark out distance between an older iambographic generic identity and the new; these writers are similar in all being not-Horace. The point of specific difference between new and old is stylistic, with Lucilius the target (6–13):

> Lucilius depends entirely on them, following them
> with but altered rhythms and meters. Something of a wit,
> with a keen nose, but crude when it came to versification.
> That's where his weakness was. He would often
> dictate a couple hundred lines an hour, standing on one foot.
> He was a clogged river with a lot of stuff that should have been removed.
> A man of many words, he disliked the effort of writing –
> writing properly, that is . . .

After casting satire as a traditional modality, he attacks it, in precisely those terms, and attacks Lucilius in a manner that doesn't exactly adopt the tolerant eye of *Sat.* 1.2. Horace's own satire will not be traditional; nor will it be a modality, simply an expression of the satiric. The counter-values he proposes are the "labor of writing" (*scribendi* ... *laborem* [12]) and "writing properly" (*scribendi recte* [13]), which are the valorized terms espoused by the Hellenistic aesthetics fashionable in Horace's generation: economy valued over abundance, formal control over direct or naïve expression, labor and craftsmanship over spontaneity. These are in fact the aesthetic bearings of Horace's entire corpus. It is interesting that he need not have gone after Lucilius in these terms. Lucilius' exceptional learning, cultured sophistication, metrical experiment and invention, his own exacting metrical and compositional studies (Bk. IX), and stylistic ingenuity are all overlooked in Horace's reading, making it clear that he caricatures Lucilius here, presents him to us readers in singular, memorable, and rather down at heels dress. *This* bold, aristocratic scourge of the city has something of the vulgar about him – and so the vulgar poetasters Crispinus and Fannius are made to join the company, an insinuating equation between an indubitably great poet and the scribblers. The rhetorical gambit fools no one but the most naïve (for instance, those he defends himself against in *Sat.* 1.10, *adversarii* for the occasion); Horace rather *shows* us the process of Lucilius's antiquing, painting over the yellow glaze so thickly that only broad, prominent outlines show through. And behind that film, another layer, with just the shadows of Aristophanes and his generic kin – all but some vague family resemblance gone. The art is in the doing it, demonstrating all the while how it is done. Horace, among Lucilius' other readers, cannot but know what is left out in this portrait; and so a doubled perspective, literary portrayal as a kind of negative allusion "intended to" but of course not able to disremember a literary antecedent. The reader recalls Lucilius in some greater wholeness, despite the obliterating caricature, and the distance between Lucilius and his Horatian version corresponds to that between the poem's Horace and the poet himself. Each writer, as represented in the satire, plays a role, stands for a certain kind of satire, even while the poem foregrounds the omissions necessary to enable the fictive contestation. But in immediately homing in on "style" Horace hints at a more radical shift. This style will not be just how Horace writes, as opposed to Lucilius, but fixes any literate Roman's attention on the conception of genre, that is on the formal distinctions among poetries. Horace in effect declares that he is now writing satire as genre – and that is new.

It is surprising, then, to hear what he says in lines 39–44:

> First, I'd exclude myself from those I might properly call
> poets. Nor would *you* say it were enough simply to write
> something in meter. Nor, if someone wrote the way I do,
> in a style more akin to prose, would you call him a poet.
> Whoever has the genius, a higher mind, a voice capable of
> great things; this one you'd call a poet.

You can easily see irony here, especially in that last line, and it is
certainly possible if you look closely, as many have done, to see the
artful arrangement of this *sermo* which does, in fact, distinguish it from
comedy, despite the generic consonance on the level of poetic diction
that Horace takes rather elaborate pains to point out. It may well be
that Horace intended readers to see through this apologia. Yet
declaring what "real" poetry is – though he is not quite up to it – is
again to valorize the kind of aesthetic qualities that distinguish dog-
gerel from poetry, and quite possibly modal satire (Lucilius & Co.)
from the more finished, polished work, satire as genre, he aspires to.
And that modesty, that negativity, has a point as well. He has constructed a speaker's identity defined through a conspicuous counter-
typology: not forerunner Lucilius who swashbuckled his way through
Roman rascality; not contemporary Stoic-poetaster Crispinus who, like
the prolific Lucilius and vainglorious Fannius (see lines 14–22),
shamelessly churned the stuff out. Instead we have (thus negatively
described) shy and modest "Horace," too abashed to swashbuckle or
even recite publicly, too dim to have any really interesting thoughts.
And he's happy about it, for it keeps him off the spot (17–18; 21–24):

> The gods did well by me, making me timid,
> seldom speaking and even then saying little ...
> ... Fannius is happy with his offer of free bookcases
> and self-portraits to readers of his verse. But no one reads mine;
> I'm a little afraid to recite publicly for this reason:
> there are those who dislike this kind of writing ...

This Horatian persona is a functional element of the fabric of the
poem. It is a portrait that scarcely disguises a carefully plotted critical
mapping and marks out generic ground in relation to established
authority and school.

Horace's new formulation creates its own foundation myth. Having
established a congruency of satiric spirit between the writers of Old
Comedy and Lucilius, he establishes a similar relationship between

New Comedy and his own satire. Again, not, as in the earlier case, just to establish generic identity, but to develop its idea, that is to show how it is a created, modeled world of language, within which selected aspects of reality and experience are configured coherently. Horace manages this through his talk of fathers. Lucilius is the rejected father figure, Horace's strong precursor, and his speaker's anxiety of influence is conspicuous. Later in the poem (103ff.) Horace will instance at length another filial relationship, where he explains how his father's assiduous ethical training has led him to write as he does (103–115):

> ... Yet if I
> speak rather too freely, if I get a bit jokey, I hope you'll
> grant me this excuse: my good father accustomed me to this;
> so that I might avoid vice, he'd warn me away by noting bad examples.
> When he'd urge me to live sparingly, frugally, and
> content with what he himself had saved for me, he'd say:
> "Don't you see what a wretched life young Albius leads and how Baius
> is down and out – a salutary warning not to be so quick
> to squander one's inheritance." Steering me away from a squalid attachment
> to a prostitute he would say: "Don't be like Scetanus!" To stop me
> chasing someone else's wife when legitimate sex was available:
> "It isn't nice to get a name like that of Trebonius – he
> was caught in the act" ...

Sometimes this passage is read naïvely, as genuine autobiography; more usually, it is pointed out that the passage derives from New Comic roots.[16] For Horace's father, as presented here, is a character drawn from comedy, specifically Demea from Terence's *Adelphoe* (see especially 441–443). But just as Lucilius' satire is not Old Comedy hexametered, Horace's version of all this is not New Comedy, with its very different literary objectives and appeals; instead, and precisely, it is a catalogue of the subject matter, the *res*, of his art, drawn from the various corners of the related literary past and reconstituted in *satiric* idiom: prostitutes, other men's wives, squandered inheritances, scandal, gluttony, and the rest. Thus, satiric father leading satiric son (and his readers) through this poetry's brave new world, pointing out the things satire, or the new satirist, should notice – and the things it shouldn't: no criticism of Caesar's foibles here. Moral edification, or reminiscence of same, or even the moral force of satire's overt criticisms, then, is not the point. Rather it is the making of a world in which such characters – glutton, lecher, dissolute heir, upright fathers, pious if somehow compromised sons – live. And how that world reflects, in its artful way, upon the real.

But the objective in *Sat*. 1.4, it is important to point out, is not realism, or illusion or persuasion, but rather the fashioning of a poetic place in which things fit. That "fit" is genre, the *formulated* thing. Here re-formulated: brazen Lucilius yields to this amusingly modest, but literate little chap Horace presents, and he too can do satire, for he's got the pedigree – just look at his father, not the literary fathers Lucilius or Aristophanes but this better-than-newcomic-Daddy, re-habilitated for the occasion, laying down the generic rules this satirist and all of us readers of satire will live by.[17]

Satire 1.5 is a natural sequel to the programmatic 1.4, particularly in 1.4's emphasis on Lucilius, for 1.5 is an imitation of what was a well-known Lucilian poem recounting a journey to Sicily.[18] Horace's excursion is one he took in the company of Maecenas, Cocceius Nerva, Fonteius Capito, and Horace's literary friends, Vergil, Varius, and Plotius, from Rome to Brundisium on the southeast coast, the heel, of Italy. The embassy was of cardinal importance, as Maecenas and Cocceius Nerva and Antony's representative Pollio were intended to broker an agreement between Antony and Octavian, rivals poised on civil war. In the event the agreement, forged finally at Tarentum rather than Brundisium since Antony was prevented from landing there, staved off that war for six years; as Ronald Syme describes it, "the armed confrontation of the angry dynasts at Brundisium portended a renewal of warfare, proscriptions and the desolation of Italy, with a victor certain to be worse than his defeated adversary and destined to follow him before long to destruction, while Rome and the Roman People perished, while a world-empire as great as that of Alexander, torn asunder by the generals struggling for the inheritance, broke up into separate kingdoms and rival dynasties."[19] This portentous political element curiously gets scant notice in the satire. The sum is just a few lines (27–33):

> Here Maecenas, most excellent man, was to come,
> and Cocceius, delegates sent on great affairs,
> men accustomed to reconciling quarreling friends.
> At this point I daubed my inflamed eyes with ointment.
> Meanwhile Maecenas arrived and
> Cocceius and Fonteius Capito,
> a cultured man and trusted intimate of Antony.

And that is the poem's chief puzzle. No contemporary reader would look into the poem without wondering what light it could shed on the thoughts and ambitions of people upon whose actions the fate of Rome itself depended. It sheds precisely none. Proffered reasons for the occlusion vary; the best reading will be the closest guess. But Horace is not coy about his coyness; he flaunts his blindness to the political bright lights, in the image of his own inflamed and bleary eyes. This satirist can/will see only so far, and he tells us so explicitly. Can this be an admission of his own status as lowly friend of the high, and along with that the assumption of the trusted, discreet confidante role that Lucilius before him had tried on? If so, it is likely a metapoetic statement as well. We don't imagine that Horace was really privy to state secrets, or better, to the psychological details, the human side of that tense drama. His poetry, then, will demonstrate the limits of his personal access. In contrast to Lucilius, this is the satire of the uninvolved, the peripheral. But also a literary tour-de-force, in dashing off a tight, economical version of Lucilius' long, baggy travelogue: the literary principles of *Sat.* 1.4 exemplified.

The poem then does not give us politics or loose words. What, on the other hand, do the bleary eyes, blind to big political machinations, see? A view from a pub at day's end, followed by tedious, slow travel on a barge, squabbles and nighttime serenades of boatmen, bad water and its consequences, mosquitoes, frogs, a pretentious local praetor puffed up for the occasion, the warm greetings of good friends, Plotius, Varius, Vergil, as they join the troupe, ball games of a lazy afternoon, a shouting match between two locals done up mock-epic style, another host whose pretentious cookery nearly burns down the house, a view of Horace's homeland, Apulia, a disappointed assignation followed by a wet dream, then rough roads to Canusium, where friend Varius takes his leave, Rubi, Barium, Gnatia, and finally, end of the page and road (*longae finis chartaeque viaeque est*), Brundisium. The pulse of life, small life to be sure, but precisely that missed by focus on powerbrokers. Fatigue, thirst, rest, illness, sex, friends welcomed and seen off, people big and small doing necessary things. Horace's innocent formulation of precisely the incidental and quotidian stands in itself as an indictment – not of Horace's "limitations" but of the murderous quest for power. Along the way of this journey – and Horace knows that any journey has metaphorical relation to life's course – things link up to the unspoken, the unseen. Personal friendships, undecorated ("Vergil and I had a nap" [48]), gloss the provisional alliances of

Octavian and Antony, "friends" dividing the world and necessarily divided themselves. The two yokels, Messius Cicirrus and Sarmentus ("Harvesty Cock" and "Faggoty"), mock-epic clown-warriors right down to their low lineages, shout a wittily witless battle at one another; the analogue to that could scarcely have been overlooked.

Then there is that wet dream (83–85).

> Here like a fool I stay awake waiting for a girl,
> til midnight; finally sleep takes me still all strung up for love;
> then, dream prompted, I soil my belly and robe.

It is modeled on a passage in Lucretius (4.1030–1036), dryly analytical in good Epicurean style. But Horace's dream comes to him as he passes by, though not through, Venusia, his home-town. Horace's Latin, *somnus tamen aufert / intentum* **Veneri** (84), allusively echoes or names the home Horace just misses, and misses, but cannot go back to.[20] This lust is not so simple. The indirection *Veneri/Venusia* enacts for the reader the poem's logic: literally pronounces the relation between the spoken and unspoken. Between satire's quotidian corporeality and movements of politics, idea, and emotion. Horace knows too that Venus is Lucretius' chief bearing; it is she whose praise opens his long didactic poem. For Lucretius she is Nature's goddess, author of life's profusion, and mother of Romans (*Aeneadum genetrix*); the poet explicitly asks her intercession to bring her lover Mars' war-making to an end, to bring peace, for "in this troubled time of my country I cannot work with steady mind" (41–42). Horace longs for Lucretius' Venus as well as his own, but misses her and wastes his longing on a dream (*somnus*). This peace-bringing mother of all Romans finds another name, Nature herself, in the satire's final lines (101–103):

> for I've learned that the gods pass their time serenely,
> and if nature should do something odd, angry gods
> did not send it from the high home of heaven.

This is Horace the good Epicurean realist. Neither gods nor Nature punish foolish men for folly; this they manage quite well enough on their own. That last line, then, beginning with the place name that is the end of this journey but finally not the site of the forged peace, "Brundisium, end of the long page and journey," designates disappointment (is this the promised end?). We should feel it too, but not because Horace has told us too little.

Satire 1.6, the final satire of the "autobiographical" group *Sat.* 4–6, brings temporary closure to the theme of self-presentation and signals a transition into new territory. Horace's father assumes again, as in 1.4, a conspicuous role, so the poem can be said to resume some of the paternity as well as self-presentational themes of the earlier poem. At the same time, the opening line's invocation of Maecenas, placing the name in the same position in the line, echoes 1.1: *non quia, Maecenas, Lydorum quidquid Etruscos* (1.6.1) / *qui fit, Maecenas, ut nemo, quam sibi sortem* (1.1.1). The move marks a new beginning to the book's second half. Then, too, the poem looks through satirical-fabular vignettes, 1.7 and 1.8, to the two more self-referential satires that close out the book. More than any other, 1.6 highlights the design of this entire first collection. And develops ideas adumbrated earlier. Horace began by writing satire's script, initially diatribe, the scathing complaint of the paradigmatic outsider. But there was the problem of that "Maecenas" in line 1; how did Horace get to be on a first name basis with *that* company? Satires 1.4 through 1.6 explain that progress, how Horace wrote his way in, and more. How satire gets to be a good deal more than diatribe, for instance, how, just as Horace is positioned within Octavian's circle, it is positioned in the political and social world of his day.

The poem has been seen as a response to Maecenas' recommendation that Horace stand for office.[21] Horace's response, "real" or not, is roundabout: Maecenas' noble lineage is contrasted with Horace's freedman father; while he is technically eligible his background would give scope for sniping; better to be content with one's own (comfortable) lot – look at the pretenders like Tillius who were not; Horace's position is in the end more desirable; freedman father, yes (reiterated twice), but the son did command a legion under Brutus and through the intercession of Vergil and Varius won an audience with and, after a bit, patronage of Maecenas, who approved of him as much for his character as anything – that owed to freedman father; and what a life now, leisurely Epicurean industry, stress-free, unpretentious diversions, simple comforts: better this than a hallful of quaestors' busts.

Nothing very exciting happens in this poem; the most we can take from a fairly literal reading is an impression of Horace's complacent satisfaction at having arrived. This is then the denouement of the chronicle, begun in *Sat.* 1.1, of the writer Horace making it in

Rome. The mild critique of political ambition is the only "satire" noticed in most accounts. Its autobiographical details are the poem's greatest attraction for most readers, though we have for some years realized that there may be next to no reliable information here: Horace's father was certainly no poor farmer but a landowner sufficiently wealthy to pay for his son's very expensive education; as we've noted, he was probably no freedman in the usual sense but a free south Italian captured in the social war then freed to make his handsome living as landowner and broker; Horace's own life was neither as leisurely as this potted Epicurean formulation of the good life indicates, nor his resources quite so constrained.[22] As to the veracity of his account of schooldays, or any features of Horace's real life – we just can't know. Still, we are interested in this self-portrait. It represents how Horace wanted Maecenas and his readers to see him and establishes certain understandings for reading the satires, poems meant to be seen as written by *this* sort of man who must *mean* the sorts of things such a man thinks: rules for reading.[23] Political controversy is, thus, understated, fairly buried, in fact; Horace is content with the way things are falling out in the mid-30s; he's done his service with Brutus and been given his second chance with the other side; he's proud to call Octavian's friend his friend; politics is a mug's game anyway, pandering, exposing oneself to censure and abuse (this from a *satirist?*); "it" is all about, now, the good (writer's) life. So the poem ends with a set-piece on the relaxed, Epicurean day, strolling of an evening past the circus and forum ("haunts of chicanery"), home then to (all-too) simple meal, unfretting sleep, late rising, reading, writing ("something for my own pleasure"), baths, lunch ... An ideal life, ideal enough in fact to be quintessentially ideal, having very little connection with reality: the tableau is a recognizable specimen of "happy life" formulae common in classical literature.[24] The obvious fictionality of that trope colors the closing lines (128–131):

> ... This, then,
> is the life free from cares and grim ambition;
> I console myself with this: I live more pleasantly
> than if my granddad, father, and uncle were all quaestors.

Is the close a fictional set-piece too? Is Horace really content to push all thought of the quaestorship, and all it entails, the political firestorms of the 40s and 30s, the memory (and the poem ends with a turn to memory) of wars lost, the indignity of dependence, all that lurks between the lines of 1.5? In (Horatian) satire, it's hard to tell.

But for the curious circumstance of Horace's bad joke, **Satire 1.7**. "Circumstance" is about right, for the complacent 1.6 comfortably rests between two circumstanding poems of civil war memory. *Sat.* 1.7 has always been considered the odd creature out in Horace's first book. Set in 43 or 42, it describes a legal contest before Brutus, then governor of Asia (minor), done up mock-epic style. The two antagonists, a scarcely remembered former praetor called Rupilius Rex and a wealthy half-Greek businessman named Persius, have let their law case devolve into a slanging match, and Horace plays it up with comic parallels to Hector and Achilles, Diomede and Glaucus – though an earthier heroism is instanced in the gladiators Bithus and Bacchius. In the exchange between the principals as Horace describes it, each has his manner: Persius is noted for his wit, Rupilius "the king" for his scurrilous abuse. Closure comes when an exasperated Persius, "soaked in [the] Italian vinegar" of Rupilius' invective, cries out to judging Brutus, "by the gods, Brutus, please, you're accustomed to doing down kings; this job's for you; slit this King's gullet." Horace's poem is consciously set up as a joke. Only 35 lines long, shorter than any other satire, it begins with a standard joke-opening: "everyone knows, I suppose, the story of ... " and ends with a punchline pun on *Rex*.

Reading it from the perspective of 1.6, as Horace wants us to, we see that it is in bad taste. It is not very funny; most critics agree on this. Its yuck-up appeal is not one the posh, precisely well-bred, Horace of 1.6 would expect to be (seen) trading in, and making jokes about the assassinated Caesar as this does is simply impolitic. One of those uncouth pissings of Maecenas' couch, a friend's indiscretion Maecenas and we are meant to forgive?[25] Or perhaps a specimen of the vulgarity satire can get away with, rather like 1.2 and the poem that follows this one, 1.8, another joke, whose punch line is a fart. If that is so, and surely it is in part, then satire explores what "getting away with" entails. Horace himself got away with service on the losing side of the civil war and now has got away with a rise to prominence on the other side. The poem is fraught with the complicated problematics of complicity – condescension, transference, regret, shame, guilt, fear – and (maybe) seeks to resolve it all with a laugh. That's a laugh Horace himself must have had when witnessing the scene, as he surely did.[26]

Between that laugh then and that of the poem's "now" are blood, death, and irrevocable loss. That is finally the trick of the satire: it brings us back to a time when a lowlife joke about killing the Caesar was a lot funnier, when Republican hopes were alive and Brutus and Cassius had respectable reputations as "liberators"[27]; then back around to the brave new world after Philippi, where Brutus, defeated by Octavian and Antony in 42, committed suicide. Do we laugh at the odd irony of that? Or at the more perverse irony of history repeating the pattern, apparently inescapably? The Athenian Demosthenes' (384–322) rhetorical attacks (his *Philippics*) on the Macedonian tyrant-king Philip led to a death sentence; Cicero's rhetorical attacks on Antony (**his** *Philippics*) led to another death sentence; Brutus' assassination of Caesar led to his own death at … *Philippi* – and where does this end? In the shadow of this poem's bad joke lurks virtually everything troubling to a Roman of the mid-30s.

Civil war dead are ghosts, ghosts haunting remote battlefields and suburban cemeteries. **Satire 1.8** is a tale of one such cemetery, though its dead are said to be merely slaves or the poor (believe it?), a human junkyard. This poem too is cast in the form of a joke, though *Horace* doesn't make it: for the first time in his satires, though not the last, a figure other than the Horatian persona, a wooden garden figure in the shape of the fertility figure Priapus, narrates. This deflection of the narrative makes for a good story and perhaps makes what he says a little safer for its author, but it is true that this Priapus sounds an awfully lot like our friend Horace. Specifically, like the Horace of 1.4 who talks about real poetry and the potency of real Lucilian satire, only to dismiss his own work as non-poetry and not all that threatening. So too this Priapus speaks of his lowly lineage ("the trunk of a fig I once was, an unpromising chunk" [1]), his lucky lifepath ("a stool or a Priapus" [2]), and a career not unlike a triumphalist (1.6), self-ironizing (1.5) satirist's ("a god I became, biggest bogey of thieves and birds" [3–4]). The satirist-conceit continues in this garden statue's priapic swagger: "my right hand cows thieves, / so also my red-painted prick sticking out from my groin" (4–5), and we are back in the sexual politics of 1.2. There the Roman male's gendered power enjoyed free play even while (unbeknownst) it came in for a good deal of second guessing. Here, perhaps precisely because male gendered power stands as the armament of a neutered (i.e., non-Lucilian) satire, this Horace-Priapus' swagger is soon enough neutralized by some scary women (23–26):

> I myself saw the witch Canidia, black robe
> tucked up, barefoot, hair let down,
> howling along with the crone Sagana; their pallor
> made them both frightful to look at.

The witches are there to work a little black magic in order to call out some spirits of the dead, magic black enough in its details as to frighten out of the poor statue a panicked fart (44–50):

> [but why go on about] how I, terrorized witness to the words
> and deeds of these two furies, was avenged?
> I farted – loud – like an exploding bladder,
> opening a crack in my rear. And *they* ran into the city.
> Canidia's dentures popped out, Sagana's wig flew off,
> herbs and woven rigmarole scattered from their arms;
> you'd have laughed, hard, at the joke.

Both the disabling of satire's priapic swagger and the victory precisely by means of that disability are significant: there could hardly be a clearer statement of the turn from Lucilian satiric principles. Horace will in *Sat.* 1.10.14–15 famously say that wit is better than acerbity in sorting through tricky issues, and here is perhaps a demonstration, but there is more in this joke. For Horace's laughter, or the laughter he asks for, is nervous laughter – the laugh of relief when something very frightening has been avoided. Surely part of this relief, thinking back to *Sat.* 1.2, is the Roman male's close encounter with the subversive power of woman and his own anxiety. Canidia, who appears in six of Horace's poems[28] and nowhere else in Roman literary or other documents, is usually associated with threateningly dominant sexuality: she is ugly, foul-breathed, old, and horny; she concocts love potions out of bits of animal, even bits of children; she poisons, she transgresses in every way – and gets her way. She frightens the establishment man, who in turn detests her. That loathing is frequently figured in Roman invective – they had a talent for it. Catullus' short invectives on repulsive, sex-mad crones are laden with grotesque anatomical and scatological imagery. Literally, negative retrojections of manhood's fear and loathing. Horace's Canidia is just such a creation, a locus of hate and insecurity that needs to be defeated in order for Horace's (and Rome's) Roman dream to fly. An index of the stakes is the very vulgarity of this solution. A minor irritant might be sent off with a subtler joke, delicate wit; Canidia needs to be blasted away with low scatology, excremental abuse.

Horatian satire, then, has its dark side. Not just a smoothing over of Lucilius' rough corners or a transposition of acerbity into disarming politesse, this satire will plumb some of the nastier anxieties author and reader share, glossing them over with the most transparent of jokes. And back to that cemetery, Canidia is more than a projection of men's sexual failure, loss of control. She is, precisely, digging among the dead in order to talk to them.[29] She stirs up the past, an ugly past of dumped bodies, wasted lives. There is no overt reference in the satire to the civil wars, but Horace's Priapus stands guard over the gardens Maecenas created over this body tip. The new prettified suburban garden, Maecenas' and therefore Octavian's image of new Rome, overlays a past that, here, Horace associates with death. Canidia breaks the gardeny illusion; beneath it all are rotting bodies. Canidia doesn't let us forget. So of course she has to be chased away, symbolically, literally, somehow, the more disgraced the better. We might say that Horace does that with deft cleverness, an amusing fable with a properly ironized champion. And satire knows that a fart is always funny, so to ridicule the witches offstage. But the deep indignity they suffer is an index of the Roman male's urgent need to keep the illusion of his own control and the idea of the new Rome alive. Futilely, as Horace surely knows, for just as excremental retribution abuses supremely, it too designates the abuser's own mortality, the smelly corporeal self *inside*. Maecenas' Esquiline garden, new Rome's dream, *really is* a graveyard and this fable's champion, Horace-Priapus, will end up there, along with his master and all of Rome's dreams of transcendence.[30]

Satires 1.5, 1.7, and 1.8, then, centered by the focal and pivotal 1.6, *dig* down, into, under Rome – and back into the turmoils of recent history. The "anecdotal" trilogy, 1.7, 1.8, and now 1.9, those poems that tell comic stories, trace out a related pattern: 1.7 refers to and comically mutes the heroics of Brutus and Co.; 1.8 exposes and comically mutes the terrors lurking beneath and behind Rome's sunny, new (triumviral) day; 1.9 reintroduces Horace as a character on a stroll through Rome, now as an established literary figure. That fulfillment, his sense of having arrived, is comically muted too by a genuinely funny self-irony, but beneath it, the shadows haunting *Sat.* 1.7 and 1.8 have not gone away.

Satire 1.9, like its immediate predecessors, is cast in the form of a joke. This time, as with many of the best, the joke is told on its teller.

Looking back on the progress of the book thus far, we can see that the last time we saw "Horace" was in 1.6; that poem was an expression of the self-satisfaction of his just having "arrived," crediting, like an award winner at a banquet, Maecenas, his father, "all those who have made this happy life possible." **Satis**fied satire, in short. And a paradox. Where *could* satire go once the satirist has everything he could hope for? Away into anecdote is one answer, into literary places where Horace-the-satirist is hidden or disguised; thus 1.7 and 1.8. In 1.9 Horace sneaks back into view, but the question of what to do with the full-fed satirist trails along with him: the satire enfigures that issue.

The (ostensible) story: the Horace we recall from the banquet of 1.6, humble poet laureate, is out on a stroll through town, along the Sacra Via to be precise, between the Palatine and the Forum: a fashionable sort of place in which to mutter over a few ideas for poems (*maybe this very one*). Suddenly he is overtaken/interrupted by someone "known to me only by name" (2), though, crucially, unnamed here. From this point on, the story is simple. The tagger-along won't let go; he's after an introduction to Maecenas, for he too, he thinks, has the stuff of a poet; he can, after all, write, in good Lucilian fashion, more verses faster than anyone he knows. Horace, three times, tries to shake him, to no avail: "I muttered to myself, O, lucky for *you*, Bolanus, with your sharp tongue ... my ears drooped, like an over-loaded donkey's" (11–12, 20). The only point at which Horace shows any firmness is in his denial that the artist's life chez Maecenas is a catty, competitive one: "no, we each have our place, we don't worry about rank or position" (50–52). The two chance to meet a friend (of Horace's), Aristius Fuscus, well-placed, in the know, a fellow writer. To him Horace signals – winks and nods – his desire to get free of his literary-climbing parasite (60–74); Fuscus sees and demurs (67–72):

H.:   "Certainly you said you had something to tell me in private?"

F.:   "Yes, I recall, but another time. Today's a thirteenth Sabbath and you wouldn't want me to fart in the face of the Jews, would you?"

H.:   "I'm not bothered by that; *religio*'s not my line."

F.:   "Alas mine. I'm weak, one of the many. Forgive me – some other time."

Fuscus is a good-bad jokester, *male salsus / ridens dissimulare* (65–66), and he leaves Horace in despair: "the rogue flees and leaves me under the knife" (73–74). The poem and dilemma ends in the only way it could, an *ex machina* whose agent is neither *deus* nor *amicus* – the follower's opponent in a lawsuit hunts *him* down and takes him off with Horace called to witness (75–78).

The satire has long been seen as paradigmatic Horatian entertainment. The poet tells a story on himself about a particularly bad day, humorously putting on view his own weakness, inability to show enough spunk to send this "pest" (as he was called by critics for years) on his way. Part of the charming amusement is recognizing ourselves: ineffectual, nice, middle-class liberals, maybe not quite able to deal well with frank ambition. And surely we all know people like this pest, surely ... That sort of un(self-)examined reading has been pushed aside in recent years for more nuanced diagnoses, but the poem is *supposed* to appeal to readers in just this naïve way. Horace, his readers, and Aristius Fuscus share a circle of sensibility that the pest does not. Take it, then, as that kind of good, self-effacing fun, even as you notice, as many recently have, that this ambitious, sequacious poet is rather reminiscent of Horace himself, once an outsider on the make.[31] He is introduced, after all, in a very curious way: *notus mihi nomine tantum*, which literally means "known only to me by name" but smuggles in the sous-entendre "known only by *my* name" as well. The suitor is never named; he appears, lingers long enough to put Horace through a (self-examining?) bout of misery, then disappears. He even talks the way a callow Horace might have, brash and enamored of the compositional facility of Lucilius ("I can write that fast too"). Does the poem then stage a psychic encounter, the poet confronting his past self and not liking what he sees, but not being able to escape him(self) either? Can one escape the self, the satirist seems to ask; the answer being "no," unless by another's agency: a litigant, a friend, a Maecenas. And even then ... Horace has been called back to witness, to trial – and hasn't this been, isn't all of this life we (Horaces) live, a protracted and recursive (self-) trial?

We might see the poem therefore as a kind of reprise, enacting in a painfully comic way the progress of one Horace from outsider-diatribist to the establishment figure we see in *Sat.* 1.6. But it also plays out some of the themes of the satires that follow 1.6. The anecdote poems 1.7 and 1.8 turn attention away from the poet's self, and refractingly explore national anxieties, speak of the disquieting past, the brash, young Horace's own past. Horace in *Sat.* 1.8 assumes the role of comic, flawed guardian of Maecenas' garden; in 1.9 he is a comically flawed guardian of Maecenas' inner sanctum. The fart appears, or doesn't, on cue as well: what worked to chase away those nasty witches, with all their psychic and historical baggage, is here merely verbalized by Fuscus as allusion, almost too cleverly: "you wouldn't want *me* to fart in the faces of the crowd" (69–70). Nor can Horace so express himself, anymore. Say satire was that lame Priapus, that comically coarse, just-potent-enough fart; what can it, or the satirist, do, now? Not even fend off an unpleasant little social climber – like Horace!

To claim there is guilt latent in this apparent bagatelle would be to ascribe an emotion to it the author wouldn't recognize; but there is an unblinking regard at the distance come, its gains and losses. Horace has made it through history's messes and misses, its blood and sorrow; he has not played a big role in any of that, but he has lived through it and seen it – with those eyes sore and bedaubed in 1.5. By the mid-30s the new way is clear; there really *is* only Octavian and Antony left, and Antony is far away; Vergil and the other poets of Maecenas' circle are writing poems about a new Rome – something Horace can't satirize. Nor should he in prudence; he is the new Rome's protégé; his special position, and therefore special predicament, is obligingly laid out in *Sat.* 1.9. But failing overt "satire," failing even that symbolic flatulence of 1.8, Horace is inventive enough to make a poetry that embraces, makes satire of, satire's impotence. So to answer that question posed by 1.6: how does a satisfied poet make satire? He, first, stages a re-enactment of the past in the present (mumbling to himself, as per his wont, one day while walking down the Sacra Via): "what if, *now*, I were to meet someone very like my old self? what would that feel like? what would that *mean?*" It would mean, for one, that the satire he once could write is no longer possible; the sated banqueter doesn't do diatribe. Nor does he tell tales on his high-placed friends ("there really is no rancor, politics, envy – really" [51–53]). The satire he can write, then, turns back on the writer ("these are my trials"), safe and amusing. Yet we have seen that Horace's self-satire stages a remembering-back, and here maybe in the darkness of memory, the old edges of satire come out again. The poet's alter ego is a (grudgingly) honest impression – there was, *is*, just maybe, ambition, rancor, politics, and envy in Maecenas' little world; the poet's persona doesn't tell tales, but this recall of where he's come from recalls also what he *has* heard and seen – in the heady, idealistic days of Brutus (surely not forgotten), on that crucial trip to Brundisium, on the streets of Rome where the *satura* (medley) of urban voices generate the stuff of resistance, discontent, mockery, satire. It is where Horace goes to listen and mutter. Horace's new satire cannot *say* any of that – it wouldn't be seemly or prudent – but it can stage its not-saying. And that may be the point.

Satire 1.10 flows naturally from the concerns of 1.9: Horace's place as a writer in the literary-political world of the triumvirate. This poem, 1.10, however, functioning as it does as closure to the first book of satires, is almost entirely programmatic, that is, about the art of writing satire. In this it corresponds to *Sat.* 1.4, answering fairly precisely, as some see it, questions raised there. How does one write post-Lucilian satire? What is the place of satire in the Roman literary tradition? Is satire really non-poetry as 1.4 seems to suggest? Horace designates 1.10 as response by referencing 1.4 in the opening line: "Of course I did say that Lucilius' poetry ran roughly ... and yet on the very same page he's praised for scouring the city with his wit" (1–2, 3–4). The (probable) fiction the poem sustains is that this second programmatic satire is a riposte to criticism leveled at Horace for attacking Lucilius. It is just possible that people were upset; Lucilius was a favorite of some, and he seems to have been popular even in trendy poetic circles; Lucilian free speech was also cherished among anti-Caesarians.[32] Yet as the close of this poem demonstrates, with its gallery of illustrious names, Horace is not insecure. He raises the Lucilius issue for a reason, and that reason is almost surely not to placate literary opponents. Rather, it seems that it is precisely to re-stage that "fight," not so much to put Lucilius in his historical place – though he does that – but to set the terms for satire's composition and place in contemporary society. It is tempting to see parallel, agonistic revolutions underway, between old Rome and new, between the anti-Caesarian sympathies of the Lucilius camp and the Caesarian sympathies of Horace's crowd, between old satire and new. Seeing things that way might oversimplify Horace's position, but there *are* literary wars being waged. A set of eight lines that comes as prologue to this satire, clearly spurious, but also nearly contemporary in origin, testify in blunt language to these wars: "Lucilius, what a blunderer you are; Cato, your own advocate / proves the case by setting out to fix / your badly composed lines" (1a–3a). Horace himself, never so crude as the author of these lines, takes the opportunity of evident literary contestation in these triumviral years, to craft the terms of his own literary innovation. So this is a fight designed to purpose – to highlight features of literary styling in satire: tone, word choice, verse construction, "level," economy of expression.

A brief summary: lines 1–15: "yes, I criticized L., praised him too for his salty wit; but that's not enough. You need a modulating style, changes of tone and manner, sometimes orator, sometimes poet, sometimes jester"; 16–35: "writers of old comedy got it right, not the fops who now lisp on Calvus and Catullus, guiding lights of the fashionable crowd; you say they wrote in Greek as well as Latin? Not impressive; I was warned away from that toy by Quirinus in a dream [said dream being a stock device of the Hellenistic set]"; 36–49: "me, I got into satire because other genres were taken by my betters, Varius, Pollio, Vergil; I could do satire, though the prize for inventing it belongs with L."; 50–71: "but, sure, I did criticize him for roughness, and why not? He'd surely change his tune if he were around nowadays"; 72–92: "the thing to do is write carefully and avoid popular vulgarizing: stick to the tastes of the tasteful: not carping nonentities, but readers who matter (see Lucilius' original profile for *his* readership of choice: p. 21): Plotius, Varus, Maecenas, Vergil (remember them from 1.5), Valgius, Octavius, Fuscus, Viscus, Pollio, Messalla, Bibulus, Servius, Furnius. There, that's settled; go on, laddy, add these lines to my little book."

Arguing in these terms in effect makes satire a legitimate poetry; this is, in fact, what you *do* to make it so. By the poem's end, Lucilius has dropped off the radar; it is the reception of *Horace's* satire that now matters. Horace comes out here, declares authority, lays down the law. For good reasons, we have believed him. This poem has duly been read as Horace's artistic manifesto: on these principles his satire, maybe his poetry as a whole, will stand. Those principles include an up-to-date Alexandrian concern for slow, careful composition, formal perfectionism, and a limited, refined readership (72–74):

> Be sure to use the eraser, often, and if you're going to write
> something worth reading twice don't work for the crowd's approval
> but be content with a few (good) readers.

But he will be no mere disciple of Alexandrian Callimachus, like those "apes" who can "sing nothing beyond (the neoterics) Calvus and Catullus" (19). You need humor, sharp wit, clarity of expression, and dignified restraint of expression (8–17). Readers ever after have been grateful for this codification of Horatian poetics, but one suspects that the essential elements noted here would have surprised none of his contemporaries; the modified Alexandrian program would have been the default aesthetic for most new poetry in Horace's day. Horace is, then, not revolutionizing poetic program *here* (he had done that far more subtly in 1.4). Rather, he seems to be establishing the currency of satire within the poetic cosmos of the age, as if to say, "satire will be a player in this constellation of new verse, written by the (stellar) likes of Fundanius, Pollio, and Vergil."

It is curious and significant that this poem, perhaps more than the other programmatic satires, 1.4 and 2.1, has been read almost exclusively for its aesthetics.[33] Yet focus on the literary-programmatic aspects of the satire tends to elide both socio-political background noise and the functionality of this poem as satire. One might legitimately ask if this is "just" about Horace's laying his poetic cards on the table for us all to see. We might in response think back to the "unsaying" of *Sat.* 1.9; what does this programmatic poem allude to without delineating it explicitly? Critics thinking into the politics of this satire have suggested that Horace draws a parallel between Lucilius' political role as partisan of Scipio Aemilianus and his own role as partisan of Maecenas and Octavian;[34] that Horace's position here may be seen to play a role in the tension between republican and Caesarian sympathizers; that the closural litany of powerful names both answers the threat jestingly made in *Sat.* 1.4 ("a great throng of poets will come to my aid and force you to become one of our party" [141–143]) and executes a power play.[35] Indeed, those crowning names show Horace playing *between* his bashful persona ("you see, I must not be so bad a poet with *these* friends") and canny barrister decisively closing his case with unquestionable authority (if your friends are not mine, you lose, no appeal).

But that language of coercion leads to further conclusions. *Sat.* 1.10, closing the book, resolves its beginning: Horace, back in those first diatribe poems, fashioned himself in an outsider's rhetoric; the book has tracked his course from that position to the ultimate insider – one of *this* group. The book has also tracked a course for satire, from an identifiably satiric register, and therefore affinity with the Lucilian tradition, to a place this poem explicitly says Lucilius doesn't belong (56–61):

> What prevents us, reading Lucilius' poetry,
> from asking whether circumstances or his own nature
> kept him from writing smoother, more finished verses

than if someone were content to enclose a line in six feet
or be happy having written two hundred lines
before dinner, or as many after . . .

Or if he did want to belong, would have to change his ways (68–71):

> But if fate had dropped him into our age,
> he'd have to chop away much, cut back
> what ran beyond the perfected, and in making verse,
> scratch his head, bite his nails.

Not the Lucilius we knew, in short: bold, careless teller of hard satiric truth. No place for *that* in the circle of Maecenas, and it may be just this image of a cringing, cowering, nitpicking Lucilius that is meant to haunt us in this closing poem. This is finally, then, less about style than it is about persona, voice, approach, about what kind of language is possible in triumviral Rome. Or rather, it is about the complicity of style – those rarified, learned, Hellenistic aesthetics in a poetic discourse that agrees not to speak in the old, Lucilian ways.

The obvious question, then, is whither satire. Those closing names hang like a great, ominously decisive shadow; how could satire function in what has amounted, in this end poem, to an end-game for the genre. You don't criticize this lot, especially if you are a pardoned ex-member of the opposition. But . . . say you are as clever as Horace is, and you have refashioned a genre out of the pieces of what was once a brazen voice of *libertas*. In this new re-fashioning, you build in echoes of the old Lucilius, or rather show him in the process of making himself over for the new age, cutting, crimping, fussing. It all can be read ambivalently, can't it? Hellenistic subtlety too has its edges, relying as it does so much on nuance. This is the image of satire Horace leaves us with at book's end, a Lucilian ferocity now sublimated into a new idiom, one of whose chief qualities is its capacity for ambivalence, for being read as carefully, and suspiciously, as it has been written.

Book 2: Writing Satire Down

Horace's second book was written in the years 35–30, a period in which he was also writing his iambics, the *Epodes*, and some of his early lyrics based on Greek precedent, the *Odes*. A period, in short, in which

Horace's career as poet was in full, prolific swing, and also a time when the poet was trying his hand in different generic modalities. After this book he will write no more satire. The second book, then, writes satire to its Horatian conclusion even while casting it in another mold. The new formulation is highly self-conscious as such. It begins with a satirist's voice and persona that are the natural outcomes of developments in the first book; it employs a predominantly dialogical mode of presentation; and it appears carefully structured and organized. If Book 1 was linear in general exposition – its groupings indicated by proximity within the book and their thematic relatedness – Book 2 is dialectical in structure, two halves of four poems each breaking up into corresponding pairs of thematically related satires: 2.1 ~ 2.5, 2.2 ~ 2.6, 2.3 ~2.7, 2.4 ~ 2.8.[36] The structural balance, even apart from the substance of the satires, bespeaks closure; the tight ordering precludes accretion. And, as we will see, the final poem ends with a dying fall.

Satire 2.1 is the last of Horace's programmatic poems. Like *Sat.* 1.4 and 1.10, it engages Lucilius as model, satiric father-figure somehow to be dealt with, and, as in the others, Horace here discusses satire's "right" register, its aggressiveness, its suitable targets, its risks. Yet there is something profoundly different about this poem; Niall Rudd memorably put his finger on it when he called it "the most brilliant piece of shadow-boxing in Roman literature."[37] His observation rests on Horace's apparent engagement with Lucilian-programmatic issues that turn, consistently, to evasion and misdirection. The Lucilian example is raised to view, but this time not for criticism; the threat of aggressive satire is raised and then dropped, the satirist's fear of retribution – the central dramatic setting of the poem's dialogue – is lengthily discussed, only to be dismissed at poem's end with a joke. In many ways then, just as the book will constitute a sign-off to satire, this opening poem turns itself into an anti-program, a resignation from a certain kind of satiric writing.

We see it from the beginning: whereas the opening lines ("to some I seem too rough and to take my work beyond the 'law,' to others I seem too slack and facile" [1–4]) might be the entrée to a discussion of just the right satiric pitch, we find in lines 4–5 that Horace has already retired – to a consultation with the jurist Trebatius. Horace, in this staged dialogue, asks the lawyer to prescribe (*praescribe* [5]) safe limits within which he might conduct his art. Trebatius' reply is surprising: "drop it!" This leads to a lengthy interchange in which options are debated: to be really safe from retribution Horace should turn to eulogistic writing, of Octavian particularly (10–12); Horace, however, claims not to be up to the task of writing epic and, besides, he is a bit leery of Augustus Caesar's reaction to outright flattery – in a remarkable image (12–20) comparing Octavian to a nettlesome horse (epic animal) and himself to an ass (Flaccus ∼ flop-eared). Still, Horace, in a priamel, a formulaic preamble, that recalls *Sat.* 1.1, declares he must *write*, and he states his intention to follow Lucilius – not, as we might expect, in savaging society but in entrusting his private thoughts to his books (21–34). Horace then shows a little ancestral bravado, claiming descent from one or the other side in old border wars – it is unclear which, but in any case, he corrects himself: he'd as soon leave his sword a-rusting in its scabbard (35–42). Yet watch out: Horace is a dangerous writer when provoked, like witches and jurists (!) (43–59). Warned himself again by Trebatius, Horace once more raises the ghost of Lucilius, terror of Lupus and Metellus, and friend (here the tenor mellows) of Laelius and Scipio – why, they used to unwind together, at ease while dinner cooked (60–74). Finally we see where this is leading: just as Lucilius had his Scipio, Horace has the (clinchingly) high-placed friends of 1.10, and now, to trump all, the support of Octavian himself, before whom all (libel) law (*solventur risu tabulae* [86]) crumbles (81–87):

T: If someone should compose libelous verses / evil spells (*mala carmina*), there is the law and judgment.

H: Fine, if they are bad (*mala*); but if they are good (*bona*) and Caesar himself approves ...

T: the laws will be dissolved in laughter, and you set free.

The satirist's problem crumbles too, before a pun.

The "programmatic" opening poem turns out, in short, not to be a metapoetic commentary on satire at all, but rather a discussion of the predicament of the satirist, of *this* satirist. We are treated to a satirist's-eye view of writing's challenges from *his* side of the desk: the criticism, provocations, obligations of faction and patronage. Or so it would seem – for the overriding impression the reader takes from this satire, recurring again to Rudd's acute diagnosis, is that none of this is serious. Horace had earlier staged a quarrel with Lucilius in order to make genuine distinctions between the old and new satire; here he stages a transparently artificial interview with his lawyer to discuss the difficulties and dangers of his position as satirist. Those difficulties are on the face of it trivial: the libel law Trebatius cites is no longer current,[38] the criticisms Horace cites are hardly specific to particular groups or factions, the compulsion to write is rendered in uncompelling terms ("it's my mania" [24–29]), the final solution so glib that the reader can think the preceding discussion nothing other than pretextual pose. That is a gambit Horace had used in *Sat.* 1.7 as well, and that poem, we recall, is commonly received as merely a poorly constructed, not-very-good joke. *Sat.* 2.1 is not poorly constructed, but it is difficult to escape the letdown that comes with its close: does the writing of satire, for our supreme Roman satirist, come down to a bad pun? The link to 1.7 is that the converse applies: the pun in each being the trapdoor into which the assuming, and therefore targeted reader in Horace's poetic cosmos, falls. The pun in 1.7 was the means by which Horace, in short, worked his indirection, an indirection that allowed him to "speak" of things open discourse could not name. When we see a bad pun in Horace, in other words, watch out.

When, for instance, Horace invokes Lucilius ("my mania is to compose in verse, à la Lucilius" [29]) our default assumption is that he means writing aggressive satire. Instead Horace refers specifically to the hexameter verse form and presents an alternative picture of the old scourge of society: this Lucilius sits at home, entrusting his reflections to his notebooks, "as to his friends, 'having no other outlet' whether things turn out well or badly" (30–32).[39] The contrast of this stay-at-home satirist to the diatribist of *Sat.* 1.1 is striking; no public preaching, no (however fictive) streetcorner hectoring of passers-by; the new satirist of 2.1 is a satirist without options, whose literary voice is reduced to that of the diarist. Now of course Horace is about to publish this satire-as-diary, and in a program poem that pretends immunity from retribution to boot, but in doing so in this guise, he declares as openly as one could declare it that certain things said in certain ways will remain unspoken.

In line 34 Horace writes, "I follow [Lucilius], but whether as Lucanian or Apulian is open to question." The reference is to the Roman occupation in 291 of Venusia, Horace's home-town, perched between (Lucilius') Campania, Apulia and Lucania. Horace's ambivalence may be innocent ignorance of things long past; alternatively it is a statement of dubiety in the context of ancient and more recent Roman wars (the Social War of 91–87 BCE). Ostensibly, the reference is to tribal ferocity, with transference to the tribe of satirists, a theme he picks up, negatively: "but this pen will not attack anyone living unprovoked, and will protect me, like a sword in its scabbard" (39–40). Even the threat of that sheathed sword is almost instantly muted by the poet's wish that it rust away, unused; but if he should be provoked, why, that sword/pen will be like nature's defenders, the wolf's tooth, the ox's horn (52), or the less natural tools of the witch and lawyer (47–49); the oddest comparandum here is the dutiful right hand of Scaeva ("Lefty") which will care for his ancient mother – while hemlock takes her off. Is this menace, then, of malice and secrecy the targeted object of satire or threat on a par with his own deadly stylus? Horace isn't saying.

He does say that if he were to write scathing satire, like the veneer-stripping stuff of Lucilius, it would be as well received by people-who-matter as Lucilius' was by Scipio and Laelius (62ff.). Again, as we've seen, here is the reflexive retreat: think of the great satirist scouring those deserving it, while enjoying the favor of "virtue's friends" (68–70). But it is not the scouring that gets emphasis; rather, the pleasant picture of domestic tomfoolery, Lucilius and Laelius chez Scipio (71–74):

> Indeed when Scipio, from *such* a family,
> and Laelius, in his wisdom and gentleness, had withdrawn
> from public view, ties and collars loosened, used to horse
> around with him while their simple veg was cooking.

Again this comes to an affirmation or celebration of Horace's own intimacy with Maecenas, and now even Octavian. "Virtue's friends" too, no doubt; and there *is* no doubt that their backing makes any case against Horace's *libertas* (with respect to others outside the circle) risible (83–86). Thus full circle, ranging across Book 1, from Lucilian *libertas* to Lucilius/Horace as establishment figure(s). And one might leave it at that: the story of Lucilius' domestication (the story of satire) in the person of Horace in the house of Octavian. Or is there another story limned beneath these surface colors? One precisely of the glossing over of wars whose memory, Horace tells us here, is not quite dead, or of what the enfeeblement of satire, pictured in this hapless, contented writer, implies about conditions that make it/him thus. Within the silence that this poem prescribes for this and any future satire other, "possible" voices live, some of them translated into the secrecies of Horace's own books – "there's a darkness at the edge of town,"[40] and within too, in that image of Lucilius/Horace scribbling *arcana*, secrets, in his books, "his (real?) faithful friends" (30) – alone with his thoughts.

For Love of Food and Country

Yet alone is what Horace never lets himself be in this book. The satires of Book 2 are largely dialogues where other voices, interlocutors, assume prominence and Horace *qua* character gets to say less and less. The exception to that rule is *Sat.* 2.6, wherein Horace reflects on the leisure afforded by his Sabine farm, gift of Maecenas, the city and country, and much else between the lines. The country setting can be seen as well in **Satire 2.2**, which is presented as the distillation of the homespun wisdom of a character named Ofellus, a tenant farmer whom Horace claims to have known from his youth. The praises of simple country living are sung; the great goods here are self-sufficiency (*autarkeia*), frugality, equanimity. The sensibility of a rustic philosopher (*abnormis sapiens* [3]) is not inapposite as focalizer of these themes but, as readers generally observe, the poem seems more a conventional literary diatribe than the plain talk of a simple farmer. The satire's voice then recalls the opening of Horace's first book, but it has become convenient, for the now comfortably established writer, to employ another's authority for *this* message. Or rather, it has become useful to Horace to create a distance between himself and his satire for an array of reasons, plausibility being only the most obvious. One important effect of the device, as we saw in *Sat.* 1.8, is to build in a sense of the poems as constructed literary artifacts. Here, compounding that sense with the "straight" sermonizing of diatribe serves as a metapoetic wink to the reader: even in its beginnings, Horace's satire was never the simple voice of the diatribist. That awareness affects how we read even a poem seemingly as straightforward as 2.2.

For instance, beyond the farmer's homily, we see that the poem, the first beyond the opening programmatic 2.1, broaches one of satire's favorite subjects, food, and prepares the reader for the extended satires on the subject in the remainder of the book. In fact, food and philosophy (of a sort) may be said to be the major preoccupations of Book 2. The two themes come together in 2.4, a "philosophical" disquisition on cookery and eating propounded by one Catius, while the quirks and valences of Roman dining appear also in 2.6 and dominate 2.8, the failed feast that marks the end of Horace's work in satire. As we have already mentioned, food and satire are inextricably linked in a number of ways: the very name *satura*, in description of what was originally a poetic hodge-podge, comes, most probably, from the metaphor of a mixed plate, a culinary medley; the genre is associated, by false etymology and the circumstantial setting of some poems, with saturnalia's excessive indulgence, gustatory and otherwise; satire's position in the hierarchy of literary genres, down there with comedy and mime, made it the natural venue for body-talk, the vices and weaknesses (engorged stomachs, belches, vomit, gas, pus, bile, and other lovelies) of the corporeal self.[41] Horace's Rome, moreover, was very aware of the "social problem" of excessive consumption. That problem was real. Status and prestige were in fact negotiated in nearly out-of-control competitions of ostentatious feasting, leading to the progressively and perversely more arcane arts of cookery and presentation, not so very different from the scenes burlesqued in Horace, Persius, Juvenal, and Petronius. "Sumptuary" laws were passed to curb this particular fetish of the elite. But the concern with food and diet cut across society, too, in the popular philosophies of Stoicism and Epicureanism. The latter – frequently caricatured by Stoics and others as a self-indulgent pursuit of pleasure, especially as seen in sex, eating, and drinking – recommended in point of fact significant restraints on these kinds of pleasures. Both Hellenistic philosophies, in their popular rather than technical, metaphysical, and logical modalities, propounded a more or less strict regimen of living, a self-governing discipline (*askesis*) that would serve as insulation against the caprices of power, fate, and circumstance. In this kind of popular philosophical climate, feasting to surfeit, distending overconsumption, display of luxury beyond the "necessary" became highly charged activities.[42] People *thought* about such things a good deal more than most of us do . . . maybe.

Featuring the feast, then, is the natural thing for a Roman satirist to do; beginning as Horace does in Book 1 with generalized diatribe, the thematic move represents a homing-in on satire's own generic and cultural identity. The excesses thus cited and deplored in 2.2 come from the world of expensive city and country houses: butlers, posh wine and food, rare birds and big fish (peacock, ptarmigan, parrotfish, bass, mullet, oysters, turbot). Better than any of this, says Ofellus/ Horace, is plain food made tasty by a healthily worked-up appetite (7–20). As in Book 1, contrary vices come in for blame as well: the miser's wretchedly sparing diet is as bad as the gourmand's (53–69).

Somewhat unusually, this poem contains a rather full encomium to plain food and simplicity (70–93), as if this satire were to serve by way of mild hors d'oeuvre to the more bracingly satirical 2.4 and 2.8.

The poem concludes, after a parting blast at a rich reprobate, with an oblique vignette in praise of Ofellus' resilience when his land is confiscated for settlement by Caesar's veterans after Philippi in 42 BCE. Ofellus says (133–136):

> now this land belongs to Umbrenus, Ofellus' a bit ago,
> nobody's abidingly, but it slips now to one
> now to another. So, be strong,
> face adversity with brave hearts.

The equanimity Ofellus demonstrates is meant to be part and parcel of a discipline that includes the simple fare praised in lines 70–93 – food and ethics link. Ofellus is of course too good to be quite true: 2.2 gives us simple satiric fare, rather easy moralizing – but for the complication of Horace's allusion here to Vergil's first Eclogue. It is generally assumed that Horace's sixteenth Epode on the Roman civil war alludes in its lines 9–14 ("we, the impious offspring of a cursed race, shall ruin Rome, the land once again be held by beasts. ... ") to Vergil *Ecl.* 1.71 ("see where discord has led wretched citizens"). The context pertains directly to the situation of Ofellus (*Ecl.* 1.70–72):

> Some impious soldier will own these fields,
> some barbarian these crops; see where discord has led
> wretched citizens: we have sown our fields for these!

Horace, like Vergil, was displaced from ancestral land by the confiscations. And while Horace unmistakably alludes to Vergil's treatment, their reactions are different. The *Eclogues*, while ostensibly set in an imaginary Arcadian landscape, are rife with overtones of the civil disorders; the poet does not hide the tragedy of it all. Meliboeus, the evicted shepherd, finds his only consolation with his fellow shepherd Tityrus, who's been left a few acres of waste land (74–83):

> M. Be off, my little goats, away, once happy flock.
> Not after this will I, stretched out in the shade of a green cave,
> watch you clinging to a thorny cliff;
> I'll sing you no songs; not with me as shepherd
> will you nibble flowering clover and pungent willow.

T. You can rest here with me tonight
under this green shade. I have some ripe fruit,
soft chestnuts and a store of cheese;
already smoke rises from far off farmsteads
and deeper shadows fall from the high mountains.

Imaginary as these characters are, these are the voices of the little people chewed up in Rome's power politics. By comparison, Horace is facile and superficial; his "advice" condescending and unfeeling. Satire drags Vergil's lyrical tragedy into the de-idealizing light of quotidian sensibility of plain talk and pragmatic "dealing with" loss. Yet both poems suggest possible, personal refuges from larger political pressures, and in Horace's allusion there is a kind of transforming calculation, so that the full-knowing reader can read through the blunt, survivor's wisdom of Ofellus to the subtending poignancies of Vergil. And that rather makes a point.

In **Satire 2.6** Horace goes back to the farm, not precisely with a restoration of ancestral land, but via a gift of a gentrified freehold from his friend and patron Maecenas. This is the famous "Sabine farm" that will assume prominence in the *Epistles* and *Odes* later. *Sat.* 2.6 is the poem, answering 1.6's reminiscence of the beginning of that patronage, Horace writes in gratitude for this great, second favor. Yet in terms of theme and specific echo, connections to 2.2 are closer. Food once again assumes an ethical role, and a counterpart to Ofellus is found in a rustic neighbor of Horace, Cervius, who tells a tale of country wisdom (the town and country mice) and, as in 2.2, has the poem's closing words. That closeness, and the distance between the pampered, rewarded Horace and his largely if not entirely invented unfortunate Ofellus triggers a specimen of the indirect satire of Book 2. Ofellus' stalwart fortitude itself becomes a satiric barb: real reactions of the dispossessed are less exemplary, and there were plenty dispossessed by Octavian and Co. Horace merely takes note, and leaves it at that. No diatribe, no preaching. In 2.6, the closest thing to the satire of Book 1 is a mild screed on the bustle and trouble of city life, of the trials of his own obligations as busy man and Maecenas' envied (but not terribly important) client. It can all be read as a self-effacing epistolary apology for his own desire for quiet, country retirement, a "moral" capped by the countryman Cervius' concluding fable of the haughty and fastidious city mouse visiting his country cousin, then drawing him to the city where their dining on delicate leftovers is

catastrophically interrupted by vicious guard dogs. The little fable has
made the poem the most appealing of Horace's satires (106–117):

> Thus when the host has settled his country friend
> on crimson cloth, just like a tucked up waiter,
> or household slave, he produces the feast, tasting first
> whatever he serves. The other, propped comfortably on elbow,
> rejoices over his changed fortune, and plays the part
> of a happy guest. When suddenly –
> a terrible crash of doors! In fear they fly from their couches!
> They scurry about the great room, and are yet more terrified
> as the high house rings with the snarls of Molossian hounds.
> The country mouse, then: "I don't need this;
> I'm off: my woods and small abode, safe from threats,
> will console me with its plain vetch."

It has been pointed out that there is a programmatic aspect to this
amusing poem, one that is taken up in the two remaining satires of this
book set in the country, 2.3 and 2.7. The city is satire's home ground;
it is the natural site of excess, greed, envy, opportunism, rivalry, disquiet, and malice; cities are the great mixers of things, of classes, races,
religions, cultures; cities are, precisely, great con-fusions. They are
inherently unstable and hence are places where ideas of order are
paramount. Satire wallows in the city's disorientation even while float-
ing its sometimes half-hearted normative ethics, its ideas of order. To
leave the city is to return to a "natural" order, where, as our country
mouse avers, there is no disturbance, no confusion. A retreat from the
city is then a retreat from satire, and many critics have seen precisely
that in this second book of *sermones*. Put more finely, *Horace* retreats
to the country – accepting this gift (bribe?) marks *his* withdrawal from
the kind of criticism that just might make reader/targets uncomfortable: the situation as it was programmatically sketched out in *Sat.* 2.1.
There, when Trebatius advises *quiescas* ("take a break; don't write
satire"), Horace dithers and protests, "shadowboxes." But what he
does in the remainder of the book is precisely take that sensible advice,
i.e., he drops the role of society's scourge, retires as satire's hero from
the stage. Leaves town.

This can and has been seen as simple compliance.[43] That was Dryden's diagnosis ("well-mannered court slave"), following others before, and many after. Book 2 seen thus is a winding down, a writing-
out of satire into non-functionality. After all, readers correctly note,

Horace only puts "satire" in, or reveals it through, other people's voices: Ofellus in 2.2, the loquacious Stoic busybody Damasippus in 2.3, the credulous culinary disciple Catius in 2.4, the cynical Teiresias advising Odysseus on legacy-hunting in 2.5, another Stoic busybody, Davus, in 2.7, and finally the comic poet Fundanius' cold dissection of a failed dinner party Horace didn't even attend. Yet Horace is seldom if ever really absent from any of these lines. The voice and many of the satiric exempla are familiar from the first book, and it might be more accurate to see the conspicuous dialogism of Book 2, its diffraction of the satiric voice, as satire not necessarily in retreat or retirement, but rather as a complicating challenge to the Trebatiuses (and Drydens) of his world. Horace ingeniously re-invented satire in his first book; why then should he revert, in his later book, to the simplistic terms, attack or retirement, posed by the dialogue with Trebatius?

More plausible is that the terms of *Sat.* 2.1 are a set up to subtler issues. It has been pointed out, for instance, that Horace's rhetoric of law treats of the interplay and conflicts between juridical (libel) and generic law; that in the new world of Augustan power neither can function as they traditionally had; that Horace, in his friendly relationship with Octavian and Maecenas, claims exemption (from libel) and an aesthetic imprimatur. "Law" in both senses becomes meaningless. Yet 2.1 registers two things clearly: Horace very much cares how he writes satire and is still preoccupied with the place of the satirist in the larger world – these are the framing elements of the poem. The remainder of the book explores the problem Horace sets for himself. Where does satire come from and how is it received? It may, just may, come from a stock, homespun philosopher like Ofellus – one kind of normative discourse – or, better, it may come from the kind of relational discourse that foregrounds the formulaic quality of conventional normative satire against the backdrop of real human hurt. In that case, the "satire" is more difficult to pin down, but is no less provocative: not only are society (in this case, arbitrary victimization of the humble by the powerful) and the satirist (that cliché Ofellus and of course Horace himself) targeted, but they are *entailed* one by the other. Horace's second book, where, intriguingly, the word *satura* is first introduced as generic descriptor by Horace, begins to point out explicitly that *the satirist is always implicated in his world*, never writes from an island of unassailable moral integrity – that other cliché, brave Lucilian scourge of the city. The moral weakness of Horace's own position as satirist thus becomes thematic. If satire loses its edge in the bad new world of post-Republican Rome, it does so not simply because Horace is no Lucilius. Rather it is that however courageous and principled satire is or can be – and it can certainly be more courageous than Horace's – it is never entirely innocent. The new "law" of satire, post-*Sat.* 2.1, asserts that satire is never a law unto itself (wouldn't it be nice?), is always dragged into and dirtied by the laws made and unmade in the unclean world it lives in. Horace, for instance, dirties himself by writing off the land appropriations with Ofellus' glib sermon on self-reliance; but the poet's genius is knowing it and showing his readers how that writing-off happens. Horace, satire's greatest theorist, looks *into* satire like no one before or since; what he finds there is troubling, complicated, human, precisely not reducible to cliché, jingoism, formula. After Horace, the satirist is always assailable, always, with much else, its own target.

Which is exactly what he shows us in the two long Stoic screeds, **Satires 2.3** and **2.7**. In both, Horace is, *as* writer of satires, the victim of others' criticism. That criticism comes from canonical satiric sources: the acquisitive world of the city, from Hellenistic philosophy, from the unempowered, from the *libertas* of the Saturnalia. The first of the two satires, 2.3, is a very long poem built on a simple conceit: one Damasippus, a bankrupt property dealer, stock denizen of the satirical city and born-again Stoic, opens the poem by lecturing Horace, comfortably ensconced in his Sabine retreat, on his failure to write something worthwhile. The local criticism is then broadened into a general homily premised on the Stoic "paradox" that claims all fools are in some sense mad. The usually targeted vices of satire, greed, ambition, etc., are here cast as forms of madness, more or less plausibly. The poem closes, as it opens, with direct criticism of Horace himself. These passages particularly require a closer look (2.3.1–16).

> If you write so rarely that you ask for paper
> not more than four times in a whole year, dismantling
> whatever you (irritable, drugged with wine and sleep) have written,
> you write *nothing* worthwhile. What do you expect?
> But you've fled here on *Saturnalia* – sober too! So recite something
> answering to your promises. Go ahead! No good ...
> Don't blame your writing-reeds; don't pound the poor wall,
> destined, apparently, for the wrath of gods and poets.
> Your eager countenance used to promise much, and good stuff,
> if only this little farmstead would take you in, at ease.
> What good did it do you to pack up Plato, Menander,

Eupolis, Archilochus; what good to take along such companions?
Did you think to placate envy, leaving your virtuosity behind?
You'll be condemned now, poor fool. Avoid Sloth's siren song,
or give up, with even temper, whatever you've done
in your good years.

The lines are full of self- and programmatic reference. This is the first satire, beyond the thank-offering 2.6, after the gift of the Sabine farm. The poem thus serves as a first, self-conscious check on the state of satire after its move to the country. The picture is a little merciless, as we might expect if we have read aright 2.1 and 2.6: satire and the satirist himself are no longer free from satire's criticism. The verbal assault, however, has tended to be mitigated in readers' eyes by the circumstances of its presentation. This is Saturnalia, when the less powerful, particularly slaves, momentarily enjoy the *libertas* of their "betters." Damasippus is no slave, but he is bankrupt, opinionated, interfering, a monomaniacal Stoic proselyte; he is no "friend" of Horace, as those affiliations of *amicitia* have been sorted in the first book of satires; he is not so far distant in character from the pushy climber in 1.9 and hence on first reading easy to dismiss. Moreover, Damasippus plays right into artistic misjudgment in his apparent advocacy of the poetic prolixity so out of tune with the Hellenistic aesthetics Horace had taken such pains to lay out in 1.4 and 1.10. In Horace's artistic world one is supposed to erase, correct, take trouble over a precious few well-crafted lines. Damasippus' rant sounds very much like an ignorant philistine's hectoring of a great artist.

Horace's poem gives that impression to readers even while it lets disquiet creep in. What business, after all, does a satirist have fleeing the city on Saturnalia, the perfect and natural setting for its own saturnalian discourse? Horace having resigned the role of saturnalian voice, Damasippus, the Stoic ephebe, takes it up. If Horace is to displace satire from the city to the country, the maddening meddler Damasippus, the city's street preacher hunting down the satirist with his own satire, will find his target with, in some respects, surprising acuity. The chief vice instanced in this diatribe is *desidia*, "sloth" (15), a canonical target of diatribe satire. The paradoxical situation of the satirist in retirement is neatly conveyed by Horace's bookbag, the very literary stuffings of satire – philosophy, new and old comedy, invective – lying as idle as most of our own books do when we travel. Horace, if he is doing anything in the Stoic's eyes, is reading rather than writing. The farm becomes here, rather than the mark of literary and other success, emblematic of what the satirist traditionally declares himself against: wealth, comfort, retirement, sloth. It is even possible that Damasippus hasn't so radically misread Hellenistic aesthetics, in which a premium is placed on industry and pains taken over composition.

And yet this staged attack on the poet for sloth amounts to a poem of 326 lines, Horace's longest satire, a testimony to industry – and a verbal extravagance that runs all over Hellenistic injunctions about economy and control. That may be meant to characterize, and satirize, the Stoic speaker's prolixity, but there is no question but that this saturation satire on satire throws a great many things we've come to understand about his art and intentions into more than enough confusion. Is Horace presenting a tables-turned, painfully protracted moment of chagrin, staged for his readers' amusement, or is he staging a crisis?

The close of 2.3 offers no definitive answer, but we may legitimately suspect both. After three hundred-some lines of Damasippus' diatribe Horace interrupts to ask how all this pertains to him. The stand-in satirist doesn't hesitate (307–326):

> [D.] ... All right, first of all,
> you're putting up a new house, that's to say,
> you're a pipsqueak playing bigshot. And you
> laugh at the swaggering gladiator Turbo – are you
> any less ridiculous than he is?
> Or do you do whatever Maecenas does, being
> way too small to compete with him? ...
> Now, a pretty picture, toss in your poems, oil in the fire;
> if there is such a thing as a sane poet, why, you're sane!
> I won't mention your foul temper.
> H. "Now stop it!" ...
> "You mega-maniac, PLEASE spare the lesser!"

The "resolution" of the topsy-turvy satirizing is merely the poet's *iam desine*, "now stop." But those words allude to the programmatic close of 1.1: *iam satis est. ne me Crispini scrinia lippi / compilasse putes, verbum non amplius addam,* "now that's enough. So that you don't think I've plundered the desk of the blear-eyed (Stoic) Crispinus, I won't add another word" (see pp. 34–8). Crispinus was a prolix Stoic, rather like the loquacious Damasippus, so it seems that in 2.3

Horace actually performs the pilfering he refers to in 1.1. But the connections go deeper. As Freudenburg points out, 1.1 is "theoretically" concerned with questions attending the root sense of the genre's identifying name, *satura*, something varied, full, stuffed, and linked to that general notion is another Stoic paradox, this one of the *soros*, or pile: adding grains of wheat together one at a time, at which number does the whole make a "pile"? The Stoic philosopher Chrysippus was famously interested in the problem and was himself known for heaping up huge numbers of syllogisms to make a convincing argument, a Stoic pile.[44] Now, Damasippus' long tirade taking up the central portion of 2.3 is, as he says, the repetition of what he's overheard from a student of the work of Chrysippus, one Stertinius, himself the author of some two hundred books of philosophy. Clearly the close of *Sat.* 1.1 is re-addressed in 2.3. Horace's answer to the problem of the *soros* in 1.1 is simply to say "enough," *satis*. Here in 2.3, aside from making Stoic, heaping-up obsession with madness a species of madness itself ("You mega-maniac, spare the lesser!"), Horace associates the heaping up, and madness, with satire ("you mega-satirist, spare the lesser!") and declares *iam desine*, "now stop." It's all an elaborate game of ventriloquism, Horace jousting with a made-up interlocutor who is a caricature of his satirical self, one who, like Horace hasn't stopped when he should (way back at 1.1?). *Sat.* 2.3 is Horace's act of egregious overdone-satire, *satis*/satire *superque*. And his breaking-off closure functions in effect to say that there is no end to satirizing, Horatian or Stoic, good or bad, or even that Horatian, Stoic, good, bad, satirist and target are all mixed up "in the end." No one is immune, no one above satire or its possibilities.

There *is* more to go; but **Satire 2.7** is essentially a tidied up, Callimachean, even "Horatian" follow-up of 2.3. This time the meddling interlocutor is a slave, Davus, and his Stoic diatribe is built on another paradox, that all but the sage are slaves (to one obsession or another). Once again the occasion is the Saturnalia, and once again Horace finds himself the target of another's satirizing tirade. As penultimate poem in the book, it may be that Horace intended it as a recapitulating coda, thematic reprise in smaller, more polished, form of conclusions he had reached in 2.3. The central conceit of slavery or addiction nicely suits Horace's own self-manumission from the obsession of satire, a liberation that **Satire 2.8**, the book's final poem, decisively declares – albeit in a curiously unsatisfactory way. The pun in "un*satis*factory" (un*satire*factory?) is labored but apt in that 2.8 is clearly composed as Horace's signing-off from satire – but in a more general way as well, for this is an unhappy poem. The setting is another feast, this one hosted by a vulgar, nouveau-riche called Nasidienus Rufus. In attendance are Maecenas and two hangers-on he brings along with him, sundry other guests, plus a comic poet Fundanius known to Horace. Horace, intriguingly, is not invited to the dinner. Doubtless such a dinner never took place; the host Nasidienus may be a made-up name, or it may be meant to stand for Salvidienus Rufus, once a friend to Octavian but put to death by him years earlier.[45] In any case the tone of the piece would have been awkward for the principals if this were a record of a real event. The dinner is a disaster. Course after course of luxurious cookery is served up, accompanied by the host's (and helper's) pretentious commentary. The phoneyness and vulgarity of it do not escape the guests, who, for their part, do their level best to exact revenge by drinking to excess. At one climactic point, 54ff., the canopies suspended over the food collapse. The catastrophe is followed by two mock- (and mocking) philosophical "consolations" directed at the host, who recovers his spirits enough to bring on a fresh array of delicacies. At which point the guests coldly depart, leaving the food untouched.

At this feast no one behaves well; even Horace, who is not in attendance, adds his bit of *Schadenfreude*: "I like nothing better than to see such shows of foolishness" (79). Commentators often declare that though we moderns might be taken aback by the rudeness of the guests, it was not likely to have been deemed offensive by Horace's contemporaries in the face of this upstart's pretentiousness. Such figures were, after all, canonical targets of satire since Lucilius and that tradition would continue to produce others later – to gorgeous satirical effect in Petronius. But the Petronius parallel is telling; the ludicrous culinary show in his *Satyrica*, "Trimalchio's Feast" as it's commonly called, leads to genuine comic satire; in Horace the laughter is forced and artificial: "come, tell, what did you laugh at next?" (80). For a poet who can tell a good joke, it is remarkable that nothing in this poem is funny; its laughter that only of the pretentious snob. Fundanius, comic poet, is Horace's stand-in, the literary man on hand. His job is to sketch out the comedy; yet either he or Horace has failed.

I am not sure anyone has sufficiently explained what is going on in this strange closing poem. Obviously, its theme is central to the book, picking up from 2.2, 2.4 (centrally), and 2.6. The structural pattern is obvious; Horace would have needed to end his book if not with this satire with some poem on food, with its now-evident social implications. It takes up other thematic focuses from the earlier poems as well, not only in the second book: friendship, alliance, social politics, Horace's position as client of Maecenas, philosophy, hospitality, the diatribe topics luxury and simplicity, the place of satire at the symposium, the table of talk. He might have done that, and at the same time conjured a fully satisfying scene for his readers, sending them, his second book, and satire itself off with a merry pat on the back. Instead, as is sometimes pointed out, he treats this feast as programmatic, he presents satire's mixed plate so egregiously overdone that the only sane reaction is to walk away coldly. Enough, Horace thus walks out of the game – or forestalling that, does not even show up at the farewell banquet!

But there seems to be more than a convenient symbolic gesture in all this, a darker edge to the poem. As in 1.7, readers' discontent with the poem's failure to be really funny can be a hint that they ought to be looking elsewhere. Beyond the programmatic joke, then, beyond this surprise goodbye party, we might see the outcome of the crisis Horace staged for his readers in 2.3 and 2.7. His first book explores and re-invents satirical poetry even as it maps the poet's own progress into the world of patronage and protection. That book ends with an image of him fully protected, almost literally encircled, by powerful and important friends. The opening of Book 2 re-establishes that position, raising the ante by invoking Caesar himself. What had begun as outsider's discourse, the poetry of the streetcorner diatribist, is now a post-Lucilian art-form, fully theorized, decidedly within the mainstream of political favor and aesthetic fashion. What is more, Lucilius, that brazen aristocrat, has been "processed" by Horace's literary talk; he is now, fully, a flawed precursor, precisely because of the way Horace has redefined the genre. Yet I think Lucilius remains a problem. His frankness, his aristocratic confidence, his expansiveness, even his prolixity suggest something, for better or worse, beyond Horace's range. For Lucilius, the feast is always on; for Horace, subtle, ironic, self-doubting, a thinker, satire's feast begins to cloy. Especially so when the always self-conscious satirist realizes, as he does in Book 2 (and as Lucilius never realizes), that his art must implicate himself. Having become the consummate insider, he cannot but be the target of his own work. Realizing that, he offers himself up as victim of bad satirists within his own better satire. Ensnared by his own game, unable like Lucilius simply to write robustly on, Horace poisons satire's feast (93–95):

> thus we fled, avenging ourselves,
> by tasting nothing at all, just as if Canidia,
> more poisonous than African vipers, has breathed on it.

Canidia, Horace's *bête-noire* from 1.8, where she was repulsed by another foul blast, returns decisively as final expiration of Horace's art. Her blood-chilling presence harks back to the disturbing implications of the earlier satire, implications that Maecenas' green gardens were never quite able to bury – and colors the final impression of this last satire. Here are Horace's friends, after all, without Horace and rendered cold and supercilious; here is Maecenas, a silent and marginalized witness to the collapse of civility, here is the guest maligning his host (remember 1.4?), here is the "happy" society of Maecenas' circle (without envy or malice as Horace declares in 1.9?). In giving, as it were, the last word to Canidia, Horace can defer responsibility for this poison pill. But there is no evading the fact that neither Lucilius nor the artsy Callimachus are any longer Horatian satire's muses. The honor now goes to Canidia.[46] In so declaring, I think, Horace does more than resign this art. For it is not that satire's feed is too much, that he needs now to turn away sated – he'd already cried *satis,* for other reasons, in 1.1, 2.3, 2.4, and 2.7. It seems rather that Horace has come to see that this feast is *not* enough (*non satis*), that it has written itself into a dead end or an endless, pointless social-satirical round. There has to be more. Horace's escape from the dilemma he found himself in, as satirist, is to turn to other poetries, to epistle, to lyric and his finest literary achievements. He is already there, perhaps, finishing the *Epodes,* experimenting with lyric, meditating philosophically in verse epistles, while not in attendance at this last satirical dinner. His alter ego Canidia stands in, scattering the feast. A bold move for this shy and comfortable poet, for in this last, dark act his satire tells the truth.

Further Reading

There is such an abundance of material on Horace's satires, even when confined to English, that this summary can only offer highlights; follow the bibliographies and notes of the works noted below for much more.

Begin, for general orientation, with N. Rudd, *The Satires of Horace* (Cambridge, 1966), E. Fraenkel, *Horace* (Oxford, 1957), 76–153, and E. Gowers, "The Restless Companion: Horace, Satires 1 and 2," in K. Freudenburg, ed., *The Cambridge Companion to Roman Satire* (Cambridge, 2005), 48–61; then move on to the ground-breaking articles on Horace in W. S. Anderson, *Essays on Roman Satire* (Princeton, 1982). There are a few more seminal articles that any student of Horace should read: on Book 1 of the *Satires*, J. E. G. Zetzel's "Horace's *Liber Sermonum*: The Structure of Ambiguity," *Arethusa* 13 (1980): 59–77 and, ranging more widely, "Dreaming about Quirinus: Horace's *Satires* and the Development of Augustan Poetry," in T. Woodman and D. Feeney, eds., *Traditions and Contexts in the Poetry of Horace* (Cambridge, 2002), 38–52; on the politics of the satires, I. M. le M. Du Quesnay's "Horace and Maecenas: The Propaganda Value of *Sermones* I," in T. Woodman and D. West, eds., *Poetry and Politics in the Age of Augustus* (Cambridge, 1984), 19–58. A book-length, fresh perspective on issues raised in these articles, and more, is E. Oliensis, *Horace and the Rhetoric of Authority* (Cambridge, 1998).

For background on ancient literary theory and the satires, see K. Freudenburg, *The Walking Muse: Horace on the Theory of Satire* (Princeton, 1993). Freudenburg's later study takes a different, more politically savvy approach: *Satires of Rome* (Cambridge, 2001), 15–124. For a variety of stimulating perspectives on particular satires, J. Henderson, "Be Alert (Your Country Needs Lerts): Horace, *Satires* 1.9" in *Writing Down Rome: Satire, Comedy, and Other Offences in Latin Poetry* (Oxford, 1999), 202–27, and "On Getting Rid of Kings: Horace, *Satires* 1.7," in *Fighting for Rome: Poets and Caesars, History and Civil War* (Cambridge, 1998), 73–107; F. Muecke, "Law, Rhetoric, and Genre in Horace, *Satires* 2.1," in S. J. Harrison, ed., *Homage to Horace: A Bimillenary Celebration* (Oxford, 1995), 203–18; along similar lines, T. McGinn, "Satire and the Law: The Case of Horace," *Proceedings of the Cambridge Philological Society* 47 (2001): 81–102; E. Gowers, "Horace, *Satires* 1.5: An Inconsequential Journey," *Proceedings of the Cambridge Philological Society* 39 (1993): 48–66; K. J. Reckford, "Only a Wet Dream? Hope and Skepticism in Horace, Satire 1.5," *American Journal of Philology* 120.4 (1999): 525–54; K. Freudenburg, "Canidia at the Feast of Nasidienus (Hor. *Sat.* 2.8)," *Transactions of the American Philological Association* 125 (1995): 207–19; B. Dufallo, "*Satis/Satura*: Reconsidering the 'Programmatic Intent' of Horace's *Satires* 1.1," *Classical World* 93 (2000): 579–90. This list could go on.

The best generally available translation remains that of N. Rudd, *The Satires of Horace and Persius* (London, 1973). If you are reading Horace in Latin, there are good commentaries in English by P. M. Brown, *Horace: Satires*

I (Warminster, 1993) and F. Muecke, *Horace: Satires II* (Warminster, 1993); commentaries on the two books of satires for the Cambridge Greek and Latin Classics series are in preparation. Fuller commentaries exist in German (Kiessling and Heinze, eds.), Italian (Fideli, ed.), and French (Lejay, ed.). On the afterlife of Horace, C. Martindale and D. Hopkins, eds., *Horace Made New: Horatian Influences on British Writing from the Renaissance to the Twentieth Century* (Cambridge, 1993) is essential. For verse renderings by English poets and translators, see D. S. Carne-Ross and K. Haynes, *Horace in English* (London, 1966).

3

Persius

Literary celebrity followed Horace as he left satire's egregious feast. His lyrics (23 and 13 BCE) and epistles (20 and 18–13 BCE) won immediate favor and were the objects of subsequent literary imitation. His satires were of course still read, their manuscripts copied through the centuries, until they – surprisingly, rather than lyric or epistle – were the means of re-introducing Horace to European letters in the fifteenth century. After Horace left off satire, Romans appear to have followed his lead in this as well, and it is not until nearly the middle of the next century that the next major hexameter satirist appears. Aules Persius Flaccus, born 42 years after Horace's death and 33 or so years before Juvenal's birth, lived in the Rome of Nero (54–68 CE), no less a repressive regime than its predecessors – save for its hothouse cultivation of artistic expression, Nero believing himself rather an artist. Which situation may help explain the contemporaneity of three active satirists: Persius, Seneca, and Petronius. The latter two did not write satire in the style of Lucilius and Horace, that is, in Lucilian hexameters (these formal parameters being decisive in Romans' conception of literary genres). But they did compose satirical tracts mixing prose and various verse forms in the manner of Varro (116–27 BCE), a scholar and writer, younger contemporary of Lucilius and older contemporary of Horace. Varro himself claimed to be imitating the Cynic Menippus (*c*. 300–250 BCE), who established the formal model of mixed prose and verse. The fragments of Varro's *Saturae Menippeae*, some 600, show an imaginative intelligence – he invented some of the wittiest titles in literary history – ranging across a variety of subjects, many of them shared with verse satire. His Neronian imitators Seneca and Petronius adopted Varro's formal model: the former composing his *Apocolocyntosis*, or *Pumpkini-fication of Claudius*, a cruelly witty burlesque of the just-dead emperor; the latter penning his long *Satyrica*, a much broader satire of life under Nero. More on both authors in this book's final chapter, but it is important to recognize at this point that Persius, who consciously writes hexameter satires in the tradition of Horace and Lucilius, was not in his day alone in cultivating the satirical muse. In fact, as Persius' immediate popularity testifies to (a little perplexing to a posterity that has struggled with his difficult Latin), his day may be the most satirically fruitful of Roman literary history. Yet the politics of power were to have their say: before Nero was forced out and driven to suicide, these three satirists and many others associated with them were dead, only one of them, Persius, by natural causes.

Of Persius there are intriguing glimpses in his ancient *Vita*, though these later-composed biographical "Lives" are nearly always to a degree fictive. He is said to have lived from 34 CE to 62, dying young of an intestinal disorder (*vitio stomachi* – apt end for a satirist). A native of Etruria and born into a wealthy equestrian family, he lived and died on his own estates, though he surely saw much of Rome and was thoroughly educated by several prominent tutors. The last of his teachers – and father-figures, for his own father died when Persius was only six – was the Stoic freedman Cornutus, to whom Persius was very close. Under his tutelage, Persius became something of an adept in Stoic thought himself and he is said to have amassed a large collection of philosophical writings. His mother and sister too were close to him. We have thus a picture of a sickly, somewhat introverted, educated, philosophical, country-living patrician with no political ambition, perhaps effeminate (*verecundiae virginalis*), repelled by Rome's seamy decadence. What emerged from these (perhaps unlikely) circumstances and cloistered life is some of the most original poetry in Latin literature.

Persius had none of Horace's obsession with "making it" in privileged patronage circles; in this he was like Catullus, another of Rome's strikingly original poets. But unlike Catullus, who eschewed patronage but clubbed with the "new poets" (*neoteroi*) of his generation, Persius was attracted to a sodality of philosophically inclined intellectuals, many of whom were associated with the Stoic resistance to Nero – most either exiled or killed as a consequence.[1] The apparent political silence of Persius' satires, as we shall see, is therefore not unimportant. Initially we can observe that lack of overt political statement in his poetry is less surprising in Persius than in Horace; an old-blood Etruscan with a rural estate might not be expected to embroil himself in public affairs, though Persius' interest in the state of Rome is obvious in the satires. Persius saw Rome as ripe for satire from a perspective quite other than Horace's. Obviously Stoic philosophy is one part of that perspective, and as a consequence Persius has been known for many years chiefly as the "Stoic satirist." For reasons that we'll see develop in reading the poetry, this is too simple a designation, but Persius unquestionably took (Stoic) philosophy seriously in ways that the genial Epicurean Horace could not.

Another part of that perspective is entailed in Persius' sense of audience. While it is clear that Horace wrote for friends within Maecenas' patronage circle, Octavian himself, as well as to a broader Roman audience, Persius explicitly claims (following a disarming line in Horace, *Sat.* 1.4.39–40) to be writing for very few (1.2–3): "Who will read this stuff ?" "Are you talking to me? No one, by god." "No one?" / "Well, maybe one or two" (compare, too, Lucilius, p. 21). His satires were never published in his lifetime, so his "intended" audience as he composed them can only be the literary-cum-philosophical intimates to whom he would have recited and circulated his incomplete drafts. Only later, when Cornutus and Caesius Bassus had edited and posthumously published the satires, did they enjoy anything like a popular vogue.

Finally, a third feature of Persius' very different poetic perspective is, ironically, his conspicuous dependence on Horace himself. Persius draws upon Horatian lines, phrases, words, situations, and themes pervasively.[2] It is not just that Persius is "bookish" or "allusive," as he is often called; Persianic satire would not be possible but for, specifically, *Horace*'s precedent. Nearly every line has something of Horace in it, yet – here is the paradox – Persius is (usually) nothing like Horace in literary or satiric effect. Whereas Horace's casual *sermo* is conversational, urbane, clear in syntax and intent, Persius' satire is dense, abrasive, difficult, obscure in language and structure, experimental in imagery. These factors not only make Persius' Latin much more difficult to read, but they show how he uses Horace as a necessary counter, simultaneously a point of inspiration and radical departure. Horace's generic struggle had been with Lucilius; Persius' agon is with Horace – the difference in procedure being that Persius does not announce his differences programmatically, but demonstrates them through radical deformation of his literary father-model.

Persius has left us only six hexameter satires and one introductory prologue in choliambs, or "limping iambics" based on the example of the Greek invective poet Hipponax. Here are its entire fourteen lines:

> I neither dipped my lips in the horsey fountain
> nor do I recall dreaming on two-headed Parnassus,
> so that I might suddenly emerge a "poet."
> And I leave the maids of Helicon
> and pale Pirene to those whose images
> the clinging ivy licks. A half-rustic,
> I bear my song to the rites of the bards.
> Who dictated to the parrot his "hello"
> and taught the magpie to try our words?
> Master of art and benefactor of genius,
> the Belly, fashioner of forbidden speech.
> If hope of deceitful cash should sparkle,
> you'd believe crow-poets and magpie-poetesses
> capable of singing Pegaseian nectar.

These are deceptively simple lines, if a little bewildering to a first-time reader. The "horsey fountain" is Hippocrene, the spring of poetic inspiration, struck open by Pegasus' hoof, said to be on Mt. Helicon. Persius is alluding to and denigrating the venerable old tradition of poet's claiming inspiration from the Muses, "so that I might suddenly emerge a poet." He does the same in line 2, mentioning poetic dreaming, the sort of poetic-conversion experiences claimed by Hesiod, Callimachus, and Ennius, reiterated (not always seriously) in Lucretius, Vergil, Propertius, Ovid; here Persius not only denies the experience, but he dismisses it by mislocating the customary place of the dream: usually Helicon, here Parnassus. As if he didn't know. The "maids of Helicon" Persius leaves behind are of course the traditional muses, and in lines 4 and 5 Helicon and Pirene, Corinthian twin to Hippocrene, get their due, dismissive mentions. The point is to satirize the artsy-poetry game by overplaying its rules: Persius is here every bit as allusive and subtle as the rarified Hellenistic poets he mocks. In this he is sometimes said to be following Horace's lead in denying satire poetic status, being himself no poet but merely a *semipaganus* (half-rustic). That would be nice, but far too easy for Persius. He goes on in line 7 to declare his serious artistic mission: "I bear my song to the rites of the bards," that is, to the real poets. And here his point comes clearer: he has not been going after Hesiod or Callimachus or Ennius, but their legions of imitators whose busts decorate the ivy-growing gardens of the rich. This becomes especially evident in the second section of the poem where magpies and parrots stand for mimicking followers of popular schools of poetry. We suspect here that more is involved than a general broadside against imitators of popular (poetic) fashion. The artistic rage of the day was a kind of neo-Callimachean-ism, a hangover and extension of the poetic principles that operated in Horace's day emphasizing careful workmanship, subtlety, metrical polish, and learned allusiveness. It sometimes went to mannerist ex-tremes: extensive use of Greek themes, polysyllabic Greek words, arch versification, even end-rhymes. There is evidence that Nero – not only emperor but chief patron of the arts – fostered precisely these prin-ciples and may even have composed the poetry in that mode that Persius singles out for satirical attention in his first satire. That belly, then, of line 11, good satiric organ that it is, becomes rather charged with implication. Is it meant to be the generic "belly," greed, avarice, of multitudes of would-be poets angling for the favor and patronage of the imperial circle? Or is it meant to indicate, too, the corpulent presence of Nero himself – the big belly that crow and magpie poets, in their mimetic yawping, aspire to? Persius never names Nero, but certainly he is "there" in the satirist's world, calling the shots that Persius *will*, with specificity and precision, deplore.

He will do so with a vengeance in his first satire, but one or two questions about this prologue linger, as must already have occurred to attentive readers: specifically, where is *satire* in this short introduction? Unlike the programmatic poems of Lucilius and Horace, Persius does not set out specifically satiric principles here, does not tell us what *his* satire will be like or strive for. Nor does he launch into the catalogue of the usual satiric sins (avarice is evident, but in very specified form), the *mempsimoiria* trope used by Horace in his opening poem, or a rem-iniscence of the ways Horace and Lucilius used to do things. Nor, finally, though he is indubitably writing "satire," does he even give us the customary, identifying, hexameter verse form. This is satire with a difference, and there is palpable ambition in the move. While Horace will ever be for Persius a point of first reference and even imitation (twistingly), Persius is not concerned with superseding his master or winning a generic contest. Rather satire is for this later satirist a necessary *poetry.* He throws it into the mix, with these (satirically) unmarked choliambics – associated only with the grumpy verses of Hipponax, not satire proper – a mysterious little package that blows up in the faces of the posturing poets of his day. It is an act of aesthetic sabotage. The few lines here trade in skepticism, sarcasm, insult, insubordination. They are not pretty, nor are meant much to amuse. One could write this way only if one felt, deeply, that poetry matters. This little fourteen-line grenade, then, is an attempt to clear out much that is bad in art: tired, old, imitative, uninspired, without purchase in life. It is also a personal manifesto. Persius does not say here what his satire will be like, but he declares who *he* is – a *semipaganus*, an outsider (remember Horace 1.1) who means to stay that way. To remain outside the artsy games(manship) of the Neronian circle, to be one's irascible, mildly inscrutable self (and no one really knows precisely what *semipaganus* signifies: "half-rustic" or "half-clansman" or even "half-poet"[3]) – this will be Persius' unHoratian ambition, not to be the accepted insider but the self-delared outsider, poet in exile.

Satire 1, like the prologue, is all about poetry. That fact, in itself, is neither terribly unHoratian nor a surprise: much of satire's talk has been about its nature and status as poetry. But Persius' is no abstract or aesthetic critique of Lucilian loquacity or the relative crudity of earlier versemaking. Rather, throughout this first satire, poetry is indexed to public morality. Opening in the most artificial – and difficult to follow – dialogue form imaginable (he shatters any naturalistic illusion in line 44: "whoever you are whom I've just made up to be my adversary"), Persius immediately reveals his dramatically new satiric persona: an irascible, disillusioned teller of unvarnished, even ugly, truth. That truth pertains to Rome whose taste in poetry is a function of a degraded, even louche, general sensibility: effeminate, illusion-addicted, pretentiously puffed up with Greek aesthetics. In this busi-ness of poetry, and precisely in this Rome of Nero, who's praised and why become important questions, not least because politics and aes-thetics were closely related. The neo-Callimachean artistic values broadly cultivated in Rome under the mentorship of the emperor himself were a mainstream holdover from the revolutionary, bad-boy poetries of Catullus and his ilk a century earlier. Their originality was long-dead, and Persius offers an extended parody of their derivative, hyper-cultivated mannerisms in lines 63–106. Further, poetry has become a vulgarized mode of popular entertainment (13–21):

> We compose in our studies, some in meter, some not,
> stuff big enough for inflated lungs to bellow out.
> And you, all combed and washed for the public,

gleaming, wearing birthday ring, sit on your high seat
having gargled smooth your supple throat,
languishing with that leering eye.
Then you'd see huge Tituses groan,
neither seemly nor serene, when those verses
enter in, and scratch their inner parts.

There follow substantial sections on the superficiality of crowd-
pleasing rhetoric and scathing parody, bewildering to a modern reader
unacquainted with the conventions under criticism, of the sophisticated poetics popular in literary circles close to Nero. Persius' straw-
man interlocutor takes its part, dismissing the opening of the *Aeneid* as
passé (92–97):

"But sophistication and smoothness have been added to raw verses.
So, 'Berecynthian Attis' has learned to close a line,
and 'the dolphin that parted cerulean Nereus'
and 'we drew a rib from broad Apennine.'
'Arms and the man' – what crusty stuff's that?
Like an old, overcooked branch of cork."

Persius then goes on to quote examples of Hellenized, mannerist verse
whose effect booms best in Latin (99–102):

"torva Mimalloneis inplerunt cornua bombis,
et raptum vitulo caput ablatura superbo
Bassaris et lyncem Maenas flexura corymbis
euhion ingeminat, reparabilis adsonat echo."

("Rough horns they filled with Mimallonian
booming, and the Bassarid about to take the
haughty calf's head and the Maenad ready to
turn the lynx with ivy-vine alternate 'Evoe!'
and echo doubles the sound.")

Notice the Greek words and end-rhymes, explicitly pointed out in that
adsonat echo, which combined with certain features of meter make this
not Persius' cup of tea (103–106):

Would this kind of thing be around if we had any balls left?
This weak-kneed stuff swims on saliva-wet lips
and the *Maenad* and *Attis* are wet too –
no evidence of pounded desk or bitten nails.

What Neronian poetry does not do, Persius tells us, is say the truth, and the last lines of this poem make *his* case for doing precisely that. But it is an odd sort of resolution, claiming as it does the precedent of "sly" Horace and vice-crunching Lucilius (115–117), his own urge to speak out, if only to a hole in the ground: "can't I speak? not in secret? not into this hole? not anywhere?" (119). The pressure for silence the poet feels is surely the sheer force and prevalence of the odious fashions he has been railing against; surely too that Belly, *venter*, lurks in the background, the scrupulously unnamed sponsor of what Rome has become.

Satire 2, written very likely earlier than the first, is less idiosyncratic, though it shares the same general sensibility. Its theme is the vanity of human wishes, of prayers specifically, and the poem was doubtless to some degree a model for Juvenal's much larger, more accomplished tenth satire. In its smaller way, however, Persius 2 is impressive: it is more coherent than Juvenal's poem, more focused, and runs its course nearer a consistent moral point. The poem breaks into fairly clear sections: after an opening invocation to Macrinus (it is a *genethliacon* or birthday poem addressed to that figure), lines 2–30 show ostensibly virtuous public and surely corrupt private prayer followed by the poet's wondering about what sort of deity such duplicity must presuppose; 31–40 illustrate the superstitions and naïve prayers of grandmothers and aunts on behalf of newborns; 41–51 present the inconsistency between desired goods and the foolishly counterproductive behaviors of those desiring them; 52–72 examine the strange and consequently nearly universal idea that because humans are fond of gold, the gods must be so interested as well; the work's last three lines return to the spiritual health embodied at the poem's beginning in the figure of Macrinus. There are lines here as inventive and searing as any in poetry (61–68):

> Oh, souls bent to the earth, bereft of anything of spirit,
> what good does it do to let these ways of ours into the temple
> and from this corrupt pulp of our flesh conclude what pleases the gods?
> This fleshy pulp, to please itself, dissolved cassia in oil,
> this pulp stained Calabrian wool in corrupting dye,
> compelled us to scrape pearl out of oyster and dig out
> veins of ore from raw earth. This pulp sins
> and sins again, yet turns its crimes to use.

Satire 3 is a considerably longer and more substantial accomplishment. The outwardly directed moralizing of *Sat.* 2 is supplanted in this work by a more contextualized and nuanced moral scope. Persius here takes inspiration from Horace *Sat.* 2.3 and 2.7 in presenting himself as the victim of another's diatribe – with a characteristic twist: rather than setting up a scene of Horatian near-retirement in the country, Persius presents himself as a lazy student, a bit hung over, rudely awakened by a more senior student (1–7):

> "So, this is how you study! Bright morning's breaking through
> the shutters and widening their slits with light.
> And we snore away, enough to ventilate that strong, stale
> Falernian. The dial's already touching the fifth hour,
> and what are you doing? The dog star has long since
> been cooking the crops and the flock is sheltering under elm."
> So, one of my comrades . . .

The intruding outburst turns into a long diatribe, à la Horace's Damasippus' or Davus' lengthy screeds in Stoic mode. Persius' ingenious variation on the theme is at once to register the tiresomeness of the Stoic sermon and to seem to take its general import seriously. This satire contains some of Persius' most inventive imagery ("you're all mud, wet and soft; you need to be hurried on the wheel / continually to be fashioned" [23–24]) as it dances between serious diatribe and disarming nods to Horatian skepticism. There are compelling lines on both sides (35–38, 77–85):

> Great father of the gods, if only you'd punish savage tyrants
> with nothing but this: when vile lust
> laced with poisonous venom stirs their minds,
> let them look upon the virtue they've lost, and waste away.
> here someone from that hairy crowd of centurions
> will say: "what I know is enough for me. I don't care
> to be like Arcesilas and sickly Solones;
> heads bowed, glowering at the ground,
> they chew mumblings and mad silences to themselves,
> and balance their words on protruding lips,
> pondering the dreams of some old sicky, 'from
> nothing nothing can come, into nothing nothing can return.'
> Is this why you go pale? Is this reason to miss lunch?"

In the end, this satire mirrors the slugabed student's inability to get things resolved – for little *is* resolved through this superb poem's complex course – but becomes all the more intriguing and humane because of that.[4]

Satire 4 is sometimes said, like Satire 2, to be another early poem to judge from its rough edges and startling obscenity, yet it is in some terms the most adventurous extant satire prior to Juvenal and there may be other indications that it comes late – more on which below. The poem takes inspiration from a pseudo-Platonic dialogue, the *Alcibiades I*, where Socrates takes Alcibiades, his sometime protégé, to task for want of self-knowledge. Persius develops that theme into an eccentric diatribe on criticism of others that seldom comes home to roost (23–32), the start of which is phrased memorably (23–24):

> Look how nobody, I mean nobody, dares the descent into oneself,
> but instead gazes at the packsack of the fellow going in front.

But soon comes the rough stuff (34–38):

> . . . a stranger is likely to elbow you and spit out harshly:
> "Some morals! weeding out your penis and groin
> the better to exhibit your withered balls to the crowd!
> When you comb out that perfumed crotch-mop
> why does that shaven tool of yours stand out alone?"

It continues in similar vein, causing readers to both blanch and wonder what could prompt such images in a poem about the relatively tame philosophical topics of other-directed criticism and self-knowledge. It is a subject we'll return to, noting here only that the poem quickly turns back, in closing, to the safer ground of moral exhortation – again, though, in remarkably original language (51–52):

> Reject what's not you; let the crowd take back its honors.
> Live with yourself: soon you'll discover how poor are your belongings.

Satire 5 is Persius' flawed masterpiece. His longest poem, it goes on for 190 lines. Its first section, 1–51, beginning with a portentous, epic call for "a hundred mouths" with which to cry out his theme, is an extravagant tribute to Annaeus Cornutus, cast as a Socratic mentor for the young Stoic writer. After a short transitional section, also addressed to Cornutus but including a standard-introductory priamel ("some prefer this, some that, but you prefer philosophy and teaching the young"), the remainder of the broken-backed poem is given over to a lengthy sermon on freedom – which is not an accident of birth or a gift but something to be earned by studying philosophy. Whence the loose connection to Cornutus' profession. The long latter section becomes a Persianic version of the same Stoic paradox that informed Horace *Sat.* 2.7: only the Stoic sage is free. The remarkable point here is the contrast between this and the diatribes of Horace 2.7 and Persius' own Satire 3, which structure in ironic perspective by casting the speech in another's voice: Horace's boorish slave or Persius' almost equally boorish senior companion. In fact there are some curious reversals of perspective here: a twin of the lazy student of *Sat.* 3 is awakened in this poem not by a meddling senior Stoic, but by the seductive voice of Avarice (132) whose counterpart is the equally seductive Luxury (142) urging quietistic enjoyment (*carpamus dulcia*) of life's goods. The siren songs of sex and religious superstition follow, only to be cut short by the contemptuous snort of another centurion – a concentrated self-reference to Persius's own *Sat.* 3. That rude-interruption-as-closure is too sudden for many readers wondering what is *resolved* in this conclusion (189–191):

> ... dixeris haec inter varicosos centuriones,
> continuo crassum ridet Pulfenius ingens
> et centum Graecos curto centusse licetur.

> ... Just say these things among varicose centurions
> and straightaway huge Pulfenius roars
> and offers a clipped penny for a hundred Greeks.

But William Anderson has pointed out the clever self-allusion to Persius' own opening in the centurion Pulfenius' crude dismissal, observing the verbal play on the "hundred voices" (*centum voces*) in lines 1–2 and the *centuriones, centum,* and *centusse* of the last three lines.[5] Just as Cornutus had objected to those *centum voces* in the poem's beginning, the crude Pulfenius sarcastically butts in here – and shuts the satirist up. In both cases there has been a failure to understand; satire meets a wall of incomprehension. After nearly 120 lines of seriously undertaken diatribe, there is chagrined resignation in this conclusion, a resignation that echoes ideas about his audience expressed in the prologue and first satire. The harsh ending amounts to an unwriting of satire.

And the final poem, **Satire 6**, possibly even composed last, seems to confirm that sentiment. Its form is that of a letter (to his literary executor Caesius Bassus), so Persius seemingly follows Horace out of satire into epistle – and lyric, for Bassus specialized in Horatian-styled lyrics: Horace in a nutshell. Here is Persius in Horatian ease, on holiday in northern Italy sending back a postcard to his friend, just to let him know how much he is *enjoying* himself. Suddenly, enjoyment becomes a "theme" and Persius is off in diatribe-style comparing misers and spendthrifts (18ff.), espousing a Horatian middle way in expenditure – even, in lines 22–26, borrowing the phrase "use it" from Horace's *Epistles* 2.2.190–191:

> ... Use it, I say, use it,
> though not so as to serve turbot fashionably to freedmen
> or subtly sniff out the delicate savors of thrush.
> Just live up to your harvest, and (it's all right)
> mill your grain.

The openhandedness extends to helping out the less fortunate ("a friend's ship has sunk ... slice off a portion of your capital and give it to him" [27–32]). The thought prompts a response from another hypothetical interlocutor, this time his heir ("my heir, whoever you may be" [41–42]), regretting the loss of inheritance; a rhetorical setup for a progressively more vituperative riposte. Persius threatens in extravagant scenarios to give it all away, or to find a substitute heir. There is a real ethical issue in all this; the heir's clutching dependency is the antitype of Stoic self-sufficiency, the basis of Persius' "use it," i.e., use what is one's own, no more, no less. And the idea of an heir inheriting more than is necessary leads Persius, one last time, into imagery of decadence and repellent sex (69–73):

> ... Should my holiday meal
> be nettle and smoked pig's jowl, split eared at that,
> so that playboy of yours can glut himself on *foie gras*,
> and, when the touchy vein of his cock coughs,
> empiss some patrician bag?

This is the kind of sneering vitriol we see in *Sat.* 4 and elsewhere, possibly modulated here toward something darker still. The dialogue between Persius and hypothetical heir has been rough, full of bluster, overstatement, and threat; this *is* the way satire talks in its nastier moments. Persius' twist on such a convention is the sub-tenor of disappointed bitterness – here, framed in the language of trade (75–80):

> Sell your soul for cash, then. Do your trade; cleverly shake down
> every corner of the world, lest someone else beat you at
> making slaps ring out on the hard platform of the slave market;
> double your cash. "I've done that." Now three, now four times,
> now ten times the profit. Tell me where I should stop,
> and we've found the man to define Chrysippus' "heap."

Commerce, cash, accumulation – all in exchange for the simple good of one's precious soul. In pre-Christian thought, the notion is not yet a commonplace, but the sense of "soul" as both life-spirit and ethically contingent element of being can be found in classical thinking from Plato onward. The Stoics, Persius' "identity-group," borrowed heavily from Plato in this and other regards. Following his Stoic inclinations and developing them further in this regard, Persius makes it the intrinsically identifying thing, the self's *logos*, whose absence haunts the broken discourse of *Sat.* 4, finds responsive chord in the filial relationship with Cornutus in 5, and informs the satirical textures of 6. One sees at moments its fleeting shadow – idealistic, angry, sad, disappointed – in the pattern of acid invective and negative definition the poem displays. That elusive soul matters more to Persius than to any other satirist.

What *Can* Satire Do?

It seems a simple question with a number of possible and predictable answers: criticize, moralize, preach, entertain, burlesque – these and others like it are common understandings of satire's functional outcomes. But oddly in its Roman (hexameter) incarnation, satire after Lucilius tends to underplay these functionalities and to see and present itself as a "literary" discourse. Horace rewrites it as an ostensibly harmless genre that, as *Sat.* 1.4 insists, does not offend, does not over-aspire, does not reach many ears. As we have seen, such a coloring is far from entirely accurate, but it is largely true that Horace's innovations in the genre were designed to make satire "say" in a certain way rather than affect people in (another) certain way. Juvenal too, as we'll see, innovates massively in terms of a literary tradition, importing the language of epic and rhetoric, while insisting, as he does at the end of his first satire, that it will criticize only the dead. Auden put the case of poetry in pessimistic, if not entirely negative, categorical terms ("In Memory of W. B. Yeats"):

> for poetry makes nothing happen; it survives
> in the valley of its saying where executives
> would never want to tamper; it flows south
> from the ranches of isolation and the busy griefs,
> raw towns that we believe and die in; it survives,
> a way of happening, a mouth.

Robert Elliott, writing in the particular case of satire in a study that examines the practice of satire in its early magic and ritual contexts, claims that as satire becomes an art form its efficacy "in the world" is extinguished:

> In such a sophisticated literary genre there is small place for the kinds of power wielded by an Archilochus or Aithirne. When Horace or Juvenal hurls threats in Archilochean terms, we understand the threats in a special sense: language which was once believed capable of magically inflicting death, now kills in a metaphorical sense only.[6]

Literary satire becomes a thing read, admired, appreciated perhaps, living on in the quiet backwater that executives and their ilk pass by unnoticing in the course of their pursuits. Not a thing that does (anything).

Persius in claiming virtually no audience for his poetry ("perhaps one or two" [*Sat.* 1.3]) can scarcely be said to be an exception to the general rule in at least this respect. Both Horace and Juvenal have had far the greater share of literary history's reception; the hardy souls who brave Persius' Latin or even read his dense and concentrated language in translation have not been so many. And yet... *aspice et haec, si forte aliquid decoctius audis* ("look also into this, if you would hear something strong and concentrated" [1.125]). Persius offers his poetry as a dare – "here you'll find none of the harmless stuff Horace was talking about; see if you can stand the heat": *inde vaporata lector mihi ferveat aure* ("my reader, ears scoured, should feel the burn" [1.126]). This passage follows another in which Persius adapts Horace on the relationship of satire to Greek Old Comedy (1.123–124):

> You, whoever is taken with bold Cratinus,
> who studies angry Eupolis and grand old Aristophanes,
> look also into this...

Horace had mentioned the same trio in the opening of 1.4 (see pp. 46–8):

> The poets Eupolis, Cratinus, and Aristophanes
> and the other authors of Old Comedy,
> whenever someone deserved to be branded
> as a thief or sex-fiend or murderer or
> something notorious, used to go right after them.

Horace then goes on to change terms (1.4.6–9):

> Lucilius entirely derives from them; he followed them,
> altering only his meters. He was clever all right,
> and perceptive, but a bad verse technician.
> That was his real problem.

Horace has jumped ship: from satire as condemnation of the deserving bad, it is to become a verse form whose technical merits matter. Persius, in adapting precisely this passage, tellingly keeps silent on Horace's point, style. Or perhaps not entirely silent: Persius' curious metaphoric word at 125, *decoctius* ("cooked down, concentrated," a metaphor drawn from wine-making), must, it seems to me, entail a stylistic implication. The overt analogy is strength, strong brew in these satires, strong enough to slip into the related metaphor of vinegary ear-wash. But "concentration" is one of the standard descriptors, too, of Persius' style, his way of saying. His metaphors come full-strength, undiluted, fast in sequence, frequently jolting the sensibility; his interlocutor-scenes come at us with rapid-fire compression and with barely distinguished indicators of just who has what lines; his narrative logic often seems gnarled, twisted, condensed. His metrical habits explicitly eschew modern taste for finish and polish. A line assigned an anonymous interlocutor could have come straight from the Horace of 1.4 (Persius 1.92): "But elegance and metrical juncture have been added to crude verses."

Persius' response is a scathing burlesque of just such technically finished poetry (1.93–106). This *decoctius* satire of Persius then comes to us, just as the vinegary metaphor implies, in a *style* that is rough, abrasive, irritating, dense, and – difficult. Consider just a few lines from his first satire (1.22–25):

> Still gathering scraps for others' ears, old man,
> to which you, a ruin in skin and joints, would say "no more!"?
> "But why learn all this if this froth, this wild fig,
> once conceived inside, not break out from burst liver?"

Metaphor is piled on metaphor with scarcely a pause to capture the developing thought; the poetry composed by the targeted modern poetaster is rendered as gobbets of junk-food, ruination of his own health, to be tossed down auditors' – ears; the poetaster responds with the traditional plea of the creative soul – I *must* write, deflatingly qualified by "or what's the point of all that schooling" – couched in such tortured metaphoricity (gassy froth and/or the weedy, stone-and-liver-bursting wild fig) as to render the whole ambition ludicrous. Even the poetaster's poor health is put in terms requiring the reader's diagnosis, "a ruin in skin and joints" for gout and dropsy. And still, having sorted those images out, we may not have it right: the manuscripts have *auriculis* (ears) rather than *articulis* (joints), the latter being some modern editors' hypothesis about what Persius originally wrote. If they are wrong about that, Persius intended to write something like "to which you, ruined in your own ears and skin, would say 'no more!' " or "ears to which (to whose flattery) you, already swollen with their attentions, would have to say 'no more!' " or "ears to whose attentive desire for (sexual) titillation you, already ruined in joint and foreskin, would have to say 'no more!' "[7] All these readings are possible. And the process of entertaining these options becomes characteristic in Persius. Even when textual matters are not so vexed, the originality and difficulty of the metaphors, the compression of language he employs, and problems in adjudicating speakers involve the reader in a process of (interfering) diagnosis, simply to make meaning.

And often the meaning we want to make ("let's have a little plain sense here") runs hard up against imagery or language that challenges our expectations or comfort. Take the lines just preceding these just discussed (15–21, see p. 93 above):

And you, all combed and washed for the public,
gleaming, wearing birthday ring, sit on your high seat
having gargled smooth your supple throat,
languishing with that leering eye.
Then you'd see huge Tituses groan,
neither seemly nor serene, when those verses
enter in, and scratch their inner parts.

Here Persius puts on show a poetry recitation as verbal fornication. Not merely "titillating" or "risqué" poetry, but language in lines 19–21 that forces visceral images into the reader's mind, just as the poet's words work their seductive way into those "huge Tituses." Reading from line 15, we might have expected (hoped for?) something milder, but when we get to line 18, Persius shakes us up. *Patranti ocello*, which I've discreetly translated as "leering eye," means literally "orgasmic eye." The image is both more concrete and more perplexing than what we might have expected. We are put on notice that there will be no mincing words here and we are challenged, once again, to put together the logistics of this mutual, poetic orgy. The whole is meant to revolt readers, for he does not like this kind of poetry, but not without drawing us into the process of making that revolting meaning.

This abrasive verse Persius produces is to be *his* poetry, the real stuff – bearing in mind that the burden of that real stuff is what we've just been reading. The boldness of his ambition is another turn from Horace, whose falsely modest denial of that status for poems he had labored much over has made *Sat.* 1.4 such an intriguing puzzle (see pp. 50–2). In Persius' prologue there is no such ambiguity. Disavowing the standard clichés of poetic inspiration and production, he nonetheless employs unambiguously valorized language to describe his work: *ad sacra vatum carmen adfero nostrum* ("I bear my song to the rites of the bards" [*Prol.*, 7]). The real world clatters and cackles all around; the siren songs of the muses have become the belly-growls of poetry on the make for patronage, best of all from the biggest *venter* in Rome, Nero, who was both patron and artiste, gluttonous for fame. Even the reclusive Stoic, the semi-attached, *semipaganus* Persius, has *noticed*. Noticed that the corrupt, climbing, real world of Rome makes poetry in its image, infects it to its core. Persius' remarkable statement in the prologue, claiming to present his verse at the rites of the bards, does not so much announce a verse that will remain pure of all Rome's infection; the nastiness one sees in patches of Persius in fact starkly and designedly reveals it. What it does instead is announce a satire that will hit back.

One way of doing that is to attack poetry precisely as a product not of romanticized inspiration but of an economy of values situated in place and time; that is the explicit job of the first satire. Horace in his way had noticed the same general situation, and his reaction was to adapt his art form to the social realities he lived in. Which is not to say that his satire is toothless, but that it expresses what it does by way of comment and criticism from within the value and patronage structures of Augustan Rome. Persius, *semipaganus*, locates himself (at least semi-) without. Yet his technique is anything but obtuse, and his means of engagement with his targeted Neronian world is, paradoxically, deeply intertextual. An example is Satire 3, whose dramatic logic, as we have noted above, is based on that of Horace *Sat.* 2.3 and 2.7. All three poems feature some version of the poet's self in leisurely situation, interrupted by an aggressive Stoic interlocutor whose remonstrations of the poet-figure develop, or devolve, into a lengthy diatribe. Commentators link Persius 3 most closely to Horace 2.3 – the majority of the identifiable allusions are located there. Each focuses initially on the relatively narrow subject of diligent writing and/or study, and moves out into a general ethical remonstration that will occupy the main body of the satire. But there are differences in tenor and effect as well. Immediately apparent is the light, ironic touch of Horace's lines. That quality proceeds not from any inherent absurdity in the matter of Damasippus' speech; the ethical material is standard stuff (the point is that it *is* standard stuff). Rather, the fun comes from Horace's presentation, which makes Damasippus comically absurd in his gaucherie, his own poor intellectual equipment, his relentless, tiresome badgering. But Horace, too fine a writer to rest contented with straight parody of Stoic diatribe, broadens the irony to include himself, or his persona in the poem, so that this celebrated and accomplished poet is reduced to helpless exasperation before this puritanical onslaught. And, as we've seen (see pp. 80–1), after suffering his interlocutor for those nearly 300 thudding lines, Horace has had enough, *iam desine!* (2.3.326): "you mega-maniac, PLEASE spare the lesser!"

Horace's cry of exasperation puts the finishing touch to a masterful self-presentation: a good-natured fellow just human enough to be rendered appealingly helpless by the relentlessly droning attack of this stoical acolyte. Yet Horace's endearing surrender *authorizes* his self-deprecating, skeptical view, a neat victory in seeming defeat. The very appeal of Horace's self-vindication at the close of *Sat.* 2.3 ensures that Horace the victim is one of "us," Horace's largely well-to-do audience; Damasippus is not. We recognize the common sense of Horace's lesser madness, which is of course only everyday weakness, but also balance and, finally, sanity. The Stoic paradox at the heart of Damasippus' diatribe, that all but the Stoic sage are insane, is confounded in its very exposition – for the Stoic preacher is the one seen here to have gone off the deep end.

But Persius will contend, in his own close of Satire 3, that none of this is right. Seen as an answer to the glib resolution of Horace 2.3, Persius' interlocutor is not ironized by the author's knowing wink. His conclusion is straight (3.115–118):

> When bristling fear or desire spur you on
> blood boiling, eyes fiery
> you'll do and say things
> mad Orestes would call crazy.

He sets up counterpoint in referring to Horace's resolution without seeming to endorse the disarming humor: Persius' speaker's diagnosis of the unfinished Stoic as madder than a hatter is meant seriously, that is, as a conventional Stoic diagnosis of the lack of personal control and insight. In taking that position, Persius not only stands up for a kind of philosophical integrity, but also pulls the rug from under Horace's neat closure to 2.3. Horace's *iam desine* ("now stop!") followed by the comic turn of the poet's virtual surrender satisfies the reader that she's got to the end in both thematic and formal terms. But the diatribe of Persius' speaker *could* go on indefinitely; there is nothing resuming or finalizing about his last words. Perhaps the poem is not finished, but then it is difficult to see where it *could* stop. What we see in Horace is neatly controlled by the directing consciousness of the poet's persona; the dialogic drama never escapes the containment of the mind through which we hear the diatribe and which has the final and definitive say. That is quite possibly Persius' point; his poem, radically contrastive despite its pervasive intertextual connections with 2.3, ends without its model's formal closure and neat symmetries. Or rather, ends with the ghost of closure, alluding to Horace's trick without effectively duplicating it. Persius' ending presents its readers with the model of poetic experience that does not end when/where the words stop.[8] If

Horace's satire can be read as an Audenesque "saying," a finely crafted and resolved verbal coherence, Persius's poem is a deliberate unsaying – of Horace 2.3 certainly, perhaps even of the Horatian project as a whole, or, one might venture, of satire. Its end is disruptive of (Horace's) satire as aesthetic object; rather it draws the satire out into the reader's experience – a reader who is never comfortingly assured by the poet that he is "one of us." Who "we" are and what this speaker's diatribe is to mean to us is left, precisely, up to us.

Satire 4 is initially less problematic in that it does have an almost Horatian symmetry and structure. It is composed of three sections: 1–22 introduce a railing monologue of sorts by an unusually brusque Socrates directed at his sometime student Alcibiades; 23–41 crystalize the poem's theme by presenting a series of vignettes on the notion of self-knowledge; 42–52 offer a concluding "moral." Throughout there is a structuring pattern of incident followed by a resuming statement: "how no one dares the descent into himself (23)...we strike each other and in turn offer our limbs to others' arrows (42)...live with yourself" (52). We can also see obvious connections between this poem and its predecessor in the book: this also is the record of an intruding, hectoring master finding his student not living up to his promise. Alcibiades, ward of Pericles and student of Socrates, was the brilliant and dissolute Athenian politician and general whose deeds and misdeeds were at the center of the Peloponnesian war at its most crucial time. An adept rhetorician and politician with brilliant appeal, he almost always landed, through a series of remarkable reversals, on his feet. Thucydides, in his account of the war, clearly despises him, but grudgingly grants him the respect nearly all at one time or other felt. This satire, modeled in part on the pseudo-Platonic dialogue *Alcibiades I*, fictionalizes an encounter between teacher and sometime pupil after Alcibiades has begun his mostly charmed public career.

Like the Persius-figure of Satire 3, this Alcibiades gets rough treatment (1–5, 14–18):

"Managing the people's affairs?" (imagine the bearded philosopher, whom that nasty dose of hemlock disposed of, saying these things) "Depending on what? Tell me that, ward of mighty Pericles.
Genius of course, and a worldly wise mind have come
even before your beard, clever in speech and silence ...
Your beauty's only skin-deep; why not stop flaunting that tail
of yours to the sycophantic crowd when you'd be better

advised to take a dose of hellebore?
What for you is the highest good? To dine on rich food
always, and lie out in the sun?"

Despite this reminding us of Satire 3's rude interruption of the student's (Persius') hungover sleep and that in turn reminding us of the Stoic proselytizers' rude interruption of Horace's holiday relaxations, there is an unsettling novelty to this satire. For one thing it does not settle into the long diatribe on conventional foibles that has become the staple of this mode of satire. In fact, there is just the barest nod to that element in the formula, some ten lines, 23–32, picking out a conventional miser-figure for critical attention. But almost immediately the diatribe slips once again, in that passage already partially quoted above, into an exceptional nastiness beyond anything in Horace (33–40):

> If you hang around sunbathing, all oiled up,
> some stranger is likely to elbow you and spit out harshly:
> "Some morals! weeding out your penis and groin
> the better to exhibit your withered balls to the crowd!
> When you comb out that perfumed crotch-mop
> why does that shaven tool of yours stand out alone?
> Though five trainers pluck away at that plantation
> on your quivering ass with hooked forceps,
> no plow will ever tame that weedpatch!"

This is nothing like the voice of any Socrates we recognize from Plato or Xenophon, nor even like the tirade of a Stoic acolyte. Persius has cast the critical attacks we make on one another, while ignoring our own sins, in the voice and manner of a very bitter, very dirty old man. The pathic sexuality criticized here is clearly tied to the political prostitution that "Socrates" had earlier noticed. Alcibiades' pandering to the crowd, exhibiting himself, is a fair satirical read on Athens' demagogic democracy – as well as of Nero's theatrical tyranny. For if the depilating, homosexual preening is meant to gloss Alcibiades' political preening, as seems inevitable, extension to the artistic emperor is natural. Founder of the arts festival he called the *Neronia* and frequent performer on stages in both Italy and Greece, and so sensitive of his artistic reputation that failure to listen to or appreciate his work could mark one as suicidally disloyal, Nero incurred intense disgust with his artistic mania.[9] Most resentment would have been felt by the élite, which would have seen artistic and athletic competition as a betrayal of their class, of the *gravitas* of their station in life. That seems silly enough to us, knowing what we do from satire and elsewhere about the doings of the upper crust, but the open, public nature of Nero's pursuit of applause would have been cause for real chagrin, even shame. Translating that feeling into an image of palpable disgust, at least to the proper young Stoic who dreamed it up, would have been both courageous and the kind of acid critique of those that "matter" in Rome that we have not seen in Horace. There are problems with this notion. Persius is dead in 62, and most of Nero's over-the-top performances took place after that. But Tacitus has a description of Nero reading out his poetry to a small group in 59 (*Annals* 14.16), and he founded the *Neronia* in 60, clearly, subsequent events tell us, with a view to providing a public platform for himself. There is no way to date *Sat.* 4, either; it may be early, may be late. But the poem's very brevity, and its intense bitterness, could be an indication that it was composed near the very end, as the world around Persius and the poet's health and life were beginning to slip into darkness.

The passage is difficult to understand otherwise. To see it as merely an instance of ill-tempered sniping at others' faults without looking into oneself simply doesn't account for its shock value. This is not nice satire; rather, a poem to be read aloud only in certain settings, and then with intent to discomfort listeners. One of the more salubrious of such recitation venues might have been the small circle of literati, mostly Stoic and certainly not members of Nero's patronage circle, whose public and political concerns would have tracked the coded obscenity. Read this way, the poem's Socrates attacks a politically ambitious Alcibiades, while an unknown bystander, *ignotus prope te*, attacks a generalized "you" for a spot of somewhat over-exposed sunbathing that becomes, in the critic's rhetoric, a startlingly obscene pub(l)ic display. That "you" is thus anyone in that audience who could stand a bit of moral bucking-up, and Alcibiades, rendered in such a way as to remind us of no one so much as the biggest fool for public attention in Persius' day.[10] This goes a step further than the vague wish, also conceivably expressed with Nero in mind, in *Sat.* 3.35–38:

> Great father of the gods, if only you'd punish savage tyrants
> with nothing but this: when vile lust
> laced with poisonous venom stirs their minds,
> let them look upon the virtue they've lost, and waste away.

Things have got bleaker. Yet, ultimately, anti-imperial venom is not the final point of this acid satire. For more than most, this poem constantly reminds us of its moral: "how no one dares the descent into self" (23); "live with yourself" (51). Whatever the excess or ugliness without, the Stoic is concerned chiefly with what's inside. Inside you and me, good reader. For that "you" of the dirty old man's critique is not only Alcibiades/Nero or the small group of auditors that happened to be present of an evening as he read out his draft of a poem: it is oneself, where this satire doggedly, persistently, directs regard. The nasty imagery of this satire makes for an uncomfortable grimace on the reader's/auditor's face, followed by hard exhortation to take care of things at home. This attention to self, self-care in a Roman imperial setting, has been discussed by Foucault in his *History of Sexuality*, and has been glossed in Persius' case by John Henderson:

> From the workings of the fourth century Socrates with his Platonic cast of the Athenian *jeunesse dorée*, the "Care of the Self" developed a preparatory, ephebic, imperative to inspect an Inner Self into a whole way of living, regimen for a civic existence. Especially in the Platonic *First Alcibiades*, the "Inner Turn" is enjoined upon the budding class of citizen leaders (and models) to strengthen and stiffen their adult civic performance.[11]

That is, in a world seen to be spinning out of the hands of the traditional institutions of Roman society and government, there could be seen, as scripted by the popular ethical philosophies, a compensatory increase in the importance of private, personal *mentalité*, a stress on the centrality of self-care and -knowledge. Under Socratic aegis, this meant getting the self ready for public life, and, as Henderson points out, the very *Alcibiades I* that is the source text for Persius's fourth satire served such an admonishing function. Persius then savages that model. The destructive, bitter vehemence of the verbal assault on the poem's "Alcibiades" figure takes civic pedagogy right out of the picture. Public involvement has become pubic display. What is left then for us readers is ... merely us – the integrity of our inward lives. For Persius' immediate audience, educated, of traditionally influential families now largely disenfranchised, this conclusion is precisely right. It may still be right for some in the twenty-first century. The way, then, Persius contextualizes his satire tells us how this *isn't* Horatian satire. We see a designed assault on the idea of satire as aesthetic object and an attempt to requicken some of poetry's channels to the self-in-the-world.

There is a test for this. How do you feel when reading Persius? (Pulled in, suckered, disgusted, mocked, challenged, upset, bewildered?) How do you *not* feel (pleased, delighted, amused)? In the end, Persius can send only words our way, not missiles or barbs or sweets. But Persius renders – *for* his readers – a strenuous exertion of language. Language that seeks to do something, even save a soul or two, as opposed to language that is art, an aesthetic object that lies there on display for our delectation. That is certainly too facile a construction that does justice neither to Horace' accomplishment nor to Persius' own artistry. But there *is* something of the aesthetic vandal in Persius' pervasive, almost destructive imitations of Horace, twisting the master's passages out of context, often uglifying their expression, showing us his dismantling of the great Horatian project for satire, even while confronting, affronting, his own audience. To what end? Maybe to reflect, embody, the nastiness of the world as he saw it and to connect that world to those, as he puts it, with the gumption to listen.

Further Reading

Often, though not always, it is the case that some of best critical material on a classical poet is quite recent; in the case of Persius, going back to the 1960s and 1970s is the place to start. K. Reckford's article, "Studies in Persius," *Hermes* 90 (1962), 476–504 remains the finest short study of Persianic metaphor, and is a wonderfully lucid entrée into this difficult poetry. J. Bramble's *Persius and the Programmatic Satire: A Study in Form and Imagery* (Cambridge, 1974) in some respects takes its lead from Reckford's work but develops a more comprehensive analysis of Persius' style, underscoring the importance of physical, visceral, and sexual imagery to that style. W. S. Anderson's two articles from the period are still essential: "Part versus Whole in Persius' Fifth Satire" and "Persius and the Rejection of Society," both collected in Anderson, *Essays on Roman Satire* (Princeton, 1982), 153–93. R. G. Peterson, "The Unknown Self in the Fourth Satire of Persius," *Classical Journal* 68 (1972–73): 205–9, is perceptive. Other discussions from the 1970s repay reading: N. Rudd, "Association of Ideas in Persius," in Rudd, *Lines of Inquiry* (Cambridge, 1976), 54–83, and J. P. Sullivan, "In Defense of Persius," *Ramus* 1 (1972): 48–62. The most accessible general introduction to the satires as a whole is another book written some time ago, C. Dessen's *The Satires of Persius: Iunctura Callidus Acri* (Urbana, 1968 / 2nd edn., Bristol, 1996). Dessen's book is insightful, reliable, and remains important. Another solid general introduction with some useful focus on the afterlife of the satires is M. Morford, *Persius* (Boston, 1982). The most recent book on Persius, D. Hooley, *The Knotted Thong: Structures of Mimesis in Persius* (Ann Arbor, 1997), treats Persius' intertextual compositional techniques in his many adaptations of Horace. K. Freudenburg's chapter on Persius in *Satires of Rome* (Cambridge, 2001) gives us a more political Persius than seen in earlier studies.

Recent valuable work on a smaller scale includes A. Cucciarelli, "Speaking from Silence: The Stoic Paradoxes of Persius," in K. Freudenburg, ed., *The Cambridge Companion to Roman Satire* (Cambridge, 2005), 62–80; P. Connor, "The Satires of Persius: A Stretch of the Imagination," in A. J. Boyle, ed., *The Imperial Muse: Ramus Essays on Roman Literature of the Empire, to Juvenal through Ovid* (Victoria, 1988), 55–77; and E. Gowers' "Persius and the Decoction of Nero," in J. Masters and J. Elsner, eds., *Reflections of Nero: Culture, History, and Representation* (Chapel Hill, 1994), 131–50. K. Reckford has written insightfully on the third satire: "Reading the Sick Body: Decomposition and Morality in Persius' Third Satire," *Arethusa* 31.3 (1998): 337–54; taking another tack on that poem is D. Hooley, "Persius in the Middle," in S. Kyriakidis and F. De Martino, eds., *Middles in Latin Poetry* (Bari, 2004), 217–43. The most stimulating read on Persius you'll come across is J. Henderson, "Learning Persius' Didactic Satire: The Teacher as Pupil," in Henderson, *Writing Down Rome: Satire, Comedy, and Other Offences in Latin Poetry* (Oxford, 1999), 228–48.

Persius has been blessed with good commentators (maybe because he needs them). The standard, authoritative commentary is written in German, W. Kissel, *Aules Persius Flaccus, Satiren* (Heidelberg, 1990). But the English commentary cum translation by W. Barr and G. Lee, *The Satires of Persius* (Liverpool, 1987), is excellent for its size and scope. Similarly scaled, and good, but a little more difficult to use is J. R. Jenkinson, *Persius: The Satires* (Warminster, 1980). The most readable translation is N. Rudd, *The Satires of Horace and Persius* (London, 1973). On Persius' afterlife in literature, see W. Frost, "English Persius: The Golden Age," *Eighteenth Century Studies* 2 (1968): 77–101.

4

Juvenal

In Juvenal's fourth satire we are treated to the spectacle of a mock Privy Council, a kind of cabinet meeting called by Domitian to discuss what to do with an enormous turbot that has been presented to the emperor. This fish is so large that it spills over the edge of the largest plate. One adviser suggests that rather than cut it up they make a new vessel to contain it; of course a new Prometheus must fashion it as it will be like nothing made ever before. There is an edge to this foolery, as the poem goes on to contrast it with some of the crueler excesses of Domitian's reign. The satire lies in that contrast, just as it does in obvious parallels between the big fish on the plate and the other Big Fish the imperial advisers are gathered around. Domitian too, soon to be cut up in fact (in 96 CE), needs a bigger stage than all the world has yet provided. Monstrosity in many of its forms runs all through this poem, and we get the impression that language is straining in its attempt to capture the horrific magnitude of what Domitian's reign has meant for Rome. Yet the poem is, in the end, up to it; indeed the *Satires* as a whole are up to it, for as bad as the Domitianic world has been, or has been seen to be, Juvenal has answered with a magnitude of words unprecedented in Roman satire. Five books, all but the last full to bursting. A big fish of a satiric corpus, or a big corpus of satiric feasting. Any way you cut it, this is the fullest and fattest satire (*satis superque*) we have, or are likely to have. This body of satiric work, then, is that Promethean "new vessel," unprecedented and unsurpassed, a wondrous monstrosity.

All this *is* a little surprising. One might have thought the genre of Roman verse satire about to peter out. After the lavish verbal extravagance of Lucilius, Horace prunes and cuts; more than that, he admonishes his irrepressible forebear for being too prolix of words. Still, Horace wrote two full books, while Persius, his major successor, wrote only the one, partial at that and never published while he lived. It might have been possible to see Persius as satire's dying fall. He surely, in some sense, thought himself a closer, writing satire to end satire: "who will read these things? ... nobody, by god!" (*Sat.* 1.2). Answering Horace's complaint about small readership in *Sat.* 1.4.22, he exults in yet less, which is to say he writes as if *that* satiric audience were gone. And he was right for a time. Little satire of note appeared in Roman letters for decades – just a few names remain, Turnus, Silius, Manilius Vopiscus.[1] Horace and Persius had as well presided over a radical curtailment of satire's scope, its generic appetite, what it takes in; the vast Lucilian world is first reduced to the domestic space of Horace, his friends, and patronage circle – with implications, always, of the threatening world of real Rome – and reduced yet further in Persius to an interior moral landscape. Persius' is almost lyrical satire. Then, around 115 CE, Juvenal's first big book, with that big fish stuffed into it, hit the shops; it was from the very beginning extroverted, symphonic, and hugely comprehensive, taking in all of Rome itself, in fact, in the centerpiece satire (3) of the first book.

This radical shift in satiric modality is a poser. But fifty or so years after Persius' death, Rome was a changed place. Nero's suicide in 68 CE precipitated the crisis of "the year of the four emperors," a situation finally stabilized when the general Vespasian, fresh from success in subduing Galilee and Jerusalem, returned to Rome to wrest power from Vitellius. Vespasian's pragmatic approach to government contrasted radically with Nero's, and restored something like a stable peace to the city. His son and designated heir, Titus, succeeded in 79 but died in 81, leaving the throne of empire to his younger brother Domitian, who ruled until his own assassination in 96. Domitian was autocratic, disdainful of the senate, and as he grew to inhabit power he retreated to an inner circle of advisers. His later reputation for outright evil may be exaggerated, but this self-described *deus et dominus* did not hesitate to kill enemies when he saw fit. Under his rule, the aristocracy and senate were profoundly weakened, the latter's exercise of traditional powers curtailed – as indeed was the case under most post-Augustan emperors. But the memory of old prerogative still remained, along with the faint hope of its restoration, making the fresh pain of Domitianic repression particularly exquisite. The ancient ruling classes lived in fear, resentment, and suspicion, and Juvenal's satire, looking back on those days, is a somewhat distorted index of the way many felt. Nerva succeeded in 96 and ushered in the years of the so-called "good emperors," Trajan (98–117) and Hadrian (117–138). Under the more open and tolerant rule of Trajan, Juvenal finally published his first book of satires – retrospectively regarding the painful days of Domitian with particular bitterness. There is the sense in these satires, artificial or not, that with Domitian gone, the floodgates could open: Juvenal seems to have had a lot of resentment to unload, a lot to say. This would not be the day of sotto-voce, background mutterings, but of satire shouted out to the streets, literally as declamation.

Still, it would be a mistake to characterize Juvenal as a political idealist, or even activist. The tough days for the senatorial class under Domitian offered only one of several targets for the satirist. And the big, outgoing manner of the *Satires* is as much determined by current aesthetic taste as by politics. For as these political events unfolded, in fact, one of the few outlets for educated Romans' anxiety and creative energy was declamatory rhetoric, a traditional aristocratic competence in forensic and deliberative contexts. Under Flavian restrictions, with power concentrated in the imperium, rhetoric saw less use in civic debate than in literature, which became increasingly rhetorical, and in the schools, with their cultivation of the artificial rhetorical exercises called "declamations." The subjects of this speechifying were stock-in-trade and trivial – "Should Agamemnon sacrifice Iphigenia?" and the like – but they provided the occasion for demonstrating rhetorical skills and display, and for addressing issues of general concern, sometimes subtly. The practice, at first restricted to school training, became something of a literary genre unto itself in public oratorical presentations intended not to persuade their audiences but to please, and, sometimes, provoke them. There is some sketchy evidence from Martial (7.91.1–2) that Juvenal, prior to his career as a satirist, may have been such a declaimer. No surprise, then, that when Juvenal composed his poetry he did so in step with his literary times and his own practiced competence. Scholars have isolated in his poetry figures, topics, tropes, types of rhetorical characterization, rhetorical "kinds" (*theses, suasoriae* or persuasion speeches, *controversiae* or debates etc.), stock questions and categories. Also frequently noted are Juvenal's use of rhetorical questions, *loci communes* (commonplaces) on riches, on contemporary corruption, on fortune, etc., dramatic shifts in stylistic level, and *exempla*. Then there are the pithy, summarizing *sententiae* (aphorisms) theorized in Quintilian 8.5, so prominently a feature of

Juvenal's work: "bread and circuses," "few tyrants die abed," "a sound mind in a sound body," "push on, madman [Hannibal], right over the Alps, to please schoolkids and become a declamation," "the bronze head of mighty Sejanus ... melted ... for basins, pans, and pisspots," "the world was too small for Alexander ... , yet arriving at Babylon, a coffin was big enough" – all these from only one satire (*Sat.* 10).

Under these stylistic parameters, satire becomes a public genre characterized by big, dramatic effects setting out to please, contra Persius, a large audience. But it *is* satire, not just rhetoric, and so, living up to its stuffed-to-the-gills name, it packs in more. Juvenal more than any other satirist builds his poems out of a massive inter-textuality comprising rhetoric, tragedy, epic, and philosophy. Tragedy, and epic in particular, have worked their way back into this hexameter, and the Horatian pursuit of the aesthetics of the Callimachean mini-ature, radically deconstructed in Persius, is cheerfully forgotten in Juvenal. Epic allusions abound, epic manner and voice are every-where.[2] This is satire to end (Roman) satire; satire after satire, perhaps after Roman literature as a whole. Juvenal's tone is apocalyptic; every-thing is old, and Rome has reached the end of days. Even the current performance of "literature" is rendered as a wor(l)d-weary dismissal (1.7–13):

> Better than my own little house I know the grove of Mars
> and the cave of Vulcan neighboring the Aeolian shoals;
> what the winds are doing, what shades Aeacus tortures,
> whence somebody carries away the gold of that furtive wool,
> what huge mountain ashes Monychus tossed; the plane trees of
> Fronto, and his marble halls resound and even the columns
> crack with relentless reading.

The old genres, literature's old lines, are here merely a dull, oppressive, pounding echo. Juvenal's answer to the problem, implicit in the lines above, is appropriation, reintegration, absorption, and recasting of the whole – as monumental satire. This response is somewhat different from that of the epigrammatist Martial – of the very little we know of Juvenal's life, it is known that the two poets were friends – who gave Juvenal the model for these opening lines (Martial 10.4.1–10):

> You who read of Oedipus and Thyestes, shaded in darkness,
> of Colchian witches and Scyllas – of what do you read but monsters?

What good is the rape of Hylas, what Parthenopaeus and Attis,
what the sleepy Endymion?
Or the boy without his falling wings, or Hermaphroditus
who hates the amorous waters?
What use is the empty twaddle on cheap paper?
Read this, of which Life can say: "it is my own."
Here you won't find centaurs, nor gorgons and harpies;
My page smacks of people.

Both poets (Martial first in 98 CE, in the new dynasty's honeymoon period) lament the overuse of cliché themes, the redone myths of Greek literature. Nothing fresh in that, writes Martial; "if you want something real and current, read my epigrams." Juvenal's take, in turn, is not only an extensive building on the theme, with variations enough to carry the poem through 171 lines, but an ingenious reversal of Martial's "point": the real monsters are not in myth but have come to life in Rome – here are the flesh and blood gorgons and harpies we all need to fear. Juvenal's apocalypse *appropriates* the monsters of myth, both claiming there is nothing fresh in the old stuff and then turning the claim on its head by inventing their analogues in the world around him. While dismissing the epic and tragedy of the recitation hall, he creates an epic and tragedy, and comedy too, of satire.

A poetic corpus as large and omnivorous as Juvenal's requires a hefty volume of commentary, but we will have to settle here for a whirlwind tour; hold tight. **Book 1, Satire 1** considers the problem of poetry and the ways of the world – just as Persius had in his first, a poem little appreciated as background to Juvenal's. Where Persius had seen contemporary poetry as a reflection of Rome's corruption, Juvenal sees literature and declamation as worn, pallid shadows, made the more pathetic by the spectacular corruptions all around. Rome is where the great satiric themes lay: marrying eunuchs, spear-chucking matrons, upstarts from the fringes of the empire displacing "real Romans," new litters bloated with their one-man cargo, swindlers, opportunists, spendthrift playboys, schoolboy adulterers, poisoning wives, swaggering freedmen, gluttons, and all the rest. One could hardly not write satire in such circumstances (*difficile est saturam non scribere* [30]). You will have noticed that Juvenal's early targets, broad as they are, are not always those who might be designated by a generous, progressive consciousness. Upstarts, new-moneyed outsiders, women, foreigners, Greeks and Jews – these are bogeys of the reactionary mind, complacent in his traditional privilege, jealous of position, resentful of change and displacement. Whether Juvenal the man was seriously such a bigot has been a matter of long discussion, and it is a question you will need to think about, for taking Juvenal at face-value will prove to be dangerous; let us withhold judgment for the nonce and observe the question as we proceed.

Whatever the case of Juvenal's personal disposition, **Satire 2** has enormous, retrograde fun with homosexuality, though what is most condemned here is (the relatively fair game of) the hypocrisy of the machismo-posturing, closet sort. But hypocrisy casts a wider net: stern moralists (and emperors) who sin in secret or who wear risqué dress to the courtroom, effeminate devotees of Cybele, gay marriage – and, as we shall see, the satirist himself "performing" his stern morality. All Juvenal's stock targets are contrasted with old-blood Romans, the dead, founding heroes and veterans of Cannae. Ancient virtue and modern decline: too easy, one might say, though traditionally the poem has been admired for the force of critique leveled in precisely these terms. Someone less convinced that the old virtue ever quite existed as portrayed here might begin to observe that Juvenal, or his speaker in this poem, spends rather a lot of time doting over these sins of effeminacy, and that the narrative serves to sketch out a portrait of the observing consciousness as much as the things observed.

The same is true of **Satire 3**, where Juvenal might be said to take the next step in this manner of presentation by putting the poem's critique, just as Horace does in Book 2, in the voice of another – in this case one Umbricius. Umbricius is leaving town. Meeting "Juvenal" at the Capuan Gate, he discusses his reasons why, and the resulting diatribe becomes a comprehensive satirical portrait of the city. Finding his income decreasing, his talents in progressively less demand, Umbricius has many and much to blame: Jews, tradesmen, opportunists, informers, street thugs, upstart freedmen, foreigners of all stripes, traffic, night-time noise, fires, tenement housing – above all, Greeks (meaning Greek-speaking immigrants from the wider Hellenistic world rather than the more respectable Greek mainland). They are slick, learned, talented, willing to do any work, they flatter shamelessly, they inform for advantage, they climb the ranks of society displacing native Romans, they seduce wives and grandmothers. Those put in their shadow, like Umbricius, whose name means "shadow-man," are the ordinary, Roman-born, poor, luckless, ill-equipped to meet the unsettling challenges of cosmopolitan Rome. Yet to read this poem, to process it rather than simply accept its terms, we have to think about this character Umbricius: shadow-man, shade of old Rome, or shady-man, partisan, bigoted, "the manifestation of the petty greed and jealousy that haunts the city of Rome"?[3] Or perhaps another kind of shade: the poisoned, dispirited shadow of a better human possibility? Juvenal gives no easy answer. But he hints that the satire means more than what it manifestly claims to be, a rhetorically overwrought diatribe on urban life. The Third was the model for Samuel Johnson's great imitation *London*.

Satire 4 is, as we have seen already, the story of a fish. That it is not only about a fish is made clear at the outset, when one Crispinus is brought on stage, a very "monster" (*monstrum* [2]). Crispinus, Juvenal's analogue to Horace's Canidia, incarnation of the detested and feared, is a recent arrival from Egypt, a fish-seller who rose to a "cabinet" position having been given the status of *eques* by Domitian.[4] There are points of connection here: his foreignness and common origins as well as his non-traditional rise to power make him the natural target of the sensibility already presented in the character of Umbricius; his fish-mongering background offers the occasion for another egregious fish-story, this the purchase of a huge mullet at an extravagant price – for only himself (11–33), the unnatural self-indulgence of which action is used to set the stage for the privy council's deliberations over Domitian's fish – hence, real, if anachronistic, Roman politics. The poem, while seemingly trivial in its detail, is one of Juvenal's most serious works.

Satire 5, the final poem of the first book, contains yet more fish. This satire is Juvenal's first variation on the satiric feast *topos*, and the excess usual to such satiric settings is fully present in the lavish and outsized dishes (mullet, lamprey, boar) served to the laird Virro. Juvenal, clearly modeling his poem on Horace's closing satire (2.8), saw the generically identifying flawed feast as a natural way to consolidate themes appearing earlier in the book and at the same time suggest a sense of ending. But the focus here is on the mistreatment of ordinary guests, those invited to fill out the table. The poem's long-suffering protagonist Trebius and the other ordinary guests endure abuse by arrogant servants, wine so bad a mop won't drink it, crusty, moldy bread, fish dredged from the sewers, no meat, and dubious mushrooms. This imbalance was not an uncommon theme, as Susanna Braund notes, appearing as it does in Martial, Pliny, and Lucian.[5] The feast is the domestic analogue to society as a whole. Virro, called *dominus* and *rex* several times, is clearly a type of Domitian.[6] The inequities he presides over are paralleled by more serious inequities outside the dining-hall doors. The satire's speaker, then, condemns both the likes of Virro and the enabling complacency of Rome's many Trebii, especially the latter in the satire's closing lines (170–173):

> He knows what he's about, who uses you thus. If you
> can take it all, then you should. You'll offer your shaved head
> for a beating, nor will you run from the whip,
> and you'll be worthy of just this dinner, just this "friend."

Rome's citizens have become its slaves.

The sheer scope of the Juvenalian satire-project is emblemized in his **Book 2** (of five), comprising a single poem of 661 lines, **Satire 6**. The poem is a diatribe against women – not unsurprising given what the reader has seen of Juvenal's persona, or speaker's attitude, thus far. The Juvenalian voice has been focalized through a conservative, "old Roman" sensibility, anxious, resentful, and more than a bit bewildered by changing times. Targeting women is a perennial reflex for express-ing that angst; and the topic is a traditional one in classical letters. Semonides, a Greek writer of iambic verse dating to the seventh or sixth century BCE, has left us a portion of another in that tradition, a catalogue of bad women, and Seneca is said to have written a work on marriage, possibly of similar character, now lost. The obvious thing to say about Juvenal's poem is that it is an example of a prevailing and pervasive misogyny in Graeco-Roman societies. The portrayals of women in this poem range from the amusingly ironic to the cruel and disgusting. Traditionally readers have enjoyed it for what it is, a specimen of malicious caricature within a context of other such poems. Seen thus (and suspending scruple), the satire is indubitably a great one. Beginning with an address to a hypothetical friend Postumus, who is planning to marry, Juvenal's satiric speaker initially pretends incredulity: how could any sane man *think* of marrying when a fair, chaste, and sensible woman is simply not to be found on the planet? Oh, once there were a few, before Chastity and Justice fled the earth; but then women were certainly hairier than their men. Then begins the catalogue of the womankind he sees out there: ladies swooning in ecstasy, and worse, at a mime's performance, noble matrons abandon-ing family and home for a broken and scarred gladiator, the emperor Claudius' Messalina stealing away to work in the whorehouse and loving it more than the professionals, the proud, the rich, the arrogant, the Greek-speaking, the dominating, those that love to fight in the arena – all of course unfaithful. Feminine accomplishments are turned on their head: a musical, learned, or politically informed woman troubles a man. Juvenal's poem escapes being merely a catalogue by his quick pacing, outlandish anecdotes, and lively *variatio*; short blasts and examples are balanced by longer vignettes and portraits; the satire never settles into tedium.

But there is a structural problem inherent in a long catalogue poem like this – there is no easy way to end it. Of course, the satire is intended to show us that this long list of misbehaving women could go on forever, but as a poem it clearly wants a resolving closure. Juvenal engineers this masterfully. After a section on blue-stockings (444–456) there follows a sequence of scenes depicting the extravagances and follies of a woman's day at home. Juvenal then launches into a dark picture of a woman's household tyranny (479–484):

> ... The cane is broken on one servant's back, another
> grows bloody from the whip, yet another feels the lash. Some have
> torturers *on salary*: he beats while she does her face, talks
> with her friends, gives advice on the hemming of a dress,
> he beats, while she reads through the day's news,
> he beats, until he's exhausted and she orders him "Out!"

The appalling scene transcends its domestic frame, suggesting perhaps nothing so much as representations of the icy calm of Apollo flaying alive the satyr Marsyas (or the cold sadomasochism of *The Story of O*). Vice in the household merges, in its scope and scale, with myth. Even in the less dramatic scenes that follow, expensive consultations with seers and priests, leading to women's fondness for abortives, love potions, and poisons, it is not hard to see the speaker's mind spinning nearly out of control. The poem has become a tempest of loathing, fear, and lurid imagining. The connection with tragic myth is explicit in the closing lines, where Juvenal declares that the doings of Medea, Procne, and the rest pale in comparison to what happens in Rome every day: "Every neighborhood has its Clytemnaestra" (658). The satire appropriates the worst the tragic imagination has on offer, children butchered and cooked up for offending fathers' appetites, or slaughtered before their parents' eyes. Greek mythologizing plays with these kinds of human depravity in its fuller exploration of the extremes of human psychology. This satire disposes of that larger aim, transposing mythical extremes into quotidian Rome, maybe asking us what it would mean if these things were to become real, or if they already have. The result is not only a kind of "supreme" closure for this poem, but a programmatic statement: this diatribe is also a supreme fiction, an act of powerful invention.

Book 3, Satires 7–9, is again something new. The voice is recognizably the same as the writer of Books 1 and 2, but there is less dramatic urgency of incident, and the book is designed with a conspicuous *variatio*, as if this were an author trying out for size some available topics rather than an impassioned and despairing poet who must needs (only) satirize. **Satire 7** is a protracted lament on the wretched, patronless state of the contemporary man of letters – poet, historian, orator, jurist, schoolteacher. Surely the patronage situation had changed from Horace's day, when young poets could aspire to membership in one of several patronage circles, some quite close to the hub of political power as well. "Who now will be your Maecenas?" (94) is Juvenal's question in this poem, clearly a rhetorical one, for the point seems not to reflect reality. There is evidence from other sources that patronage, albeit of a different nature, was to be had for some at least, and Juvenal's opening makes an exception of the potential generosity and encouragement of the newly ascended emperor – probably Hadrian. We know nothing about Juvenal's patronage situation, but Martial, like others, advanced to equestrian status via imperial patronage and enjoyed ups and downs with private patrons. But the cry of poverty and the empty promises of patrons had probably become conventional by this time, as it had in Samuel Johnson's day when a patron could be resentfully defined in Johnson's dictionary as "a wretch who supports with insolence, and is paid with flattery." Juvenal's poem is his own riff on that theme, laced with resentment of flatterers like Statius and the fortunate-in-wealth like Quintilian.

Satire 8 is another general indictment, this time on the frequent disconnect between noble birth and noble nature ("virtue is the only nobility" [20]). The poem begins in almost Horatian tones: it is cast in the form of friendly advice to a young, rising politician named Ponticus; the tenor of the satire is, especially early on, duly muted to the occasion, though acid invective breaks out in places, and the poem builds to a crescendo as the tirade becomes more relentless until it ends in a classic Juvenalian epigram. In cataloguing the sins of the aristocracy, plundering the provinces, cruelty to provincials, demeaning misadventures, yet more demeaning stage and arena performances leading nicely to the artsy and murderous Nero – all neatly contrasted with virtuous "commoners" (loosely interpreted) like Cicero, Marius, and Servius Tullius – Juvenal mentions a great many important Roman families. To the extent that Rome's history is embodied in those names, this satire can be seen as an indictment of the Roman project: what has Rome made of itself? A puffed-up parade of failed, aristocratic potential. The poem's closing lines render the seriousness of this satiric attack with a characteristic wry bitterness (269–275):

> I would rather Thersites were your father, so long
> as you, like Achilles, could wield the weapons of Vulcan –
> rather than you, born of that hero, grow up like Thersites.
> As far back as you want to trace your family name,
> you'll see that it leads to an asylum of outlaws.
> The first of your ancestors, whoever he was,
> was either shepherd or something I'd better not say.

Satire 9 is another experiment, though it owes more than a little to Horace's imaginary dialogue in *Sat.* 2.5 between Odysseus and Teiresias. Whereas the former poem dealt satirically with the unseemly matter of legacy-hunting, Juvenal's raises the stakes in unseemliness by centering it on the fortunes of a worn-out male prostitute. Cast in dialogue form, it begins with a vulgar jauntiness it never loses (1–4):

> I'd surely like to know, Naevolus, why, as often as we meet,
> you come across like Marsyas, just having lost out to Apollo.
> Why the expression so like Ravola's when he was caught
> *in flagrante*, beard still wet from Rhodope's crotch.

Naevolus confesses his woes. For all he has done for his patron, keeping sir and madame happy, providing children, preserving the marriage (all it takes is a lover), he is treated shabbily. Ageing and poor, he feels his creeping obsolescence. As a satiric figure, he is at once an image of "something rotten in Rome," a gloss on modern aristocratic life – following the sterner critique of *Sat.* 8, and a self-reflexive commentary on Juvenal's own persona in Books 1 and 2. For Naevolus takes the same aggrieved line, performs the same *laudator temporis acti* routine. As Freudenburg puts it: "the joke's on us for ever having been taken in."[7] But there is in Naevolus a delightful humanity as well, as he blurts out his long, grotesquely detailed sexual adventures only to realize that he has been indiscreet and begs Juvenal not to let on that he has divulged dangerous secrets. Juvenal, or his voice in this poem, responds that no patron has secrets – everyone in the household tells tales, true or not. Reassured, or just moving on, Naevolus asks Juvenal's advice, which is to find a rich crone. Dismissing that as already tried, Naevolus closes the poem with an all-too-human fantasy of the wealth he'd like to have accumulated – if only he were fortunate.

Book 4 comprises Satires 10–12. The first of these, **Satire 10**, is one of the great poems of European literature, a status affirmed in Johnson's well-known imitation, *The Vanity of Human Wishes*. The satire's distinction is in part due to its distinction within the Juvenalian corpus, for this is the closest Juvenal ever gets to his popular image as a grave and moral satirist. That image was promulgated late: we see the first fashionings of it in Jerome's early, unacknowledging quotation, but critical appreciation in these terms stems from the European scholars Dryden depends on, and Dryden himself sets the terms for the Anglophone world, praising Juvenal's "vigorous and masculine wit," his "noble soul" in denouncing vice. More than literary character is at stake here; in the early to mid-eighteenth century, the major writers of the day, Pope and Johnson, were both deeply involved in opposition, anti-Whig politics and their view of the paradigm-setting Romans was colored by the needs of the time. Horace's temporizing or Persius' seemingly apolitical moralizing would not do; when an image of strong opposition was required on which to model contemporary satire, eighteenth-century Englishmen turned to Juvenal, and in so doing not only made him a strong, uncompromising voice, but made him moral as well. Johnson's versions of the third and tenth satires are transparent in these regards, *London* energetically political and *The Vanity of Human Wishes* capped with a Christian, moralizing coda. It is important to realize how locally motivated and tendentious such readings (or receptions) of Juvenal are, while at the same time recognizing that the tenth is the most amenable of all of Juvenal's satires for such treatment. It has lines in it that *could* come from a Christian moralist – among many others, 141–142:

> . . . For who embraces virtue herself
> if you take away the reward?

The poem as a whole has about it a *transferable* seriousness that is not common in the poet's other works. Its subject is the folly of extravagant, unrealistic desires – drawing its initial inspiration from Persius 2. But the satire is for all that not a philosophical meditation. Rather, wrongheaded human desires simply provide the occasion for a nicely structured and altogether fascinating series of negative exempla: Sejanus and political power, Cicero and Demosthenes and eloquence, Hannibal, Alexander, and Xerxes and military might, Priam, Marius, and Pompey and long life, a number of men whose youth and beauty were the occasions for misfortune at the hands of conniving women. The exempla cannot be summarized in a way that does not rob them of their vividness and their sardonic, epigrammatic wit. The poem simply must be read through and savored. The strength of the satire is in these factors of style and presentation; there is no philosophical coherence in it. Philosophy, such as it is, comes only at the end in the syncretic Stoic and/or Epicurean endpiece, commencing with the poem's only apparently endorsed "wish," the famous *mens sana in corpore sano* ("sound mind in a sound body" [356]). In fact, even that oft-quoted aphorism is an ironic shadow. Every desire up to this point has proven hollow, empty, delusional. The poet's ironic "solution" is in this: "if you must ask for something, duly sacrificing animal entrails and holy offerings of spotless piglet in holy chapels, pray for a sound mind in a sound body" (334–336).[8] And how further ironic that Juvenal, that intemperate complainer of Books 1 and 2, should be (seriously?) espousing temperance, restraint, and equanimity here.

Yet, in closing, a homily (357–366):

> Ask for a brave heart free of the fear of death,
> which sees long life as the least of nature's gifts
> and which is able to bear whatever sort of sorrows,
> is not prone to wrath, desires nothing, and thinks the
> trials and grim labors of Hercules better than
> the easy loves and banquets and pillows of Sardanapalus.
> These things I'm showing you, you can give to yourself; the path
> to a tranquil life lies open to virtue alone. Lady Luck,
> you really have no power; it is we who make you
> a goddess, and place you in heaven.

Philosophically vague and idealizing as he is in this ending, Juvenal writes in language that can be taken straight (your choice), without irony or complication, and centuries of readers have done just that.

Satire 11 revisits the theme of Satire 5, the feast, yet separates itself from others of this satiric kind by taking up the topic of the speaker's own humble, honorable repast in contrast to the extravagance and glitzy tawdriness of the rich. As in several other instances, Juvenal is borrowing from his contemporary Martial, whose epigrams 5.78 and 10.48 are short exercises on the notion of the salubrious dinner and clearly models for Juvenal's satiric expansion. Juvenal doesn't, however, launch into another over-the-top burlesque of the wealthy vulgarian's dinner-show. That genre had perhaps been played out in any case – after Horace, Petronius, and his own fifth satire – and Juvenal shifts focus to the positive goods of a humble repast, and along with it the broader ethical injunction to know oneself and one's place. Juvenal's feast is just possibly again programmatic, codifying the tone of the later books: restrained, vaguely ethical, espousing traditional values (dinnertime readings from epic rather than racier stuff) – and sardonic. For this is not all homespun simplicity. Juvenal's addressee in this poem is one Persicus, otherwise unknown to us, and the poet's attitude to him is ambiguous. On one hand, he seems a friend of position substantial enough to have dining options: Juvenal has to make a case for his own home cooking over other more lavish options Persicus might have. On the other hand, in pitching his chaste simplicities, Juvenal puts his case in interesting terms: his servant boys are *not* the shaven, well-endowed, naked sorts seen in the bathhouse (156–160); Persicus *won't* see ("perhaps you were expecting" [162]) lascivious dancing girls – he adds the nice detail of a bump-and-grind and carries on in that vein for quite a few lines. Finally, Persicus should put all thoughts of his own adulterous wife out of his head ("coming home in the morning, robe damp, wrinkled, and stained" [186–189]). It all reads like a sly taunting of a man whose weaknesses he knows. Or perhaps he intends a wider audience – whose weaknesses he knows.

Satire 12 is another satire in epistolary form, and like the previous satire this has a disconcerting incoherence and sardonic edge. Juvenal's addressee is a figure named Corvinus whose name, though common, is possibly fictional and significant in sense, suggesting a legacy-hunter (the "raven" who feeds on dead meat).[9] If so the theme doesn't come up until line 93 and following, where the name is repeated and the usual sins of the legacy-hunter are retailed on to the end of the poem (Horace 2.5 and several epigrams of Martial being the models). In between the opening address to Corvinus and the closing diatribe is a mock-celebration of the safe return of a "friend," Catullus (no connection to the Republican poet), from a storm at sea and near shipwreck. This Catullus is portrayed as a rich trader who, faced with a storm of epic proportions, is praised for throwing his rare luxury items overboard. The poet's celebration takes conventional form in the promise to offer sacrifices, detailed at some length, in thanks to propitious gods. Yet the incongruity of this satirist actually doing such a thing sounds the first warning that all is not serious here. The overdone epic features of the storm, the heroic sacrifice of luxurious trade goods compared bathetically to a trapped beaver's biting off his own testicles, and the epic notes and allusions in the crippled ship's safe return confirm the case. If this Catullus were a real person (a possibility), he can have been no real friend. The satirist nonetheless protests his sincerity by disavowing any personal gain to be had from his sacrifices and ostentatious joy, for Catullus has children. That is to say, he has heirs, and the poet could not, thus, be the kind of legacy-hunter he portrays in the last 38 lines of the poem – those who offer huge sacrifices to the gods (elephants, if they could!), household slaves, even a daughter (like Agamemnon's Iphigenia). Yet Juvenal has played the role of legacy-hunter perfectly, with seeming sincerity in language and images fraught with insincerity. The poem manifests no obvious target, or rather an abundance of them – Corvinus the legacy-hunter, Catullus the wealthy trader, the shifty-ambiguous speaker himself – and so may be one of the satirist's subtler experiments as "unreliable narrator."

Book 5 is Juvenal's last, and it is incomplete; its final poem (Satire 16) breaks off in mid-sentence after 60 lines. Literary historians' best guess is that Juvenal died in the early 130s, within a few years of the events narrated in Satire 15. The end must have come unexpectedly, as there is no autumnal gathering of thoughts in these last poems, merely a sense of keeping on. The first of the book, **Satire 13**, continues a practice seen in the previous poems, the adoption and twisting into novel shape of a conventional poetic genre: the satiric feast of 11, a safe-return poem in 12, and here in 13, a *consolatio*, an ancient generic type, often written with a broader audience in mind, comforting one for a recent misfortune. Quite often such poems are showcases for a particular philosophical perspective. There is no particular philosophy systematically on display here, and in many respects the poem is one of Juvenal's odder performances. Throughout its long course – 249 lines – it can never be said to take seriously its consoling function, as the satire's speaker never genuinely sympathizes with his addressee. Yet the variations on the generic theme, assuming that this is the literary game being played, are not exactly coherent either. The first section, up to line 119, reads as an interesting exercise in "*consolatio* noir"; philosophy dresses down, inhabits Rome's mean streets (19–22):

> Book learning, fortune's master, is all well and good,
> but we think those also fortunate
> who have learned from Life, learned
> to take her troubles and not fret under her yoke.

No sweet sophistries from this school of hard knocks narrator. The Rome he describes is utterly a fallen world, a place where philosophy and integrity are merely the chimeras of a deluded or hopelessly romantic mind. Honesty is as dead as the old days when the gods themselves were primeval and few (38–48), a virtuous man now would be considered a freak, and no one should expect other than to be swindled by any and everyone with the chance (60–70). This section of the poem is laden heavily with anecdotes of corruption rendered, not with Juvenal's old indignation, but in the matter-of-fact voice of a man who has made his peace with his degraded world. His impatience is not directed toward instances of corruption but toward the naively credulous.

From line 120 the "serious" advice begins (120–123):

> Accept the solaces of one who doesn't read the
> Cynics or Stoics, distinguished mainly by their shirts,
> or one who looks up to Epicurus, fussing
> as he does over the flowers in his garden.

This is not the Dame Philosophy that will appear to Boethius in his last extremity, but a tarted-up, Thoroughly Modern Philly. Yet some of the advice offered seems, in this second part of the poem, rather straightforward and serious, as when he claims that revenge only spoils the loss with hate (175–190) – only to "clinch" his case with a gratuitous sexism: "no one takes more delight in revenge than a woman" (191–192). Continuing the theme, lines 192–210 contain a less than successful elaboration of the affecting lines on personal guilt of Persius 3.35–44. The closing tableau suggests, improbably, that the guilty will in fact be plagued by remorse – night visions of the wronged that will ultimately compel him to confess. None of this consolation accords with the vision of life and of Rome in the first section of the satire. There is both (surely intentional) overstatement and platitude in this last section, as if in the debased world that is the context of the poem, philosophy too cannot amount to much.

Satire 14 is the longest of the later poems (331 lines), and it recaptures some of the fire of the first book in its rhetorical patches. Its ostensible theme is the dubious influence of bad parenting on children, an original angle that permits the satirist to run through the usual satiric sins: sex, sadistic abuse of slaves, meanness, gluttony, luxury, avarice. The governing idea put positively, parents' obligation to protect their children from vice (natural imitators that they are), is rendered with some force at several points early on in the satire, but as it progresses the poem becomes an extended diatribe on avarice alone. The first half of the poem is, in fact, the livelier and carries more satiric force in its animal analogies and short tableaux on sex, sadism, lavish gourmandism, even in the short satire on Jewish ritual. The familiar Juvenalian device of raising to view the virtue of hoary antiquity – usually tongue-in-cheek – is here too, though with less apparent irony than elsewhere.

But if Satire 14 offers a new gambit leading to old ground, **Satire 15** inverts that approach: opening up with the familiar, high-volume, Juvenalian voice of incredulous outrage, it modulates with subtle shifts of irony and misdirection into something novel. The ostensible provocation for the satire's indignation is a "news report" of cannibalism in Roman Egypt; two neighboring villages with a long history of feuding fall into accelerating violence that runs to such a pitch that one fallen foe is dismembered and gobbled up raw. Much of the old Juvenal is on view here: beginning with the irony-dipped description of Egyptian religion and its taboos (9–13):

> It is forbidden to violate or bite into onion or leek
> (O holy people, for whom gods grow in gardens!),
> every table abstains from wool-bearing creatures,
> it's wrong there to cut the throat of a kid:
> but it's all right to dine on human flesh.

Familiar too are the epic analogies – Cyclopes, Laestrygonians, and more – that are used in 13–32 by way of juxtaposing the greater horror of the "real" story he is about to tell in 33–92. The xenophobia, or misoxenia, lacing Juvenal's "anthropology" in this poem will come as no surprise to readers of the first book, and he carries it through with uncharacteristic consistency and focus through the remainder of the satire. Other instances of cannibalism, the besieged, starving Vascones, say, are noticed and explained as the consequences of unusual circumstances; only these Egyptians eat each other because of their particular depravity. Yet the more Juvenal focuses on the particular incident and particular offending race, paradoxically, the more general the indictment seems to become. Juvenal includes a long digression (131–158) on nature's gift of compassion, which leads to sensitivity to the good, care for one another, community, public safety. But "these days there is greater amity among snakes" (159). Lions, boars, tigers, bears keep the peace with one another; only men lust to kill their fellows (159–168). When Juvenal returns in line 170 to cannibalism, the lens has been widened, and we see it as an instance of a general human perversity. Which of course is all it could be, given that Juvenal's audience is the same Rome that relishes the almost daily slaughter, torture, and dismemberment of the arena – for entertainment. Indeed, the literary presentation, the loving detail in which the human feed is rendered here, the ripping and tearing, picking of bones, the last human scavenger clawing at the blood-soaked ground with his nails for just a taste, may remind a reader, and possibly Juvenal too, of no one so much as Lucan, whose over-the-top images of gory dismemberment are meant as a gloss on the disintegration, the drive to entropy, that is civil war. Romans reading of these Egyptians would have seen something of themselves.

Juvenal's last book concludes with a fragment, **Satire 16**, just those 60 lines. Not enough is here to indicate whether this would develop into an interesting satire; as it reads now, it is a tepid, civilian's complaint against the powers and privileges of the military. In law, land disputes, and much else, it is best to avoid conflict with a soldier – one will surely come away the loser. It is possible that the poem was intended to develop characterizations of soldiers, boorish centurions, in Persius (*Sat.* 3.77ff. and 5.189ff.). The resentful tone brings us back to early Juvenal, and in fact that may have been an intentional touch if he was writing what he meant to be his last complete poem. One wishes for more, for unlike Horace and even the posthumously edited Persius, there is no sense of closure or completion in Juvenal. No sense of coming to a summary perspective on his art – or anything else. At about 70 years of age, he seems simply to have wanted to go on writing: he was running out of time, not of invention.

The Ghosts of Rome

Very little is known of Juvenal's life, from beginning to end. The biographies composed in late antiquity, which cooked up stories of exile to Egypt or Britain, military service, an offended emperor, and more, are largely fanciful speculations inspired by various elements of the satires. Most scholars considering internal evidence in the satires estimate his birth somewhere around 67 CE and his death roughly coinciding with the passing of Hadrian (138 CE). He may have come from a respectable family but seems not to have been wealthy; later in his life his means seem to have been substantial enough to support a small farm (maybe) outside Rome. That is all. Which may allow us the picturesque indulgence of imagining this breaking off at line 60 of Satire 16 (*et laeti phaleris omnes et torquibus, omnes* ... ["let everyone delight in medals and torques, let everyone ... "]) as a last, spilled cup of sour, satiric wine slipping from the master's dying hand as satire's feast goes cold. However the end *really* happened, it defini-tively spelled the end of hexameter satire. While the satiric spirit would continue on in Lucian and find life again in the polemics of Jerome, the satiric sketches of the middle ages, the Renaissance Latin of Erasmus and others, and find new incarnation as splendid as satire could ever be in Boileau and the England and Ireland of the seventeenth and eight-eenth centuries, Latin hexameter satire dies with this great old man. There are myriad reasons for the passing of a genre: changes in taste and historical circumstance, migration of talent to other literary kinds. But, predominantly in this case, there was the phenomenon of Juve-nal's accomplishment itself, for he had come to possess the genre. Founders Ennius and Lucilius, re-inventor Horace, deconstructive Persius – none of these has ever *meant* satire to posterity as Juvenal came to mean it. Aside from everything else, this performance – big in all the ways we have noticed – was too impressive to follow. Juvenal had taken satire out of the (posh) backwater of Latin letters, read as it was by inner circles, coteries, friends and connections, educated readers who liked their social commentary suggestively misdirected through sophisticated literary device but without the portentous trap-pings and claims of high literature. Juvenal on the other hand made it a public performance, indeed a dominant one. His "age" – and we could stretch that to include the Flavians as well as Nerva, Trajan, and Hadrian – boasts several good, but only two great writers, Tacitus and Juvenal. The fourth and fifth centuries, when satire came back into a kind of vogue, knew that: notice, quotation, or imitation appear in Ausonius, Ammianus, Lactantius, and Servius.[10] And Juvenal continued to dominate the satiric scene as major touchstone right on through the eighteenth century up to the present day. It is an odd paradox: literary reception has placed this writer of "low" verse, about whom we know virtually nothing, in the very top rank of Roman poets.

Such a catasterization cannot be accounted for by coldly itemizing the features of Juvenal's style: its incorporation of epic and tragedy, its rhetoric, its quotable aphorisms. Or the sharp rhetorical tension created by his tendency to use elements of a "high" style in treating the low and scabrous sides of Roman life – although this is an important and original device. Or even (perhaps) by the compelling puzzle of just where Juvenal stands in respect to his satire. He has been called moralist and bigot, a resentful, down-at-heels *rentier* and brave paragon of political integrity; misogynistic, phallogocentric, reactionary, playful, bemused, indignant, despairing, ironic. All of these characterizations have been held at one time or another seriously, often simultaneously. Part of the problem is that without some biographical or literary perspective apart from the satires themselves, there is no way of knowing; part is the simple fact that Juvenal is not consistent in the presentation of his "self" or persona in the poetry. This is in sharp contrast to Lucilius, Horace, and Persius, from all of whom we can derive a reliably coherent picture – however real it may or may not be – of the poet. Thus the farm Juvenal refers to in Satire 11, with its attractive country fare, may be real and his own, or may be done up as a literary convenience for the poem following Horace, whose farm we know *was* real. For Horace that farm was emblematic, representing a certain outlook on life, a country contemplativeness and personal affiliation, that shows its traces in even the most urban of Horace's satires. Juvenal, even when thus quoting Horace, gives us nothing like the same sense. Similarly, even in the urban mode we feel is Juvenal's idiom, we cannot quite tell what exactly the poet really feels about it all, whether, for instance, the indignation expressed in Juvenal's first book reflects honest emotion or is an artful construction of what an angry, dispossessed Roman might say. This question of the "persona" of Juvenal, his self-presentation or even self-caricaturizing, in particular satires has been a vexed and controversial one for a number of years. The major premise of "persona theory," much

exploited in Juvenal criticism since the 1980s, is that since there is no
reliable way of looking behind the poet's self-performance in a particular satire, that performance itself must be the focus of critical
regard. A related analogue is that Juvenal projects several different
faces in the poetry as his books are written. The issue remains an
open and disputed one.

But Juvenal's claim to posterity's attention rests, I think, on other
factors, exemplified nicely in the first satire, his program poem. We are
accustomed to such poems by now from Horace 1.4, 1.10, 2.1, and
Persius 1, recalling that even Lucilius seems to have felt the need to
explain his venture into non-elite verse (see pp. 21–4). By Juvenal's day
such exigency was well past. Horace had made the genre respectable,
and Persius had tacked it solidly to philosophy. One needn't apologize
for satire any longer. Yet of course Juvenal goes through the motions.
Epic has gone bad – the "*Theseid* of hoarse Cordus" and others. So too
comedy, elegy, and poetry in general (1–14). This opening assault on
contemporary literature is usually discussed in the context of public
recitation and declamation, giving emphasis to Juvenal's particular,
rhetorical angle on satire. But it draws just as conspicuously on Persius
1, which was the first to target poetry satirically, as opposed to discussing the terms of satire's literary presentation. In this sense, Juvenal
is signaling his intent to begin where Persius left off. Juvenal's contempt for the current artistic scene is every bit as fierce as was his
predecessor's (1–6):

> Do I have always only to be a listener, never respond,
> so often be beat about the head with that *Theseid* of hoarse Cordus?
> Without recourse when this poet reads out his comedies to me,
> or that poet his elegies? When Telephus wastes my day
> scot free? Or Orestes, spilling out over the margins
> and back of the roll, and still not done?

But there is a difference in tone. Persius found the neo-Callimachean-
ism of his day almost personally offensive; it bespoke a social corruption in barely disguised moral terms (Persius *Sat.* 1.32–35):

> This poet, shoulders draped in hyacinthian robes,
> uttering something rancid in nasally tones,
> a Phyllis or Hypsipyle, or some other poet's weepy,
> dripping the words out from delicate palate.

Where Persius was disgusted by what he saw as a violation of an honorable man's sensibility, Juvenal's contempt is motivated by the sheer tedium of the dull repetition of canonical subjects. Roman literature has become boring, a waste of time. The psyche that registers it thus is not the moral sensitivity of Persius but a mind worn down, jaded, world-weary – but self-confident. After all, he has had the same rhetorical schooling as these "poets"; he knows whence they come and of what their words are made (15–18). His opening parody makes clear with its compressed and learned allusiveness (7–11) that he knows "the literature" as well as or better than anyone.

Not a lamentation, then, but a brag, a matter of self-assertion. Again, not a modest "would that I could write epic but since I can't I write these satires" but a claim that this satire he will write trumps epic and is far more worth listening to than anything else one might hear where poems are declaimed. Juvenal will push satire front and center, and the sheer power of his voice will cast other poetries into shadow. In a supreme reversal of generic priorities, the only "great" rival he recognizes is the mighty Lucilius, presented in explicitly epic guise (19–20):

> But why should I tread that ground where
> the great son of Arunca once drove his chariot?

Satire has grown up. And when Juvenal turns loose his horses in line 22, satire's power and momentum, quite apart from its moral correctness, is undeniable, even overwhelming (22–30):

> When tender eunuch takes a bride, and Mevia,
> bare breasted, toting a hunting spear, goes a-pig-sticking,
> when the barber who once shaved my face can now,
> with his money, challenge the whole Patriciate,
> when that glob of Egyptian low-life, that slave of Canopus
> Crispinus, hitching up Tyrian robes on his shoulder,
> waves about merely a ring of plain gold on his sweaty fingers,
> because he can't bear the weight of gems in summertime,
> it's difficult not to write satire.

It is important to be precise about Juvenal's satiric register. It has none of the caution, modesty, or reticence of Horace, nor does it have the anxiety and fervor of Persius. Further, there is no inner, psychic guide, tuned to Juvenal's moral compass, dictating what gets criticized and what does not by the poet. This is a satiric feast in which Juvenal dishes out what comes to hand, tossed and seasoned by Juvenal's own style of satiric cookery. His satire is a show of the outlandish, *made* outlandish by its presentation. Thus the sensationalism, the rhetorical overpitching, even the explicit jealousy and bigotry. These are the tools of his literary kit, as is the epic styling in its late silver guise: grand, mad passions splashed loudly and spectacularly. This, after all, is a public enamored of all the epic passions and fireworks and stageyness that he derides from the start but can't get clear of; the language they love gets built into Juvenal's rhetoric of resentment. The poet may or may not have been actually resentful and jealous of *nouveaux-riches*, or have really harbored genuinely racist feelings about Egyptians, Jews, and most foreigners. We can't know. But we can observe that Juvenal uses the rhetoric of the resentful and bigoted unabashedly, part and parcel of a larger artistic program that looks to create big effects, that writes for a public audience and plays to its sensibility – plays to, then betrays, that sensibility. For Juvenal's are *outlandishly* big effects. His sixth satire on women is, precisely, a model of excess, and excess runs right through the corpus. Juvenal is virtually impossible to follow because he has taken the materials of satire and performed them at maximum volume and pitch. Which not only creates for us this great, unprecedented, megaphonic show (we adore, playing as it does on all too common human dispositions), but puts on display its own overplaying. We *see* and *hear* that this is a performance, and thus realize that as performance it cannot be a heartfelt cry of outrage. The important consequence is that readers realize they have been caught out, that they've been taken in by satire's show of earnest moralizing. Juvenal, moralizing to excess, destroys the illusion for once and all.

So too, we see as *Sat.* 1 progresses that Juvenal is not at all interested in argument. If Horace set out to make the case (to Maecenas, to his literate and relatively privileged audience) for a certain kind of (satiric) writing, Juvenal blithely ignores any such concerns. His satires do not argue; there is really nothing *to* argue. Hence, instance follows instance, broken only by aphoristic asides to his reader, even when invoking Horace (51–57):

> Should I not believe these things worthy of the Venusian lamp
> Shouldn't I go after this stuff? But what? You'd rather hear
> epics about Hercules and Diomede or bellowing from the labyrinth,

or the boy-struck sea, or the flying *faber*, when
a husband pimps his wife, pocketing the cash
(while she gets none), good at looking away from the action,
good at snoring wide-awake in his cups ...

In this way the satire progresses. The pace and energy is masterful, even as the poet always controls the accumulation with aphoristic commentary and asides to the reader. Juvenal's artistry is nearly impossible to translate into English, as in this closure to one series of instances (77–80):

> quem patitur dormire nurus corruptor avarae,
> quem sponsae turpes et praetextatus adulter?
> si natura negat, facit indignatio versum
> qualemcumque potest, quales ego vel Cluvienus.

The first line in literalizing, explaining prose: "whom does the seducer of his own money-hungry daughter-in-law allow to sleep" (i.e., who can sleep when ...). The thought is powerfully compressed in Latin; the disturbing seduction of a daughter-in-law is twisted with yet darker irony in that line-ending *avarae*, "avaricious," an adjective in agreement with *nurus*, "daughter-in-law." The postponing effect, possible in Latin but scarcely in English, works the line to dark climax. However careful the rendering, this line and others either fall flat or do not approach the acid concentration that Juvenal manages. English struggles even to capture Juvenal's control of tenor:

> Who can sleep when a man seduces his daughter-in-law – with money
> she's happy to take, when brides are corrupt, young men adulterers.
> If genius fails us, indignation makes the satire,
> of some sort, anyway, like that of Cluvius or me.

Facit indignatio versum is so often quoted as emblematic of Juvenal, satirist of angry indignation, that we are surprised when we see how controlled and qualified this programmatic statement is in context. For neither vice nor anger drive this engine. As to the vice, Juvenal plays the old sex card, a fairly bland one at that. These shenanigans in themselves are time-honored and keeping no one awake. Nor is any of this personalized enough to generate genuine anger or indignation. Rather it is the presentation, the art, that has made the lines verbally powerful and even persuasive (for readers *have* been persuaded), even as he denies with comical false modesty his artistic competence: Cluvius, whoever he was, was no Juvenal, we can be sure.

Up to this point in the first satire, Juvenal has been offering an extended preamble, cataloguing the vice around him, an epic abundance he presents in counterbalance to the epic proper he intends not to write. At line 81 he makes a new beginning, with new programmatic declaration (81–87):

> From the time when rains were swelling the seas and
> Deucalion sailed his way to the mountaintop, consulted the Sortes,
> and life heated up the softening stones, and Pyrrha
> paraded her naked girls before the new men –
> whatever people do, their wishes, fears, wrath, pleasures,
> joys, activities, this is the stuff of my book.
> And when was there a richer abundance of vice?

There is exquisite touch here as well. Deucalion was Greece and Rome's Noah, so Juvenal returns to the beginning in order to claim a massive comprehensiveness for his satire – not only all of the world Rome knew but all of time as well. Yet that huge swath of history and experience will never really appear in the poems, and the beginning here looks strangely like the present: Pyrrha is a very modern arranger. And what follows in the satire is yet more constrained, eighty more lines or so dedicated largely to greed and the corruption of the patron–client relationship particularly as it relates to the *sportula*, disbursement of a wealthy patron's cash to his clients. Which may seem disappointing to a reader wanting Juvenal to live up to his promises, but in fact the poet delivers in his own unannounced terms. For on this relatively tiny stage of ordinary Roman life the monsters of a certain kind of Roman imagination loom large: the wealthy middle-eastern immigrant pushing aside tribunes waiting in queue, grubbing cheats, Egyptian bigshots dedicating statues to themselves while "traditional" Romans leave their patrons' door in disappointment and while said patrons feast in impossible excess. Juvenal has built a literary funhouse where middle-class Roman paranoias and resentments loom in hugely exaggerated form. He fashions it out of superbly crafted language that overwrites itself, that slips into ludicrous caricature – and thus into betrayal of its own *ostensible* project.

Juvenal, particularly in Satire 3 but in other satires as well, has for many been the poet of Roman imperial life, the writer one looked to for a realistic picture of Rome's mean streets. Yet a remarkable feature of Juvenal's satire, as we have seen, is its faithlessness to fact. The satires cannot be principally an indictment of Rome's corruption – remember, this is his explicit program – since documentation of those sins is nowhere to be seen. The instances he does present are for the most part either broadly "typical" or chestnuts from the traditional satiric stock or fantasies. Between these and the reality on the streets there will be incidental correspondence; the breadth of types and caricatures assures that. But these characters inhabit an imagined Rome, imagined not only by the poet drawing upon his stock of generic resources, but by his readers as well. He plays on *their* fears, anxieties, prejudices, and disappointments. And so the satire (necessarily) *works* for that audience. To use modern words anachronistically and somewhat inappropriately, the misogyny of *Sat.* 6, the homophobia of *Sat.* 2, the xenophobia of *Sat.* 3, 15, and most everywhere, were attitudes in place already, registers of a great many Romans' view of the world; these elements of their imagination become elements of Juvenal's art. One of Juvenal's, and therefore satire's, most significant influences on posterity is precisely this manner (or want of manners). Later English and European satire would not often trouble itself about being nice; it would on the contrary be rough, abusive, cleverly malicious, normative, sometimes reactionary, it would play on and with prejudice and "ordinary" sensibility, even when making, as did Juvenal, supreme works of literary imagination. If Roman satire had ended with Horace or Persius, the European literary landscape would look much different.

From line 150 on to the end of the first satire, Juvenal works a closing gambit that has puzzled readers (149–153):

> Every vice now stands at its extreme. Unfurl the sails,
> full canvas! But here you might say "where is the genius
> equal to the task? where is the frank honesty of days of old,
> with which they could write whatever they wanted
> with fiery spirit?"

The hypothetical questioner goes on to instance the dangers of writing satire that attacks the powerful – like Nero's favorite Tigillinus (155–156):

> ... you will soon burn, a very torch
> alongside others thus charred, throats fixed to posts ...

Further, the interlocutor continues, you can write about battling epic heroes and no one gets hurt, but start strutting like Lucilius and people begin to fret (162–167). The prospect seems dire enough to convince Juvenal, who declares, "Then I'll try my hand against those ashes that lie beneath the Flaminian and Latin ways" (170–171).

You recognize the old *topos* from Horace, *Sat.* 2.1.57–86, implicit also in 1.4.33–38 and Persius, *Sat.* 1.107–134; it has become a stock element of satire's programmatic formulae. What is troubling is the idea that Juvenal uses that *topos* seriously to back away from the politics of post-Domitianic Rome, from real issues of his day – a betrayal of the potential of that big, public voice. It is odd that eighteenth-century England so admired Juvenal's political courage, despite this apparent run for cover. The question cannot be resolved here in sufficient detail,[11] but we have seen already how this speaker's weaknesses and inconsistencies are mapped to a larger purpose of employing emotions and rhetoric already in play in Juvenal's Rome. Juvenal, unlike Persius perhaps, is not out to change his city, but to portray its ways in its own language, thus to create a satiric literature fully as sophisticated and prepossessing as the epic he summarily dismisses from the opening lines of his first poem. He plays the "dangers of writing satire" conceit in just the same way, couching it in the most sensational and incongruous terms – those wretched, human torches (so to be punished for writing *satire?*), that caricature of "fiery Lucilius" spreading fear and remorse through the land. A rhetorical bogeyman, in short, intended to (seem to) frighten the rhetorical character "Juvenal" into conventional quietism: a position, of course, he has no intention of embracing. "See how I too have backed away from the powerful" – this is one of satire's stock scripts, and Juvenal reads it out. But in so doing he says also, "see how I do it, with what color, what extravagance, what memorability – this will be how I do satire."

But, those ashes, the ghosts of Rome. Edward Courtney reads this last discussion between poet and interlocutor on the dangers of writing satire quite literally. Juvenal will use the Flavian dead as exempla of Rome's current sinners and sins; there were dangers in potential offense, though not the Neronian burning at the stake; finally, "We must infer that the grim past had so ingrained itself in Juvenal's mind that to some extent he failed to recognize contemporary realities."[12] This strikes me as incorrect, but is nonetheless suggestive. To get to more satisfactory ground we have first of all to abandon the idea that satire, Juvenalian satire particularly, has as its primary goal the flaying of vice, of taking the rascals on. What we've seen of Juvenal just doesn't work that way; rather than flay Rome, it lays it out for us readers, presents it in extravagant colors and sensational music. Some of the images he shows readers may/should genuinely disturb, but as a consequence of literary design, rather like that of the tragedy he so frequently invokes in the poetry. In such a satiric program as this, attacking individual contemporaries is simply not a primary issue. Is Juvenal just cooking up a fantasy image of Rome then, done up for delectation, where nothing "real" matters? Courtney's comment is relevant here. Rome *is* its past, the haunts of the Flaminian Way as potent as the scary grave-ground of Horace *Sat.* 1.8, where his stand-in Priapus only momentarily runs off frights sure to return with the darkness (see pp. 58–60). Civil war, those horrific executions under Nero, Domitianic repression, the sleaze of power politics, rampant luxury and greed – this is the nasty underside of power and empire, past and current. These ghosts won't stay buried in modern Rome; Juvenal digs them up and puts them on (if we are paying attention, gruesome and terrifying) display. More than that, he *processes* Rome's nasty ghosts: they are there in the targeted sinners, the gluttons and grabbers and lechers ("this is what we have become"), but they are there too in the bigotry, hypocrisy, and anxiety of the perceiving, satirizing eye/I. Rome's nastiness is everywhere, even in the language that so delights its readers; for it is *their* language, and if they are clever enough, they know it. Satire inevitably leads back to itself, betrays itself, is part of the world it portrays. *Experiar quid concedatur in illos / quorum Flaminia tegitur cinis atque Latina* ("Then I'll try my hand against those ashes that lie beneath the Flaminian and Latin ways"): Juvenal must have smiled when he penned those lines.

Further Reading

W. S. Anderson's several articles in his *Essays on Roman Satire* (Princeton, 1982), 197–486, are the natural first stop for interpretive work in Juvenal. One might do well to read, particularly, his "Studies in Book 1 of Juvenal," "Juvenal 6: A Problem of Structure," and "The Programs of Juvenal's Later Books," 197–292. S. Braund has written extensively on Juvenal, and both *Beyond Anger: A Study of Juvenal's Third Book of Satires* (Cambridge, 1988) and *The Roman Satirists and Their Masks* (London, 1996) are important.

Also, ranging over the whole corpus, and good reads, are E. Gowers, *The Loaded Table: Representations of Food in Roman Literature* (Oxford, 1993), 188–219; A. Richlin, *The Garden of Priapus: Sexuality and Aggression in Roman Humor* (New York, 1992, rev. edn.), 195–209; G. B. Townend, "The Literary Substrata to Juvenal's Satires," *Journal of Roman Studies* 63 (1973): 148–160; and C. Keane, *Figuring Genre in Roman Satire* (Oxford, 2006), passim. K. Freudenburg, *Satires of Rome* (Cambridge, 2001), 209–77, is a bracing modern treatment. On Juvenal's style, see J. G. F. Powell, "Stylistic Registers in Juvenal," in J. N. Adams and R. G. Mayer, eds., *Aspects of the Language of Latin Poetry* (Oxford, 1999), 311–34, and R. Jenkyns, *Three Classical Poets: Sappho, Catullus, and Juvenal* (London, 1982).

J. Henderson has written an engaging short book, *Figuring Out Roman Nobility: Juvenal's 8th Satire* (Exeter, 1997), and a seminal article, "Pump Up the Volume: Juvenal, Satire 1, 1–21," now in Henderson, *Writing Down Rome: Satire, Comedy, and Other Offences in Latin Poetry* (Oxford, 1999), 249–73. Less centrally "about" Juvenal, though including a good section thereon, is Henderson's "When Satire Writes Woman: *Gendersong*," in the same volume, 173–201. Of further articles beyond those mentioned above, look first to the following: W. S. Anderson, "Juvenal Satire 15: Cannibals and Culture," in A. J. Boyle, ed., *The Imperial Muse: Ramus Essays on Roman Literature of the Empire, to Juvenal through Ovid* (Victoria, 1988), 203–14; S. Braund, "A Woman's Voice: Laronia's Role in Juvenal Satire 2," in R. Hawley and B. Levick, eds., *Women in Antiquity: New Assessments* (London, 1995), 207–19; and Braund, "Juvenal: Misogynist or Misogamist," *Journal of Roman Studies* 82 (1992): 71–86; W. R. Johnson, "Male Victimology in Juvenal 6," *Ramus* 25 (1996): 170–86; C. Keane, "Theatre, Spectacle, and the Satirist in Juvenal," *Phoenix* 57 (2003): 257–75; E. J. Kenney, "The First Satire of Juvenal," *Proceedings of the Cambridge Philological Society* 8 (1962): 29–40; H. A. Mason, "Is Juvenal a Classic? An Introductory Essay," in J. P. Sullivan, ed., *Critical Essays on Roman Literature: Satire* (London, 1963), 93–176; N. Rudd, "Poets and Patrons in Juvenal's 7th Satire," in *Lines of Enquiry: Studies in Latin Poetry* (Cambridge, 1976), 84–118.

Those reading Juvenal in Latin will find the commentaries of E. Courtney (*A Commentary on the Satires of Juvenal* [London, 1980]), J. Ferguson (*Juvenal: The Satires* [New York, 1979]), and S. Braund (*Juvenal: Satires Book I* [Cambridge, 1996]) helpful. Braund particularly has good introductory material and interpretive essays. Of translations, P. Green, *Juvenal: The Sixteen Satires* (London, 1998), with its abundant supporting commentary, is a good bet. N. Rudd, *Juvenal: The Satires* (Oxford, 1992) reads well too. There is a nice Penguin collection of particular satires by English poets and translators of Juvenal, M. W. Winkler, *Juvenal in English* (London, 2001).

5

Menippeans and After

Of Pumpkins and Dead Emperors

With Juvenal the poetry we can properly describe as Roman Satire ends; nothing from classical Rome that fits satire's canonical, generic description – hexameter verse in the tradition of Lucilius – survives to us from after Juvenal. Yet almost everyone, including most readers (and the writer) of this book, think of satire as something larger than the three poets plus Lucilius (and maybe Ennius) we have been reading and discussing. We think of a broader satiric spirit, which finds grounds for mirth and dismay in the way the world runs. As we have already noticed, Roman satire reaches back into a Greek tradition of just that attitude, generically processed through invective and comedy, as well as in the Socratic and Cynic philosophical traditions. The kinds of thing that go on in jeremiad, burlesque, parody, flyting, fable, allegory, and satire of folk and literary traditions right on through the Graeco-Roman period up to the present day all share a family resemblance we can loosely describe with the term "satire." Yet most of this satire is generically unrelated to the verse satire we have been considering. That raises interesting questions. How, then, can Roman verse satire be definitive? Does it codify a certain mainstream for the expression of the satiric spirit, this broader functionality we see elsewhere? Or is it merely one instance, interesting but shortlived, among others, interesting too, and in some cases longer-lived?

These questions are challenging and worth further thought. Even what we think satire "is" precisely is not self-evident, and large books have been written, formulating large theories that attempt to sort it out. For Northrop Frye, satire is one of four major generic modalities of literary expression; for Robert Elliott, it is a primeval instinct found throughout the history of human society that develops into various species of art.[1] In both cases, satire is a register of expression traceable to our very nature as human beings, and as such assumes a huge canvas. Which might mean that the satire we have been considering is just a particular, rather artificial species of a much larger genus, one that adapted itself to the local, social, political, and cultural circumstances of late Republican Rome and flowered in Augustan and early imperial days. As such, it is still of course good material, and as we read and consider it, we will find points of connection, enactments of familiar human proclivities, formulations of human limitation that have not stopped teaching us about ourselves, and catching us out. But Roman satire may fairly be said to be more than merely this local instantiation of satirical spirit; just as Rome itself is a larger historical and cultural presence than even its long years at the center of Mediterranean life would indicate, so this literary kind, born in and for Rome, casts a long shadow. That shadow is tied to Rome's huge cultural legacy to western Europe, of course. Within that tradition, it simply does not make sense to speak of satire without reference to the achievements of Horace, Persius, and Juvenal, and literary posterity has so referred to them obsessively. In subtler ways, too, Roman satire assumes a more than local importance; for it is the first and perhaps history's most accomplished *development* of the satiric spirit. Roman satire showed that this particular angle of perspective, or register of human temperament, could not only influence or characterize literature, it could *be* literature, a literature, ironically, that grows out of its (broadly) satiric origins, questions them, rebels against them, and finally dies out of alienation from them. That story, the story of Roman satire, has proven poignantly memorable.

Yet there is much more "satire" out there, and even in Rome, the hexameter form was not the only way into this modality: comedy, philosophy, streetcorner diatribe, verse invective all did this thing we popularly call satire, if not exclusively, at least some of the time and in some ways. Scholars have, as well, conventionally talked about another classical vehicle of satire proper, that is "Menippean" satire, combinations of prose and verse, mostly the former, written in the tradition of one Menippus, a third-century (BCE) Cynic writer. Terentius Varro, a prolific Roman writer of the Republic, called his 150 books of prosimetric creations *Menippeae*. Others after, notably L. Annaeus Seneca

(d. 65 CE), Petronius (d. 66), and the Greek Lucian (d. post 180 CE), created satirical works of similar formal characteristics. Critics call all of these – and more later (Julian, Boethius et al.) – Menippean.

Doing so conceals a multitude of critical sins. For these works are at least as different from one another as they are similar. The fragments we have of Varro, a considerable number, but still only fragments, indicate writing of some wit – his titles are particularly engaging – on many topics shared by hexameter satire: moralizing, symposia and feasts, philosophy, sex, travel, the degeneration of modern life, madness, avarice, and so on. But while Seneca's only work in this "genre," his *Apocolocyntosis* ("Pumpkinification of the Emperor Claudius"), is undeniably satirical, its extended skit on the dead Claudius seems different in kind from what can be extrapolated from Varro's scraps. And Petronius' *Satyrica*, a very long work most of which has been lost, derives as much or more from the ancient novel than from satire. Lucian, writing in Greek rather than Latin, composed entertaining satiric fantasias that seem to owe little to Roman tradition. In short, the title "Menippean" may be seen as an anachronistic, literary-historical convenience, not an identity marker. It usefully enables a grouping of certain ancient works bearing a passing resemblance to one another, though seldom in the same terms.[2] Yet Quintilian may have had another thought. In 10.1.95 of his *Institutio Oratoria* ("Manual of Public Speaking"), he refers to a genre, distinct from verse satire, identified with the work of Varro:

> But there is another even older kind of satire. That most learned of Romans, Terentius Varro, founded this, based as it is on a mixture of prose and verse.

It is difficult to gainsay the testimony of a reliable ancient witness, despite the merely formal criterion specified. And, for what it's worth, Seneca cites one of Varro's Menippeans in the course of his work.[3] We might then cautiously assume a certain, broad generic identity among those works we call "Menippean" whose character we cannot fully reconstruct – Quintilian certainly does not give us much to go on. It is in any case most likely that Seneca, and to a lesser extent Petronius, built upon Varro's precedent, altering the formal characteristics of what was an open and flexible model in the first place for their own purposes. Some consistencies seem to persist into at least Seneca's work: a jaunty touch, forays into colloquial and vulgar language for comical purposes, a literary allusiveness indicating a reasonably learned audience, metrical variety, swatches of Greek, surprising inventiveness. Scholars have also extrapolated from Seneca, Lucian, and Julian, particularly, the "generic" characteristic of a fantastic voyage, a journey to the heavens, the sort of thing one sees also in Old Comedy. This narrative feature triangulates well with verse satire; Lucilius' first book is a satiric/comic "council of the gods," a trope that is picked up in modified form in Juvenal 4 and echoed, broadly, in the god's-eye view of human ambition in his tenth satire. That perspective from on-high works its way into Christian moralizing, some of which, as in the case of Jerome, is intermittently satirical as well. Seneca makes it the centerpiece of his *Apocolocyntosis.*

Seneca is an unlikely source for satirical writing, and indeed the evidence that the *Apocolocyntosis* is his is fairly thin, one ancient reference. But research has not turned up other candidates, and he did have a motive for writing this comically scathing, *ad hominem* satire. The son of a prominent rhetorician of the same name, Lucius Annaeus Seneca was born a few years before the turn of the millennium; he rose to prominence as an advocate and became an intimate of the court – possibly too intimate: he was banished to Corsica in 41 CE for alleged familiarity with Gaius Caligula's sister Julia. Recalled in 49 through the offices of Agrippina, niece, then wife, of Claudius, he became tutor, then adviser upon accession to the young Nero. The eight or so years of Seneca's influence were Nero's best, but when the emperor began to turn openly murderous, including among his targets his own mother Agrippina, Seneca requested leave to retire from the court – a little too late for the good of his reputation. A few years of retirement notwithstanding, he himself was served with a death sentence in 65, having been charged with participation in a conspiracy centering around C. Calpurnius Piso – the so-called Pisonian Conspiracy – to assassinate Nero. Tacitus reports him to have committed suicide with immaculately rehearsed Socratic equanimity.

Seneca is known to literary history for his popularizing disquisitions on Stoic philosophy, moral essays and epistles, and his wonderfully lurid tragedies. Little in his background aside from broad literary training sets him up as a satirist, but the circumstances of his exile – having appealed unsuccessfully for commutation to Claudius – gave reasonable cause for lasting resentment of that emperor. Ambitious, aggrieved, in the prime of life, and exiled from the life-blood of Rome, he (we may suppose) held a grudge, despite his public Stoicism. And Claudius was an easy target. By the time of his poisoning, he was loved by few; he had been set up in power by the Praetorian guard rather than the Senate; he was fond of passing summary judgment in private trials; he had yielded great power to his respective wives and the freedmen in his circle; he was of stumbling speech and, though something of a historical scholar, was held to be stupid.

There is no question that the *Apocolocyntosis*, written perhaps a few months after Claudius' death and public consecration as a god, is a gross, wholly amusing libel whose opening words quickly set the tone (1.1–2):

> What happened in heaven on the thirteenth of October in the new year, the beginning of a most prosperous age, is my task to record. I yield nothing to offense or favor. This is the utter truth. If someone asks how I know these things, well, if I don't want to, I needn't respond. Who is going to make me? . . . I shall say whatever comes into my mouth. Who ever required sworn witnesses for a historian?

The narrative picks up Claudius' post-mortem life, describing his attempt to gain admittance to the divine pantheon. Hercules, not known for his intelligence, acts as his advocate in the debate before a gathering of the gods, the *concilium deorum*. The decision hangs in uncertain balance until the deified Augustus speaks up for the first time as a god, as he claims, to denounce his successor in language that mimics the mannerisms of his own *Res Gestae* with touches of light comedy and dark intimation thrown in (those executions of his relatives).[4] This testimony convicts him and Claudius is sent to the underworld, where a more summary trial awaits and some ingenuity is exercised to find an appropriate punishment. It seems he will be condemned to play dice endlessly – an obsession in life – with a leaky dice-box, when Caligula, his old tormenter, appears and asks that Claudius be made his slave. Wish granted, whereupon the dead emperor is turned over to Caligula's freedman.

The central conceit of the whole is the sharp juxtaposition of parodic sublime on one hand and vulgar bathos on the other. The verse sections burlesque praise poetry while the prose, with great resourcefulness and wit, deflates everything it touches. It really is as inventive and diverting a read as you can find anywhere. Malicious jokes run from beginning to end – Claudius' dying words, "I think I've shat myself," are not atypical of the level of some of the humor. But there is subtler stuff too: allusions and quotations only the educated could recognize, parodies of contemporary literary mannerisms, and a fair amount of imbedded Greek. And the underlying strain of seriousness is palpable: Seneca does not let go of those political murders, alluding to more in the few he mentions. The question remains, however, whether the whole amounts to much more than a one-off screed on the memory of a dead emperor. There *are* hints of a broader scope. The *concilium deorum*, deriving from Lucilius's specifically satiric tradition, has at the core of the conceit the notion of appeal to a final audience where justice will be served. The gods, however partial and flawed, look down upon humans' greater follies and pass judgment. In literature the idea is as old as the opening tableau of Homer's *Odyssey*. Seneca's version of debate on Olympus has the quality of generic imitation for simple *ad hominem* purposes until the speech of Augustus, who raises the spectacle of political murder in an imperial context and brings, by his presence, the divine *concilium* conceptually back to earth, specifically as a senatorial debate – his mention that he had not spoken as a god before has some relevance here. In an imperial context such viable senatorial debate is a poignant memory, so that once again we see the ghosts of Rome being invoked. The fact that Seneca engineers Augustus' plea in such a context to be decisive is a broad hint, to Nero and this fantasia's circle of readers, that in Rome titular *imperium* is meant to have its limits.

Then there is that bit of (another sort of) purple verse put in the mouth of Apollo in lavish praise of the new emperor, Nero. The Parcae have just allotted to Nero long and illustrious life; their very threads turn golden as they're spun; Apollo can scarcely contain himself (20–32):

> ... "Cut nothing short, Parcae," said Apollo,
> "let this one, like to me in looks and grace,
> and not worse in song and voice,
> surpass the limits of mortal life. He will bring
> joy to the weary, and will break the laws' silence.
> Scattering the flying orbs like the Morning Star,
> and like the Evening Star he rises upon their return,
> or like the reddening Sun when it brings in the day,
> shining he looks upon the world and whips up his chariot,
> such a Caesar is here; Rome shall now look upon such a Nero.
> His shining blazes with modest brightness, his neck
> splendid with flowing hair."

The encomiastic excess here is sometimes explained by reference to the conventions of Hellenistic ruler-cults and of praise-poems where rhetorical parallels exist. It is argued too that Seneca's relief, and that of the courtly circle around Nero, at the passing of such a shadow along with the promise of the new accounts for the over-the-top flattery – and that stellar imagery. More than stellar, in fact; the comparison of the young Nero to the sun aligns him with his encomiast Apollo. Too much? What of the irony entailed in the fact that the new emperor is sanctified as an immortal (Apollo) at the beginning of a poem satirizing the sanctification of his predecessor? P. T. Eden registers an important, related point about the passage's style: "[The hexameters'] facile, elisionless flow presents expected images in formalized word patterns with insipid blandness. There are no formal elements of parody or satire: the author makes his literary point by holding a mirror up to uninventive mediocrity."[5] That is precisely the kind of verse-making Persius went after in his roughly contemporary first satire. And while Persius is said to have been no fan of Seneca, that antipathy had to do most likely with Seneca's philosophical compromises while serving at court – not literary style. In short, Seneca writes this way for a reason. And just as Persius had been able to take effective satire into the very heart of Nero's world, the art and sensibility the emperor fostered, Seneca seems able here to do something similar. The encomium ends tersely (4.2): "thus Apollo. And Lachesis, because she favored the shapely man, was lavish; and gave to Nero many years of life from her own store." Then quickly and bathetically back to Claudius and his scatological end.

It is in this ambiguous tension between praise and dispraise that Seneca does satire. He does it not in the way Horace or Persius had, but in a way they would have recognized. The praise/blame collocation here shows its contrastive terms far too compromised, too involved, one with the other. Add in the fact that Seneca had earlier composed the entirely laudatory funeral oration for Claudius, read out by Nero, who could not suppress a giggle, and one finds it difficult to keep the terms, or targets, apart. A cautionary nuance intended for his sometime student? Possibly, particularly with the satire's emphasis on Claudius' cruelty. At any rate, the terms of Seneca's/Apollo's flattery, in respect to Nero's artistic vanity particularly, show that this philosophical mentor knew his pupil well and didn't mind, carefully, letting others in on what he'd seen.

Satire Breaks (Out)

Petronius, yet another Neronian, has presented far more complex problems for students of Menippean satire – beginning with his title, *Satyricon* or more correctly *Satyrica*, based on different case forms of the Latin adjective meaning "satirical" or "salacious things." The word doesn't derive from the root that gives us *satura*, but from another meaning "satyr-like"; still, the close homophone would have suggested to Roman readers both the notions of "satire" and "naughty business." The ambivalence hovering about the title extends to broader confusion about the generic identity of this work. Put reductively, the work falls into either the tradition of the ancient romance or "novel" or the Menippean (satirical?) tradition. Or both. Qualifying the *Satyrica* as Menippean rests on the strictly formal element of combined prose and verse. On the other hand, it was excessively long in comparison to other extant classical Menippeans and contains virtually none of the standard generic elements found in Seneca and Lucian: no divine perspective, no fantastic voyage to the heavens, no moralizing, no explicitly satirical genre markers. In terms of general structure, it is much closer to the Greek novel of Chariton, Longus, and others, or even Apuleius' second-century Latin *Golden Ass*, than it is to any extant (ancient) Menippeans. Some scholars have noticed problems identifying it as a novel, noting particularly that the sentimental Greek Romances that have come down to us intact are not known for forays into homosexual affairs as at the heart of the *Satyrica*'s remaining sections, or for its low-life misadventures, and generally scabrous texture. But the *Golden Ass*, with its raunchy sex and sorcery, though it postdates Petronius, is founded in part on an earlier Greek *Onos*, and ancient summaries and fragments of early novels show a much wider range of subject matter than we see in the few complete novels we have. The remaining fragments of Iamblichus, for instance, indicate plot elements similar to those we see in Apuleius. Moreover, recent publication of the so-called Iolaus fragment offers a prosimetric parallel to Petronius in crucial respects. It involves one Iolaus and a male prostitute who masquerade as *galli*, castrated initiates of Cybele, among, one presumes, other misadventures, and employs the coarse Sotadean verse associated with such characters.[6] These family resemblances still leave unanswered the question about what exactly the *Satyrica* was intended to be, and many readers throw up their hands on the point and think of it as its own peculiar kind of masterpiece. It is possible that this remarkable work draws from Menippean precedent, just as it does from verse satire and, to a larger extent, the early novel, resulting in a literary concoction whose designation as Menippean satire is justified only by its later reception and influence, a matter we'll get to shortly. At the same time, it is also fair to conclude that the *Satyrica* does(-in) satire. Let us see how.

The author of the work is likely the Neronian T. (or C.) Petronius Niger described by Tacitus in his *Annals*. Tacitus' portrait is a compelling sketch of a talented administrator, but even more ingenious *bon-vivant*, quite given over to luxury and out-of-the-way pleasures (16.18):

> His days were spent sleeping; his nights with work and the pleasures of life. Just as industry leads others to fame, indolence guided him. Yet he was considered not a common spendthrift, as are many that throw away their money, but a refined sybarite. His words and deeds, to the extent they were casual and suggestive of a certain unselfconsciousness, were considered, in their frankness, all the more pleasing. Yet as proconsul in Bithynia and then as Consul, he showed himself vigorous and competent. Then, having returned to his dissolute way of life, or giving that impression, he was taken up into the circle of Nero, as his "arbiter of taste"; for Nero thought nothing elegant or refined unless Petronius had approved it.

In time, just as had Seneca some months earlier, Petronius ran afoul of Nero, in this instance owing to the jealousy of Nero's confidante, Tigellinus. Tacitus describes Petronius' end in 66 CE as a conscious inversion of the classic Socratic death scene enacted by Seneca (16.19):

> He didn't put up with the hopes and fears of delay, nor did he rush the job. He cut his own veins. Then, binding and opening them again as he liked, he chatted with his friends, but not seriously, so that he might not get a reputation for resolution. And he listened to his friends discoursing not on the immortality of the soul or consolations of philosophy but reciting light verse. He gave some slaves presents, others beatings. He even appeared at dinner, and then dozed off, so that his death, however compulsory, might seem natural. Not even in his will did he flatter, as others usually did, Nero, Tigellinus, and others of the powerful, but he wrote up a list of Nero's indiscretions, naming names of each male and female partner and the sordid details of each new thrill, and sent it under his seal to Nero.

That portrait scripts for us certain ways of reading the text. We expect irony, skepticism, a degree of superior condescension, perhaps particularly with respect to Nero insofar as traces of the man may be discerned in this text. One take on the *Satyrica* has been precisely this, that it offers a satirical view of Rome under Nero: the wanderings of the narrative's protagonists in the pursuit of pleasure and related misdemeanors as it were guided by the greater *logos* of the emperor. Similarly, we do not expect moralizing satire or a serious philosophical undertow from such an author, even while we are aware of a writer capable of subtly alluding to these possibilities, of playing with a learned but light touch with their expressive registers. In fact, Petronius is an immensely allusive writer who draws models, characters, and situations from literature, philosophy, and his own experience. From epic to mime, philosophy to verse satire, from the letters of his immediate contemporary Seneca to the quirks and habits of Nero himself – all find significant place in the huge canvas of this literary entertainment. That kind of comprehensiveness will become a paradigmatic feature of much subsequent "Menippean" satire, as we shall see. For contemporaries, it must have been a gargantuan puzzle.

Set on an epic scale, and invoking epic all along its course, it is structured in a manner that later literary history would call "picaresque." It follows a central character, Encolpius, and his lovers, friends, and rivals journeying from Marseilles through the byways of Campania and beyond. The odyssey has a vague organizing principle: Encolpius, our dubious hero, has provoked the anger of Priapus and continues to run afoul of the god, suffering impotence, and is off in search for a cure. Along the way Encolpius struggles with his associate and rival Ascyltus to keep the attentions of the fetching young slave Giton he has stolen away from the latter's mistress. Thievery, violence, and sexual misadventure constitute this trio's general activities – "criminal-satiric fiction" is one of the work's possible designators,[7] but there is much else folded into the narrative. Discussions of literature and rhetoric (one Agamemnon, a rhetoric teacher, plays a major role in our chief extract), parodic recitations of contemporary poetry (the poet Eumolpus stepping up to offer specimens of that), what look like "Milesian tales," the kind of racy narratives that will bulk out Apuleius' *Golden Ass*, and, dominating the extant text, the long description of Trimalchio's feast. New readers soon discover that even the episodes we have – from Books 14, 15, and 16 of a possible twenty-four, it is sometimes guessed – are radically incomplete and fragmented, making an understanding of the artistic place and purpose of the text exceptionally problematic.

The *Satyrica*'s prosimetric nature may disorient a reader's bearings yet further. Menippean, especially in Petronius' hands, has been called an "anti-genre," drawing as it does on a multitude of conventions and scumbling their boundaries and distinctions in this great mélange. Epic and mime, romance and satire, verse and prose, play side by side in this narrative. Not meant to be one of our clean and categorizable literatures, it works actively against conventional ideas of literary kinds, genres, that in Greece and Rome were determinative precisely because they were tied to certain, specific conditions of delivery and reception. As Stephen Nimis puts it,

> Epic, drama and lyric all deal with a multitude of themes and story types, but have a claim to being genres insofar as they were performed (or imagined to be performed) in a particular place and time and in a specific social context (festivals, symposia, etc.). Not coincidentally these are all verse genres, whose character as verse is tied closely to their performative context. The rise of prose literature represents a process of abstraction of discourse from particular contexts and audiences so that prose (with the important exception of rhetoric, which is more aligned with verse in this and other respects) is not imagined to be performed or circulated in any particular context. As such, prose is free to make reference to various verse genres for serious or humorous effects, for prose can "contain" verse without becoming verse (which is not reciprocally true).[8]

Petronius' prose sweeps up satire and much else, dislocating it from its performative contexts and recasting it into a form that, for all its traditional Menippean elements, is really quite unprecedented. To the extent that Petronius is aware of "doing satire," he conspicuously breaks it down, or away from its own traditions and precedents; in effect he breaks the mold. Thus his grand-scale imitation of satire in the set-piece at the heart of Petronius' extant text, the banquet of Trimalchio.

Petronius' is satire's last great feast. It is built on Horace's sign-off, the failed supper in *Sat.* 2.8, where the pompous host Nasidienus' vulgar pretensions are acidly related by Fundanius to Horace, who, we recall, was not present – an overt programmatic signal that the poet was moving along to other generic venues (see pp. 81–4). Scholarship has noticed sufficient parallels of character and incident to indicate that

Petronius clearly meant to build on Horace's model.[9] But where Horace had broken off the dinner by engineering a disastrous collapse of canopies followed by the guests' abrupt departure, rejecting any taste of the proffered dinner, Petronius' feast of the rich freedman Trimalchio goes on and on. If both works can be read as finales to satire's dominant, identifying trope, Horace can be said to turn away with a certain prim fastidiousness while Petronius immerses his characters, and us, in it until all are sated to sickness. Course after course of impossibly lavish cuisine presented with grotesque ingenuity, each course with its own illusion or conceit, each followed by another so that the guests' (and readers') minds reel with the cheap jokes and relentless staginess of it all as much as the stomachs of Encolpius and Co. suffer from sheer distention. Many of satire's usual targets are here: pretension, vulgarity, luxury, superstition, Juvenal's upstart freedmen and foreigners, wealth standing in for, indeed buying, social status and political distinction. There are signals too, as commentators have noticed, that Nero himself does not escape satirical notice. Trimalchio shares with him a number of quirks: both preserve the hairs from their first shave in golden vessels, both share similar tastes in their entourage, both wear golden bracelets, Petronius has a boy acrobat fall on Trimalchio, echoing an episode when a boy taking the role of Icarus fell and spattered Nero with his blood, both share a taste for music and literature, Trimalchio's of course badly learned and tasteless.[10] Trimalchio's egregious feast may be, as satire's feasts enfigure their society, a conceit for Rome at the table of her supreme patron.

But this is *satura* writ to its extreme, full and overfull, more so even than Juvenal in that it transcends satire's conceptual limits. Juvenal wrote a massively incorporating satire that was still, recognizably, satire. Petronius satirizes over-the-top tableaux of feeding, indulgence, and vulgarity, but then goes on. Or rather creates such a wide canvas that satire's feast is just one facet of something much larger. The narrative, even confined to this episode, places the dinner at its center but frames it with the disjointed drama of characters, however unlovable, the reader has come to know. So while we are sure that the educated narrator and his friends find this dinner party impossibly vulgar, we understand that the observers themselves are eminently satirizable scamps. There is no sure "moral" perspective targeting Trimalchio (though we have seen in the verse satirists that this is hardly essential for satire): instead we have an anti-authoritative narrative that morphs the emblematic scene into something else. The nature of that morphing is best seen in the calamities that befall Trimalchio – who, if he were Horace's Nasidienus, would be set up for ridicule and then left to dangle uncomfortably. Nothing like this happens. Trimalchio is inherently ridiculous, but he utterly dominates the long scene; his colorful absurdity itself is this feast's *pièce de résistance*. The whole satire, if satire it can be called, turns into an ironic celebration of its target.

Where Trimalchio is not present, as when he steps out to relieve himself, Petronius seems to guy satire in another way. Once away, the guests are encouraged to speak out, and what we get, as John Bodel has pointed out, is a parody of Plato's *Symposium*.[11] Symposium scenes – high end, Greek drinking parties cum philosophical discussion – are frequently imitated in classical literature, sometimes parodically as here, and are natural analogues to satire's feast scenes. Plato's version is an elaborate discussion on the nature of love, with each of the guests offering a disquisition on his view. Socrates, of course, sets them all straight in the end. The love theme might seem a natural fit with the erotic preoccupations of the *Satyrica* as a whole, but Petronius' imitation, set in Trimalchio's absence, is confined to the mundane grouses and gripes of Trimalchio's illiterate guests. The scene has been called an example of the real natter of real Romans; in fact it is none such, but would it be too far-fetched to say that its faux realism, a consciously intended literary effect, is meant to reduce Horatian *sermo* to one kind of absurd conclusion? The gripes of the several "philosophers" do exercise the critical function of satire in their disquisitions: follies of the rich, the price of corn, rampant atheism, malpracticing doctors, and in a wonderful parody of a Juvenalian rant, Ganymede the corn-price monomaniac has his self-incriminating say (44): "So, those at the bottom of the heap suffer, because the ones on top grind them down, and enjoy a perpetual holiday. If only we had the lionhearts whom I found living here when first I arrived from Asia!" Some complaints are more general but betray satiric ancestry – in a general slanging match among the guests that itself serves as a gloss on satire (57): "You see the louse on your neighbor but not the bug on yourself" and "You're a muddy pot, a strap soaked in water ... "

There is much else in these speeches that is merely inane gossip, but Trimalchio's return from the toilet leads him into a cheerful chat about his constipation and its remedies, ending with a magnanimous "permission to fart" declaration (47): "None of us was born solid. I can think of no greater torment than having to hold it in." The line itself may refer to Claudius' "last words" as Seneca has it in the *Apocolo-cyntosis* (see p. 145).[12] It may also function as commentary on what has been going on in his absence. In either case, satire's target becomes something of a satirist himself. The permitted fart leads finally – though this sort of thing keeps ricocheting through this massively rich text – to the spook stories of 62–63. At one point Trimalchio persuades his friend Niceros to speak up; he does so with an engaging tale about a close encounter with a real werewolf. Trimalchio swallows it whole and offers a story of his own, this about witches who steal away a comely young boy's dead body. A brawny retainer attempts to drive them off, striking one in the privates with his sword, whereupon the witches disappear, but leave the defender ruined. The broad Priapic context of the *Satyrica* and these details specifically evoke Horace *Sat.* 1.8, where a blasting fart was enough to ward away these feminine powers of darkness (see p. 59). In Trimalchio's feast, where farts are given license to fill the air, there is no such happy outcome – if you believe in werewolves and witches, or with Horace, in the darker fears and historical perturbations they enfigure.

Petronius' enactment of the satirical scene, in short, continually pulls the rug from under satire; alludes to it, plays with its conventions, mocks its seriousness, casts it adrift in a sea of other genres, themselves treated equally badly. Nor does Nero's Rome come off well – and there is the crux. If satire can be said to be a kind of social criticism rendered with a degree of artistically encoded irony, the *Satyrica* may be fairly said to qualify as satire or satiric fiction. Yet seen in the light of the generic conventions that shape the work of Lucilius, Horace, Persius, and Juvenal, the *Satyrica* is quite something else. It would seem, then, that it matters less what we call this great, fragmented work, and instead appreciate the precise strokes of its artful dismemberment of Roman verse satire, recasting its broken pieces into a shape that would influence centuries of later work.

And Then …

While Latin hexameter satire died with Juvenal, (not always satirical) satire in the Menippean tradition carried on. Both Lucian (d. 180 CE) and the Emperor Julian (d. 363 CE) wrote Greek Menippeans: the *Necyomantia* ("Dialogues of the Dead") and *Icaromenippus* ("Menippus As Icarus") by the former, *Caesars* and *Misopogon* ("Beard-hater") by the latter. Lucian was far and away the more creative and successful writer. His two satires involve fantastic voyages to hell and heaven respectively, in the latter case with the intent of trying to silence the mad, metaphysical speculations of the philosophers. Julian's efforts mark continuing interest in the form into late antiquity, a tendency that would continue through the diverse and syncretic (Latin) works of Martianus Capella's (*fl.* 410–430) *Marriage of Philology and Mercury,* Fulgentius' (467–532) *Mythologies,* and Boethius' (480–524) *Consolation of Philosophy.*[13] Despite the absence of consistent comic-satiric intent in these writers, they use Menippean conventions inventively in the context of the sometimes awkward conjoining of classical learning and Christian doctrine. Experiments in Latin with the form continue to sputter up now and again, in the twelfth century particularly, until it enjoyed a new day in the sun, along with much else classical, in the Renaissance Menippeans of Lipsius, Rigault, and others.[14]

Here is where literary history takes one of its funny turns. Menippeans based on specifically classical precedents fade from the scene after the European Renaissance. But two notable twentieth-century scholars, Northrop Frye and Mikhail Bakhtin, in their efforts to provide a comprehensive taxonomy of literature (Frye) or account for the origins of certain qualities of Dostoevsky's fiction (Bakhtin), apply the term "Menippean" to a broad range of works dating from the Renaissance that share some properties of ancient Menippeans. For Frye, drawing substantially on Petronian precedent, the genre would take in works whose characters include "pedants, bigots, cranks, parvenus, virtuosi, enthusiasts, rapacious and incompetent professional men of all kinds"; it treats of abstract ideas and sees folly not as moral failure but "diseases of the intellect, as a kind of maddened pedantry which the *philosophus gloriosus* at once symbolizes and defines."[15] Erasmus' *Praise of Folly,* More's *Utopia,* Rabelais' *Pantagruel* and *Gargantua,* Burton's *Anatomy of Melancholy,* Sterne's *Tristram Shandy,* Nashe's *Unfortunate Traveller,* Swift's *Tale of a Tub* and many more are included under such a rubric. Bakhtin found in these and others evidence of the mediaeval Carnival, Feast of Fools, and earlier, in the Socratic dialogues, counter-institutional forces that dismantle or ironize presumption and authority. Carnival, a larger cultural phenomenon than the Menippean genre it fosters, mocks conventionally empowered politico-religious institutions with parody priests and sacraments, de-coronations, and the like, while valorizing the victims of institutional authority: slaves and peasants, with their insurrectionist, (c)rude humor. On a literary level, the fantastic voyages characteristic of Greek Old Comedy and Menippeans can be seen behind a number of later works whose features also include dream-scenes, less than salubrious incidents and characters, utopian and parodic elements, a tendency to consider large "truths" or themes, and much more.[16] These qualities distort and therefore reappraise conventional perceptions of reality and become a lens for satirical re-evaluation, a function that finds use for this species of Menippean, in modified forms, on up to the present day.[17]

The Renaissance was also pivotal for the afterlife of verse satire. The European middle ages knew of Juvenal and Horace, but hexameter satire was not picked up in Latin, nor were the major satirists invoked as models for the vernacular language. The satiric tradition was carried forward largely by allegorical texts like Langland's *Piers Plowman* and by moralizing, Aesopic fables modeled on Phaedrus.[18] The latter is an interesting satiric tradition unto itself that is maintained from the middle ages through Spenser's *Mother Hubberd's Tale*, on up through *Animal Farm* in the twentieth century. But verse satire of the sort we have been looking at primarily in this book fades out of view, and would not have returned but for the curious process of rediscovery, retrieval, and imitation that was the Renaissance. Dante remembers Horace the satirist, but lesser Renaissance names – names known to few readers indeed – took up the challenge of composing in their style (in Latin): Mussatus (c.1300), Da Strada (c.1350), Corrarius (c.1430), and others.[19] Through relatively arcane neo-Latin poets like these and the scholars who edited the manuscripts of rediscovered classics, verse satire again began to creep into the popular mainstream. Alexander Barclay translated into English Sebastian Brandt's *Narrenschiff* ("Ship of Fools") in 1509, a verse satire dependent in part on Juvenal, while John Skelton (1460–1529) became the first original English satirist of note in the sixteenth century. His early work is still mediaeval in character, but *Colin Clout*, written in a bumptious, ragged style, is an extended satire on ecclesiastical abuses, and Skelton's later poems consciously invoke Horace, Persius, and Juvenal, as well as Martial. Not long after, the exiled courtier Sir Thomas Wyatt composed Horatian-styled satires (in terza rima rather than hexameters) in the 1530s, and by the 1590s satire could be said to have come back – in somewhat altered form. Names to reckon with here are Joseph Hall (1574–1656), John Marston (1575–1634), Thomas

Lodge (1558–1625), John Donne (1572–1631), Everard Guilpin (*fl.* 1598), Ben Jonson (1572–1637), Abraham Cowley (1618–67), and for a revivified strain of Martialesque satirical epigram, John Owen (1560–1622).

Each of these writers – Donne, Jonson, and Cowley not only as satirists – could and should be discussed at length, something impossible here in this summary review of the English tradition (from here on the tour of post-classical satire gets breathtakingly swift), and all of them are up to somewhat different things. But what they share is something crucial to *satire*'s range of expressivity. That is, while they all write verse satire, coming round, by the early seventeenth century, to the rhymed pentameter couplet that would become the English norm for the genre, and make self-conscious reference to the major Roman exemplars, they represent more than simply the re-activation of a literary kind. What that is has to do with their position vis-à-vis their English past. English vernacular satire, even when aware of classical prototypes, had hitherto been constrained by its mediaeval and Christian ethical frame – and often indeed there *was* a fair match between quotable *mots* of particularly Persius and Juvenal and Christian homily. As we have noted, the fables of Phaedrus provided a useful model mediaeval adaptation in just such a spirit. This is "satire" in one familiar guise, as a conservative and moralizing discourse. But post-mediaeval, vernacular verse satire, perhaps a little miraculously, re-stored a great deal of the genre's expressive pliancy and subtlety. Subtlety, perhaps, in a limited sense, for most of the satirists of the 1590s espoused an often overwrought, rough, and obscuring style they thought characteristic of Juvenal and Persius. But their attitudes were no longer simply moralizing or generalizing complaints; rather, they attacked specific targets, often each other, and concentrated their bile on the local and topical, on denizens of the city, on literature itself. London, its rivalries, corruptions, inequities, money, sin, and ambition had, as Colin Burrow points out, become a fair analogue to Rome.[20] Moreover, we see here the beginnings of satire's overt involvement in politics, a tendency that would flourish in the later seventeenth century to the point that satire would have a politically influential status far beyond anything it enjoyed in its Roman life. And whereas the "dangers of writing satire" trope seen in Horace, Persius, and Juvenal was often exaggerated, there was in England an effective ecclesiastical ban on the publication of satires in 1599 that had an appreciable, repressive effect; that issue would recur as satire's political voice became more prominent. The danger became more real. But the most interesting development of all was the fact that the energetic satiric activity of the 1590s and beyond *conceptualized* itself as satire. Even when misprizing stylistic and thematic features of their classical models, they consciously wrote in an emulative manner, aware of themselves practicing an ancient, specific, and known art form. So Donne opens his fourth satire (1–4):

> Well, I may now receive, and die: my sin
> Indeed was great, but I have been in
> A Purgatory such as feared hell is
> A recreation to, and scant map of this.

His Purgatory is the importunate "climber" of Horace 1.9 (17–23):

> Therefore I suffered this: towards me did run
> A thing more strange than on Nile's slime the sun
> E'er bred, or all which unto Noah's ark came –
> A thing which would have posed Adam to name,
> Stranger than seven antiquaries' studies,
> Than Afric's monsters, Guiana's rarities;
> Stranger than strangers ...

How unlike Horace this farrago of biblical and vaguely Juvenalian imagery. None of the self-ironizing decorum of the Horatian persona as the abusive rhetoric just piles up. In all this, Donne's satire is much of its time: (metrically) rough, rhetorical invective. Yet Donne is obviously conscious of working from classical models and of reorienting them in a generic framework or set of conventions that effects, makes for, satire in the 1590s. That is, not only a satirical poem, but something that recognizably fits into an inherited generic formula. Thus while Donne's satiric persona is not that of Horace, it *is* patently a persona, a figure and voice made up for this very literary-satirical occasion. Moreover this satirist is conspicuously placed within the world of his created satire. So, that flawed, implicated satiric eye/I we recognize from the Romans – a perspective largely not seen in mediaeval, homiletic satire. Byron, much later, puts it pithily:

> Although some kind, censorious friend will say
> "What, art thou better, meddling fool, than they?"

And every brother-rake will smile to see
That miracle, a moralist in me.[21]

There were no pure moralists writing satire in Elizabethan England. Most literary discourse, and certainly all satire, was cooked up in a climate of overt controversy, rivalry, and dispute, where writers were perforce caught up in the web of critical discourses they wove for others. This can be seen even in the work of Ben Jonson, who adapts this generic identification even to what is technically not verse satire. His 1601 satirical drama, *Poetaster*, a play set in Augustan Rome but transparently glossing England of 1601, portrays Jonson himself as Horace and Jonson's rivals, Marston and Dekker, as Horace's Demetrius and Fannius. Here is his imbedded translation of the end of *Sat.* 1.10:

Should I be worried by that louse Carper, or suffer agonies
because Demetrius sneers at me behind my back or because
I'm slandered by that ass Fannius who sponges on Hermogenes Tigellius?
I should like these poems to win approval of Plotius and Varius,
Maecenas and Virgil, Valgius, Octavius, and the admirable Fuscus ...

More than just borrowing a name or convenient setting, Jonson speaks through a Horatian mask, and Horatian *auctoritas* speaks through Jonson – or so he would have it. His versions in *Poetaster* of *Sat.* 2.1 and 1.9 are employed precisely as defensive or aggressive authority. The tactic was noted and satirized by others, notably in Dekker's *Satiromastix* a year later. This was a world where rivalry, patronage, status, and sometimes brutally hard political and social contestation were the conditions of survival – and it was very well suited to the satiric muse.[22]

That muse would take a brief nap immediately after Jonson's death, awaking rested and energetic for the English Revolution (1647–9) and Restoration (of the monarchy in 1660).[23] John Cleveland (1613–58) and Andrew Marvell (1621–78) wrote satires on Royalist and Parliamentary sides. After the Restoration, John Wilmot, the Earl of Rochester (1648–80), circulated a number of clever, sometimes scabrous, satires, "Timon," "Artemiza to Chloe," "Satyr against Reason and Mankind," and his well-known attack on John Dryden in the 1675 "Allusion to Horace" written in imitation of Horace's *Sat.* 1.10. In that poem Rochester takes up the Horatian mask, as had Jonson before, and turns the "rough Lucilius" trope against Dryden, just as Dryden himself had against Jonson, and Jonson yet earlier with Shakespeare.[24] But Rochester's satire, written before Dryden's major satirical work, must seem petty carping to a later age, for Dryden (1631–1700) is indisputably the giant of the Restoration. His *Absalom and Achitophel*, adapting the biblical episode from 2 Samuel wherein King David is confronted with the rebellion of his son Absalom, neatly fits the situation of Charles II, his illegitimate son Monmouth, and the conspiring politician Shaftesbury. Dryden's satiric exposure of the episode gave satire an overtly political and undeniably prepossessing public voice. On the smaller stage of literary rivalry, Dryden's *Mac-Flecknoe* demolished his rival Thomas Shadwell (1642–92) with a relish that puts into shadow Rochester's ingenious dissection of Dryden. *MacFlecknoe* itself leads in direct descent to Pope's *Dunciad*, and Dryden's satiric achievement as a whole inaugurates the great English age of the genre, the eighteenth century of Swift, Pope, Gay, Churchill, and Johnson.

But almost as important as Dryden's published satires is the long introduction, the *Discourse on Satire* (1693), which he wrote to the translations of Persius and Juvenal he published late in his career. It is the most substantial theoretical orientation of Roman satire into modernity. He treats at some length the "original and progress" of the genre through its major Roman exemplars and competing etymologies (*satyros / satur*) are discussed (settling with Casaubon on *satur*), as are Greek versus Roman origins, relations to drama, generic development, and salient characteristics of each of the major verse satirists. After relegating Persius to a meritorious (for his moral quality) third place, he treats extensively the strengths and weaknesses of the two remaining verse satirists, awarding the laurel of ancient satire to Juvenal who gives Dryden "as much Pleasure as [he] can bear." That verdict is in the end far less important than the influential terms of distinction he applies to Horace and Juvenal. Horace is the "better instructor," is the superior philosopher, subtler, more courtly, delicate, of "pedestrian" stylistic register, but witty and elegant; Juvenal, a "more vigorous and Masculine Wit," denounces vice rather than folly, thunders indignation in a higher rhetorical register, and offers, as we have seen, more pleasure. In a sententious and often quoted summation, Dryden adumbrates a view (we have seen before) that would influence the reception and treatment of Horace and Juvenal for the next century and beyond:

[Juvenal's] thoughts are sharper, his Indignation against Vice is more vehement; his Spirit has more of the Commonwealth Genius; he treats Tyranny, and all the Vices attending it, as they deserve, with the utmost rigour: And consequently, a Noble Soul is better pleas'd with a Zealous Vindicator of Roman Liberty; than with a Temporizing Poet, a well Manner'd Court Slave, and a Man who is often afraid of Laughing in the right place: Who is ever decent, because he is naturally servile.[25]

There are numerous and egregious misjudgments here, as Niall Rudd has perspicaciously discussed,[26] but in the history of reception misreading has not mattered: the politically engaged satirists of the early eighteenth century, even the conspicuously "Horatian" Pope, would find something of this spineless courtier in Horace, and in Juvenal something vigorous and principled. Johnson's Juvenal is the natural outcome.

Yet Dryden's view is not in the end so categorical – or obtuse. Reacting to Barten Holiday's claim that "A perpetual Grinn, like that of Horace, rather angers than amends a Man," Dryden, in defense, takes another line:

I cannot give him up the Manner of Horace in low Satire so easily: Let the Chastisements of Juvenal be never so necessary for his new kind of Satire; let him declaim as wittily and sharply as he pleases, yet still the nicest and most delicate touches of Satire consist in fine Raillery.[27]

Horace's "low satire," as Dryden describes it, teaches us the "vast difference betwixt the slovenly Butchering of a Man, and the fineness of a stroak that separates the Head from the Body, and leaves it standing in its place."[28] And that lesson too the eighteenth century would learn well.

Alexander Pope (1688–1744), Jonathan Swift (1667–1745), Richard Savage (1697–1743), Samuel Johnson (1709–84), Charles Churchill (1731–64), William Cowper (1731–1800), George Crabbe (1754–1832) together with others mark the eighteenth-century high point of English satire. Dryden had, as we have noted, laid down terms for ancient satire's reception and use, and consummate artists like Pope brought the genre to something like formal perfection. Yet politics remained an active arena for unprecedented satiric engagement, as John Sullivan describes it, contrasting the political quietism or more careful criticisms of the Romans:

The new Augustan satire, however, might call into question, or defend, the Divine Right of Kings, the relationship between government and religion, the regal monopoly of international affairs, or even one's own shifts in religious and political allegiances. The critical discussion of literature, conducted by the Roman satirist on an aesthetic level and almost in a political vacuum, for the new Augustans became a cover for political and personal animosities and friendships.[29]

A case in point is Alexander Pope. His politics, originally disinterested or vaguely Whiggish in Pope's early years as a writer when he associated with the likes of Addison, Steele, and Congreve, began to shift as he came to associate, roundabout 1712–14, with a group of Tory figures, Dr. John Arbuthnot, Jonathan Swift, John Gay and others. Upon the death of Queen Anne in 1714, Hanoverian succession (George I and II) brought a sense of alienation and disappointment to this group and to the Tories in general, especially from 1727 onward, under the strong and autocratic hand of George II's first minister, Robert Walpole. The literary controversialism of Pope's career can be traced largely to these political alignments of Whig and Tory, in the two-party system that had developed after the Restoration. Virtually nothing that Pope would write after 1714 would be immune from attack on grounds that frequently had little to do with the quality of his versemaking. And of course Pope gave as good as he got. In 1733 he composed a stinging denunciation of George II's court ("such a varnished race / of hollow gewgaws") in his *Fourth Satire of Dr. John Donne, Versified*, an attitude that wells up acidly in a number of later satires. It is no accident that much of the satire in the early to mid-eighteenth century comes from Tory hands, as they were the discontented party out of power. But even before Anne's death, Pope, Swift and others had formed the famous Scriblerus Club – weekly dinner gatherings of literary friends who eventually undertook a scheme to satirize what they saw as the absurdities of contemporary learning in a cooked-up burlesque called the *Memoirs of Martinus Scriblerus*. With this, Pope was on the main road to satire, and a large portion of his later work, particularly after 1726, would be written in satiric vein. Yet within the broad rubric of satire, Pope's wide-ranging accomplishment raises significant conceptual issues. For Pope's satire is not a singular strain, but ranged freely through a vast spectrum of tenors, manners, idioms, from the exquisite mock-epic machinery of his early *Rape of the Lock* (1712–14) through his essay on false profundity in modern poetry, *Peri Bathous* or *The Art of Sinking in Poetry* (1727), the screed against his enemies written after Dryden's *MacFlecknoe*, the three books of the (first) *Dunciad* of 1728, the several *Imitations of Horace* (1733–9), the satirically reflective *Epistle to Dr. Arbuthnot* (1735), to the dark *New Dunciad* of 1742.

Within this range, what satire *is* becomes rather complicated, which is part of the reason why so much has been written about Pope's work – far too much to go into here. It is fair to say at least that the complexity and protean quality of Pope's satire far exceeds the descriptors or eighteenth-century typologies of satire, Horatian or Juvenalian, often used to map it. Yet his *Imitations of Horace* function as an index of some dimensions of the issue. On one see, they illustrate how Pope came to see himself in his later years, that is, as a later Horace. It has frequently been pointed out that virtually nothing he wrote after 1726 or so was not in some sense dependent on Horace. But if you consider Jonson's similar adoption of a Horatian persona as his sense of personal/professional sense of writerly self, you see that things have changed. However Pope might style himself "Horatian," with his country estate Twickenham standing for Horace's Sabine farm, his circle of Tory friends to match Horace's, his preferred satirical/epistolary mode, the "fit" is clearly not right. His position in English society, his Catholicism, his Tory affiliations, the withering, personal attacks he suffered from his enemies (cruelly mocking his disease-curved spine and frail health), his ferocious ripostes, his transcendent wit – all anchor Pope to his time and place. Whereas, Jonson might have sought out the Horatian mask as a kind of affiliation and authority, Pope, who knew full well what Jonson had been up to, addresses the issue of possible satiric discourse within a conspicuous diachronic frame. So those *Imitations*, which set original and Pope's versions side by side, illustrate nothing so much as the differences between times, circumstances, poets. His *First Satire of the Second Book of Horace Imitated* (1733) functions, as did Horace's original, as a program poem:

> There are (I scarce can think it, but am told)
> There are to whom my satire seems too bold,
> Scarce to wise Peter complaisant enough,
> And something said of Chartres much too rough.
> The lines are weak, another's pleas'd to say,
> Lord Fanny spins a thousand such a Day.

The lines follow Horace's opening gambit – but unlike Horace name names. Peter Walter and Francis Chartres were known rogues, and Lord Fanny (from Horace's Fannius, *Sat.* 1.4 and 1.10) is the courtier Lord Hervey, later called Sporus, and worse, in the *Epistle to Dr. Arbuthnot*. The poem is riddled with such names. So too, while pretending Horatian discretion, the ostensible burden of *Sat.* 1.4, Pope laces the verse with sharp, uncompromising, unHoratian aggression. This satire will be a weapon (75–80):

> Peace is my dear delight – not Fleury's more:
> But touch me, and no Minister so sore.
> Who-e'er offends, at some unlucky time
> Slides into verse, and hitches in a rhyme,
> Sacred to ridicule! his whole life long,
> And the sad burthen of some merry song.

That merry song could grow ferocious, going after his old enemy Hervey (*Epistle to Dr. Arbuthnot* ["A." below], 305–322):

> Let Sporus tremble—A. What that thing of silk,
> Sporus, that mere white curd of ass's milk?
> Satire or sense, alas! can Sporus feel?
> Who breaks a butterfly upon a wheel?
> P. Yet let me flap this bug with gilded wings,
> This painted child of dirt, that stinks and stings;
> Whose buzz the witty and the fair annoys,
> Yet wit ne'er tastes, and beauty ne'er enjoys ...
> Whether in florid impotence he speaks,
> And, as the prompter breathes, the puppet squeaks;
> Or at the ear of Eve, familiar toad,
> Half froth, half venom, spits himself abroad
> In puns, or politics, or tales, or lies,
> Or spite, or smut, or rhymes, or blasphemies.

An unHoratian Horace, or Pope showing us how the mask no longer fits. Where it doesn't fit – in far more ways than the aggression noted here – is where the satire begins.

Pope's engagement with the politics of his day is paralleled by that of his friend Jonathan Swift, whose satire is surely political, but who more than any of his contemporaries, and any since, also transcends the limitation of its local bearings. Swift is primarily known for his prose satire (though he did write verse satires as well) and does not look explicitly to Roman models, so he is a little out of the tradition we are considering here. But his energetic satirical muse, seen in the religious satire *Tale of a Tub*, his literary mock-epic *The Battle of the Books* (both 1704), his amusing satire on astrology, *The Bickerstaff Papers* (1708), the political animus of *The Publick Spirit of the Whigs* (1714), the broad social critique of *Gulliver's Travels* (1726), and the more specific attack on English treatment of the Irish in *A Modest Proposal* (1729) demonstrate both the range of Swift's satiric application and a growing tendency to satirize devastatingly on a broad scale. *Gulliver's Travels*, while perennially popular as an amusing narrative, is no children's story. By turns comical, crude, tragic, and scathing, it constitutes a ferocious indictment of humanity: here, for instance, is his closing passage on the subject of colonialism (4.12):

> [T]hey see an harmless People, are entertained with Kindness, they give the Country a new Name, they take formal Possession of it for their King, they set up a rotten Plank or a Stone for a Memorial, they murder two or three Dozen of the Natives, bring away a couple more by Force for a Sample, return Home, and get their Pardon. Here commences a new Dominion acquired with a Title by *Divine Right*. Ships are sent with the first Opportunity, the Natives driven out or destroyed, their Princes tortured to discover their Gold; a free Licence given to all Acts of Inhumanity and Lust, the Earth reeking with the Blood of its Inhabitants: And this execrable Crew of Butchers employed in so pious an Expedition, is a *modern Colony* sent to convert and civilize an idolatrous and barbarous People.

Swift did not disguise his lack of faith in human kindness or rationality, which raised the charge of misanthropy even in his day; Swift denied it, claiming once in a letter to Pope, "Principally I hate and detest that animal called man; although I heartily love John, Peter, Thomas, and so forth." If one image of the satirist is of one who looks to the dark side of human potential, Swift is paradigmatic. He is in this in some sense reminiscent of Persius. And like Persius he expresses his distaste for the human animal in repugnant terms – as in the infamous *The Lady's Dressing Room*, where a young lover searching through his lady's boudoir makes unfortunate discoveries, not least in her chamberpot:

> Hard by a filthy basin stands,
> Fowl'd with the scouring of her hands;

> The scrapings of her teeth and gums,
> A nasty compound of all hues,
> For here she spits, and here she spews . . .
> So Strephon lifting up the lid,
> To view what in the chest was hid . . .
> And up exhales a greasy stench
> For which you curse the careless wench . . .
> Thus finishing his grand survey,
> Disgusted Strephon stole away
> Repeating in his amorous fits,
> Oh! Celia, Celia, Celia shits!

There are dashes of Horace and Juvenal too tossed into this misogynistic brew, and both the abhorrent, excremental imagery and Swift's presentation of women have prompted interesting discussion, and continue to do so. Which makes a point about Swift's satire; more than any of his eighteenth-century colleagues in the art, Swift's scathing pessimism, textured as it is with consummate wit, pushes this satire right under our noses. Tory and Whig controversialism, the politics of theological debate, of friendship and affiliation, of the Irish question(s), all matter deeply in reading Swift's work; but much of his satire has the power to engage and provoke modern readers immediately, almost viscerally. *A Modest Proposal*, Swift's withering attack on English policies with respect to Ireland in famine years, retains its power to shock – the radical imbalances of wealth and power that prompted it not having been much mitigated in the nearly 300 years since. Swift's speaker, a statistics-juggling social planner, proposes making Irish newborns a cash crop:

> I have already computed the charge of nursing a beggar's child . . . to be about two shillings per annum, rags included, and I believe no gentleman would repine to give ten shillings for the carcass of a good fat child, which as I have said will make four dishes of excellent nutritive meat, when he hath only some particular friend, or his family to dine with him. Thus the squire will learn to be a good landlord, and grow popular among tenants, the mother will have eight shillings net profit, and be fit for work until she produceth another child.
>
> Those who are more thrifty (as I must confess the times require) may flay the carcass; the skin of which, artificially dressed, will make admirable gloves for ladies and summer boots for fine gentlemen.

Satirical verse, prose, and theatre, as in John Gay's (1685–1732) "Beggars Opera," dominated the first half of the eighteenth century. Aside from those mentioned above, Daniel Defoe (1661–1731), Samuel Garth (1661–1719), Matthew Prior (1664–1721), Edward Young (1683–1765), Soame Jenyns (1704–87), Henry Fielding (1707–54), Edward Moore (1712–57), and Oliver Goldsmith (1730–44) all played parts in this extraordinary explosion of satiric genius. In time all that had to change; the advent of English Romanticism was the immediate cause (Wordsworth comes onto the scene in the 1790s), itself a symptom of a change in sensibility beginning much earlier. Although some (progressively less important) verse satire continued to be written even into the early nineteenth century, the genre's symbolic closing act appears just about at mid-eighteenth century in the free imitation of Juvenal's tenth satire by Samuel Johnson, *The Vanity of Human Wishes*. From its beginning the poem takes a serious, sententious, summary tone perhaps latent in Juvenal 10, but neither explicit in nor characteristic of the Latin poet (1–14):

> Let Observation with extensive View,
> Survey Mankind, from *China* to *Peru*;
> Remark each anxious Toil, each eager Strife,
> And watch the busy Scenes of crouded Life;
> Then say how Hope and Fear, Desire and Hate,
> O'er spread with Snares the clouded Maze of Fate,
> Where wav'ring Man, betray'd by vent'rous Pride,
> To tread the dreary Paths without a Guide;
> As treach'rous Phantoms in the Mist delude,
> Shuns fancied Ills, or chases airy Good.
> How rarely Reason guides the stubborn Choice,
> Rules the bold Hand, or prompts the suppliant Voice,
> How Nations sink, by darling Schemes oppres'd,
> When Vengeance listens to the Fool's Request.

By modernizing topical references (Wolsey, Villiers, Wentworth, Bacon, Galileo, and Sweden's Charles XII make exemplary appearances), recasting phrasing and arguments, and interpolating an overt Christian sensibility, Johnson creates a version remote from anything Juvenal could think or express (349–352):

> Enquirer, cease, Petitions yet remain,
> Which Heav'n may hear, nor deem Religion vain.

> Still raise for Good the supplicating Voice,
> But leave to Heav'n the Measure and the Choice.

This Christianizing "philosophical" take, however, fits neatly with Johnson's Tory-bred skepticism about human potential, and does in fact find correspondence in Juvenal. That temper, moreover, is characteristic of the century's major satirists. Educated, Tory conservatism, often critically cynical, runs right through eighteenth-century verse satire, even when, in the case of Pope, the verse sparkles with brilliant wit or, in the case of Swift, satire is written against the predations of government and power. That attitude is one feature that gave Romanticism such powerful counterpoint. Johnson's conservatism, in fact, makes this "translation" a powerful anti-Romantic treatise (before the day), cast in the mold of Juvenalian satire. For all the Christian self-assuredness and philosophical calm of the closing lines, the *Vanity of Human Wishes* is a profoundly pessimistic document, even adverting – with a pointed sententiousness worthy of Juvenal – to the sad end of the eighteenth century's paradigmatic satirist himself – and with that, his art:

> In life's last Scene what Prodigies surprise,
> Fears of the Brave, and Follies of the Wise?
> From Marlb'rough's Eyes the Streams of Dotage flow,
> And Swift expires a Driv'ler and a Show.

The End(less)

It is plainly impossible to mark a closure to the afterlife of Roman satire – though John Sullivan tries to distinguish one possible endpoint: "[t]he last resurgence of classically based satire is to be found in the writings of those associated with the Tory journal, *The Anti-Jacobin*: John Hookham Frere (1769–1846), George Canning (1770–1827), and William Gifford (1756–1826)," who composed harsh attacks on proponents of social, political, and intellectual changes prompted by the French revolution.[30] Literary targets included Coleridge, Rousseau, Southey, Hazlitt, Leigh Hunt and others. The Anti-Jacobin writers are in effect the logical and largely debased conclusion of the Tory satire of the early to mid-century, written-down to the level of party line predictability. While sometimes amusing and classically informed, they offer more to students of history rather than to lovers of literature. Yet satire as literature does carry on in one guise or other to the present. Byron's *Don Juan*, an epical satire written in ottava rima (so departing from the canonical rhymed couplet) targeting English social conditions beside much else, is only the most well-known of his forays into verse satire. From poetry, satire's muse soon migrates to the satirical prose of Thomas Love Peacock and then to the great novelists of the English nineteenth century, Dickens not least, to the satirical fiction of the twentieth century – Aldous Huxley, Evelyn Waugh, Norman Douglas, Kurt Vonnegut, Joseph Heller, Anthony Burgess, Salman Rushdie, Martin Amis, Richard Condon, Christopher Buckley, Dom DeLillo – even to the campus novels of Kingsley Amis, Malcolm Bradbury, Randall Jarrell, David Lodge, Bernard Malamud, and Richard Russo. Satire can be found in the occasional verse of a great many, if not most, major poets of the twentieth century, though for few is it a major occupation. That may change. But in the present moment, say from mid-twentieth century onward, satire's energy has been channeled into the mass media, where it flourishes and shows no signs of abatement: the standup satirical comedy of Lenny Bruce, George Carlin, Richard Pryor, John Stewart; the satirical-entertainment productions of Flanders and Swann ("The purpose of satire, it has been rightly said, is to strip off the veneer of comforting illusion and cosy half-truth – and our job, as I see it, is to put it back again"), Michael Moore, the *Onion*, *The Seattle Raptor*, *The Goon Show*, *Monty Python's Flying Circus*, *Brass Eye*, *Saturday Night Live*, *The Daily Show*, *The Simpsons*, *South Park*, *Doonesbury*, *Private Eye* – this list really is endless.

All of which is a fair distance from the aristocratic bravado and unabashed polemic of Lucilius. Or is it? Educated Romans talking down (and dirty), playing with serio-comic discourses, making mischief with "serious things," with Roman literature, politics, society, and philosophy, with pose, pretension, and authority, may seem curiously familiar. Whatever its politics, satire redraws perspective on the stuff of the world, channels resistance, reservation, second thought. It processes and reacts against the larger forces that drive events and the people pushed around or made foolish by them. A ready "anchor" of satire has always been this topicality, which means, paradoxically, that it can never stay put: the Rome of Lucilius is not the Rome of Horace, and so too with the others. Satire thus makes mischief with itself too, always upsetting its own applecart because its "aboutness" and its real and conceptualized world(s) never stay put. Rome becomes other things, other places – satire's muse hits the road.

Further Reading

On Menippean Satire

The best discussion is still J. Relihan's *Ancient Menippean Satire* (Baltimore, 1993); on Julian and Boethius, see Relihan in K. Freudenburg, ed., *The Cambridge Companion to Roman Satire* (Cambridge, 2005), 109–22. Broadening the range, and excellent, is P. Dronke, *Verse with Prose from Petronius to Dante: The Art and Scope of the Mixed Form* (Cambridge, MA, 2004). H. Weinbrot, *Menippean Satire: Antiquity, the Renaissance, Swift, Pope, and Richardson* (Baltimore, 2005) focuses on the later material, but contains a brief, informed discussion of the relevant classical texts. See also the survey by E. P. Kirk, *Menippean Satire: An Annotated Catalogue of Texts and Criticism* (New York, 1980). For Bakhtin, see B. Branham, *Bakhtin and the Classics* (Evanston, 2001).

On Seneca's *Apocolocyntosis*, E. O'Gorman's recent "Citation and Authority in Seneca's *Apocolocyntosis*," in Freudenburg (2005), 95–108 is useful. Also see E. W. Leach, "The Implied Reader and the Political Argument in Seneca's *Apocolocyntosis* and *De Clementia*," *Arethusa* 22 (1989): 197–230. P. T. Eden's text cum English translation (Cambridge, 1984) has excellent introductory material and notes.

On Petronius interesting criticism in English is considerably thicker on the ground. Two recent books are particularly good: C. Connors, *Petronius the Poet: Verse and Literary Traditions in the Satyricon* (Cambridge, 1998), G. B. Conte, *The Hidden Author: An Interpretation of Petronius' Satyricon* (Berkeley, 1996), and V. Rimell, *Petronius and the Anatomy of Fiction* (Cambridge, 2002). See also pieces on smaller scale by the same authors: Rimell, "The Satiric Maze: Petronius, Satire, and the Novel," in Freudenburg (2005), 160–73; Connors, "Rereading the Arbiter: *Arbitrium* and Verse in the *Satyrica* and in 'Petronius redivivus'," in H. Hofmann, ed., *Latin Fiction: The Latin Novel in Context* (London, 1999), 64–78. Also in Hofmann, see the chapters by G. Schmeling, "Petronius and the *Satyrica*," 23–37, J. Bodel, "The *Cena Trimalchionis*," 38–51, and G. Anderson, "The Novella in Petronius," 52–63 – all repay reading. As does S. Nimis, "The Prosaics of the Ancient Novel," *Arethusa* 27.3 (1994): 387–411. There is still plenty to learn from J. P. Sullivan, *The Satyricon of Petronius: A Literary Study* (London, 1968) and, on Persius, Lucan, and Seneca, as well as Petronius, *Literature and Politics in the Age of Nero* (Ithaca, 1985). Sullivan has translated (conveniently for us) both the *Apocolocyntosis* and the *Satyricon* in a single volume for the Penguin series (Harmondsworth,

1977). P. G. Walsh's more recent translation, also excellent, for the Oxford World's Classics series (Oxford, 1997), has very informative introduction and notes.

On the Classical Legacy in English Literature

For chapter-length distillations, J. P. Sullivan, "Satire," in R. Jenkyns, ed., *The Legacy of Rome: A New Appraisal* (Oxford, 1992), 215–42; R. Sowerby, *The Classical Legacy in Renaissance Poetry* (London, 1994), 308–74; and now C. Burrow, "Roman Satire in the Sixteenth Century," 243–60, D. Hooley, "Alluding to Satire: Rochester, Dryden, and Others," 261–83, C. Martindale, "The Horatian and the Juvenalesque in English Letters," 284–98, D. Kennedy, "The 'Presence' of Roman Satire: Modern Receptions and Their Interpretive Implications," 299–308, and J. Henderson, "A Volume Retrospective on Roman Satires," all in Freudenburg (2005). At greater length, A. Kernan, *The Cankered Muse* (New Haven, 1959) and R. Alden, *The Rise of Formal Satire in England under Classical Influence* (Philadelphia, 1899). Also, F. Bogel, *The Difference Satire Makes: Rhetoric and Reading from Jonson to Byron* (Ithaca, 2001); A. Kernan, *The Plot of Satire* (New Haven, 1965); C. Knight, *The Literature of Satire* (Cambridge, 2004); W. Kupersmith, *Roman Satirists in Seventeenth Century England* (Norman, 1985); D. Nokes, *Raillery and Rage: A Study of Eighteenth Century Satire* (Brighton, 1997); F. A. Nussbaum, *The Brink of All We Hate: English Satires on Women, 1660–1750* (Lexington, 1984); R. Paulson, *Satire and the Novel in Eighteenth-Century England* (New Haven, 1967) and *The Fictions of Satire* (Baltimore, 1967); C. Rawson, ed., *English Satire and the Satiric Tradition* (Oxford, 1984) and Rawson, *Order from Confusion Sprung: Studies in Eighteenth-Century Literature from Swift to Cowper* (London,1985); M. Seidel, *Satiric Inheritance: Rabelais to Sterne* (Princeton, 1979); H. D. Weinbrot, *The Formal Strain: Studies in Augustan Imitation and Satire* (Chicago, 1969), *Alexander Pope and the Traditions of Formal Verse Satire* (Princeton, 1982), and *Eighteenth-Century Satire: Essays on Text and Context from Dryden to Peter Pindar* (Cambridge, 1988). C. Keane has edited a special issue of *Classical and Modern Literature* 22.2 (2002) with interesting articles (most on particular modern authors) by Keane, H. Weinbrot, C. Schlegel, V. Vermeule, R. Rosen, and V. Baines.

Notes

Introduction

1 From the *Oxford Classical Dictionary*, 3rd edn. (Oxford, 1996).
2 A frequently cited article by C. J. Classen, "Satire – the Elusive Genre," *Symbolae Osloenses* 63 (1988): 95–121, makes the case that there is nowhere in antiquity or late antiquity a sufficient "theory" of satire and that its central characteristic, variety, prevented clear conceptualization of the literary form even while in practice it thrived as an exercise in social criticism and instruction.
3 See T. Habinek, "Satire as Aristocratic Play," in K. Freudenburg, *The Cambridge Companion to Roman Satire* (Cambridge, 2005), 177–91.
4 Some argue that the title is post-Ennian. In any case, the fact that they were called *Saturae* early on is significant.
5 See the special issue of *Arethusa* 31.3 (1998).
6 J. Henderson, per litteras, has made suggestions along these lines.
7 See E. Gowers, *The Loaded Table: Representations of Food in Roman Literature* (Oxford, 1993).
8 Per litteras.
9 See C. Keane, *Figuring Genre in Roman Satire* (Oxford, 2006).

Chapter 1   Beginnings (?)

1 A detailed consideration in English is C. A. Van Rooy, *Studies in Classical Satire and Related Literary Theory* (Leiden, 1965), 1–29. See also M. Coffey, *Roman Satire*, 2nd edn. (London, 1989), 11–23.

2   H. Keil, *Grammatici Latini*, vol. 1, 485, reproduced and translated in Van Rooy (1965), xii.

3   Van Rooy (1965), 1–20.

4   Porphyry (232/3–c.305 CE) mentions both Ennius and Pacuvius among the "certain others" who preceded Horace in the writing of satire at Horace *Sat.* 1.10.47, and he names Ennius with Lucilius and Varro as writers of *saturae* in his introduction to *Epistles* 1.3.

5   E. H. Warmington, *Remains of Old Latin* III.6–7 (Cambridge, MA, 1938/1967). Translation adapted from Warmington. As is often pointed out, Ennius also wrote *numquam poetor nisi si podager*, "I never poetize unless I'm down with gout," fr. 64.

6   F. Muecke, "Rome's First 'Satirists': Themes and Genre in Ennius and Lucilius," in K. Freudenburg, *The Cambridge Companion to Roman Satire* (Cambridge, 2005), 34, points out that the two Greek words that may be translated as "to satirize" are *iambizein* and *komoidein* – to "write iambic" and "write comedy."

7   Kirk Freudenburg, *per litteras*, suggests here a connection to Horace's *conviva satur* (1.1.119): ... [the happy man] "who parts this life like a satisfied guest." In the world of iambic poetry strong brew (the inebriated abuser) is the preferred metaphor. Horace uses that imagery (lots of times) to recalibrate the balance of his satiric enterprise towards tippling "just enough." And here it seems that Horace may in fact be making an Ennian gesture with his *conviva satur* (i.e. if Ennius' *convivat sine modo* is to be taken as somehow programmatic).

8   Van Rooy (1965), 42.

9   D. Mankin, ed., *Horace: Epodes* (Cambridge, 1995), 8.

10   Mankin (1995), 9.

11   See K. Freudenburg, *Satires of Rome: Threatening Poses from Lucilius to Juvenal* (Cambridge, 2001), 138–9, on Hipponax in Persius's prologue.

12   Frr. 1 and 14–19, Warmington (1938/1967); translations adapted from Warmington.

13   Van Rooy (1965), 40; Aulus Gellius, *Noctes Atticae* 12.4.4: *Annales*, fr. 210–227, Warmington (1938/1967). See also Muecke in Freudenburg (2005), 39 and her references there.

14   Muecke in Freudenburg (2005), 40. See Horace *Sat.* 1.3.63–6, 2.1.73–4, 2.6.40–46, and compare, as Muecke notes, perversions of the relationship in Juvenal 5 and 9.

15   Quite possibly in contradistinction to Ennius as "auctor" (1.10.66). There is debate about who is referred to as "auctor" in 1.10.66; possibly Ennius, possibly Lucilius. If the reference in Horace 1.10.66 is to Ennius, this is the only place that Ennius as satirist appears in the genre's major authors.

16 Books 22–25 are epitaphs and other short poems written in elegiacs.
17 Van Rooy's (1965) translation, xii.
18 All references to Warmington's (1938/1967) Loeb text; Warmington's translations of Lucilius or my adaptations of same.
19 See A. Barcheisi and A. Cucchiarelli, "Satire and the Poet: the Body as Self-Referential Symbol", in Freudenburg (2005), 207–23.

Chapter 2   Horace

1 G. Williams, "*Libertino Patre Natus*: True or False?" in S. J. Harrison, ed., *Homage to Horace: A Bimillenary Celebration* (Oxford, 1995), 296–313.
2 *Odes* 2.7.9–12 and Archilochus fr. 5.
3 J. E. G. Zetzel, "Horace's *Liber Sermonum*: The Structure of Ambiguity," *Arethusa* 13 (1980): 59–77 and E. Oliensis, *Horace and the Rhetoric of Authority* (Cambridge, 1998) valuably discuss in some detail this process of becoming an "Augustan" insider – and attendant issues.
4 See C. A. Van Rooy, "Arrangement and Structure of Satires in Horace *Sermones* Book I," *Acta Classica* 11 (1968): 37–72; 13 (1970): 7–27, 45–59; 14 (1971): 67–90; 15 (1972): 37–52.
5 See K. Freudenburg, *Satires of Rome* (Cambridge, 2001), 33–4 and J. Glazewski, "*Plenus Vitae Conviva*: A Lucretian Concept in Horace's Satires," *Classical Bulletin* 47 (1971): 85–8 on Horace's invocation of Lucretius 3.938–43 in these lines.
6 Freudenburg (2001), 32.
7 A. B. Chambers and W. Frost, eds., *The Works of John Dryden*, vol. 4 (Berkeley, 1974), 65.
8 M. Coffey, *Roman Satire*, 2nd edn. (London, 1989), 72.
9 On this, J. Henderson, *Writing Down Rome: Satire, Comedy, and Other Offences in Latin Poetry* (Oxford, 1999), 186–8.
10 The locus classicus for the "philosophical" satirist is W. S. Anderson, "The Roman Socrates: Horace and His Satires" in *Essays on Roman Satire* (Princeton, 1982), 13–49.
11 Commentators agree that the source must have been a collection of sayings; cf. Ps.Acro *ad* 1.2.31. Cato (censor) invokes Cato Uticensis, model of abrasive Stoic virtue.
12 J. Henderson, "Not 'Women in Roman Satire' but 'When Satire Writes "Woman",' " in S. Braund, ed., *Satire and Society in Ancient Rome* (Exeter, 1989), 104, a counter-version of the essay that appears in *Proceedings of the Cambridge Philological Society* 35 (1989): 50–80 and in Henderson (1999), 173–201.

13 A. Richlin, *The Garden of Priapus: Sexuality and Aggression in Roman Humor* (New York, 1992), 174–85.

14 This discussion of 1.2 is adapted from my "Rud(e)imentary Horace: Satires 1.2," *Electronic Antiquity* 5.2 (October 1999) [http://scholar. lib.vt.edu/ejournals/ElAnt/V5N2/hooley.html#15].

15 Among others see J. E. G. Zetzel's discussion, "Dreaming about Quirinus: Horace's *Satires* and the Development of Augustan Poetry," in T. Woodman and D. Feeney, eds., *Traditions and Contexts in the Poetry of Horace* (Cambridge, 2002), 39–45.

16 Several have discussed the allusion; see first E. W. Leach, "Horace's *pater optimus* and Terence's Demea: Autobiographical Fiction and Comedy in *Sermo* 1.4," *American Journal of Philology* 92 (1971), 616–32. C. Schlegel has written most recently on the point, "Horace and His Fathers: Satires 1.4 and 1.6," *American Journal of Philology* 121 (2000): 93–119 and most recently, *Satire And The Threat Of Speech: Horace's Satires, Book 1* (Madison, 2005).

17 This discussion of *Sat.* 1.4 is adapted from my "Generic Modeling in Horace Sat. 1.4," in C. Callaway, ed., *Ancient Journeys: Festschrift for Eugene Numa Lane* [http://zeno.stoa.org/cgi-bin/perscoll?collection=LaneFS].

18 The programmatic connection has been analyzed by A. Cucciarelli, *La Satiri e il poeta: Orazio tra Epodi e Sermones* (Pisa, 2001). The Lucilian poem is his Book 3.

19 R. Syme, *The Roman Revolution* (Oxford, 1939), 217.

20 As E. Gowers, "Horace, *Satires* 1.5: An Inconsequential Journey," *Proceedings of the Cambridge Philological Society* 39 (1993), 59–60 and Freudenburg (2001), 54, point out.

21 The Quaestorship, and with it membership in the Senate. See D. Armstrong, "*Horatius Eques et Scriba*: Satires 1.6 and 2.7," *Transactions of the American Philological Association* 116 (1986): 255–88, whose valuable analysis underpins much that follows in this section.

22 On all this see Armstrong (1986); on the father's status, see G. Williams in Harrison (1995), 296–313.

23 J. Henderson, *Fighting for Rome* (Cambridge, 1998), 95–6.

24 Martial 10.47 is a nice point of comparison; see too Tibullus 1.1 and Vergil *Georgics* 2.458ff. Horace offers variations on the theme in *Epodes* 2 and *Satires* 2.2.

25 Freudenburg's question, per litteras.

26 So Henderson (1998), 74; the best accounting of the poem to date.

27 See Cicero, *Philippics* 1.

28 *Epodes* 3, 5, and 17; *Satires* 1.8, 2.1, and 2.8.

29 Lucan's recreation of Canidia in his Erichtho in the context of civil war affirms what Horace is up to with his Canidia.

30 Horace was buried alongside Maecenas in these gardens.

31 Good on the point are Freudenburg (2001), 64–6, 70–1, and Henderson (1999), 202–27.

32 K. Freudenburg, *The Walking Muse: Horace on the Theory of Satire* (Princeton, 1993), 102.

33 I. M. Le M. DuQuesnay, "Horace and Maecenas: the Propaganda Value of *Sermones* I," in T. Woodman and D. West., eds., *Poetry and Politics in the Age of Augustus* (Cambridge, 1984), 27–31, and Freudenburg (2001), 66–71, go beyond the aesthetics.

34 DuQuesnay (1984), 27–31.

35 Freudenburg (2001), 68–71.

36 Correspondences first set out by F. Boll, "Die Anordnung im zweiten Buch von Horaz' Satiren," *Hermes* 48 (1913): 143–5.

37 N. Rudd, *The Satires of Horace* (Cambridge, 1966), 128.

38 D. Cloud, "Satirists and the Law," in Braund (1989), 67.

39 F. Muecke, ed., *Horace: Satires II* (Warminster, 1993); Muecke's translation.

40 Bruce Springsteen.

41 Gowers, *The Loaded Table* (1993), 109–126, is excellent on all this. See too Gowers' extended discussions of the food-focused 2.4 and 2.8, poems I do not substantially discuss here.

42 Muecke (1993), 9–11, offers a very good, concise summary of these matters – with attending bibliography.

43 Freudenburg (2001), 108–124, discusses "Book 2 and the hissings of compliance."

44 Freudenburg (2001), 27–31.

45 See Muecke (1993) ad loc.

46 See K. Freudenburg, "Canidia at the Feast of Nasidienus (Hor. *Sat.* 2.8)," *Transactions of the American Philological Association* 125 (1995): 207–19.

Chapter 3   Persius

1 The *Vita* mentions, aside from Cornutus himself, the poet Lucan, Seneca (whom he was said not to admire), Claudius Agathinus, Petronius Aristocrates, and Paetus Thrasea. Through Thrasea he can be assumed to have known many others of the opposition. Persius is said to have written a poem on Thrasea's mother-in-law Arria, heroine of the Claudian opposition. The largely Stoic "conspiracy of Piso" in 62 was detected; conspirators and suspected allies – some, like Lucan, ineffectually or very loosely connected – were eliminated.

2　Casaubon's 1605 edition itemized many points of contact. The list has been enlarged by others since. See D. Hooley, *The Knotted Thong: Structures of Mimesis in Persius* (Ann Arbor, 1997) for the most recent general treatment.

3　See Hooley (1997), 235 and n.

4　For detailed analyses see K. Reckford, "Reading the Sick Body: Decomposition and Morality in Persius' Third Satire," *Arethusa* 31.3 (1998): 337–54, and D. Hooley, "Persius in the Middle," in S. Kyriakidis and F. De Martino, eds., *Middles in Latin Poetry* (Bari, 2004).

5　W. S. Anderson, "Part versus Whole in Persius' Fifth Satire," in *Essays on Roman Satire* (Princeton, 1982), 162–3.

6　R. C. Elliott, *The Power of Satire: Magic, Ritual, Art* (Princeton, 1960), 129.

7　See J. R. Jenkinson, *Persius: The Satires* (Warminster, 1980), 69–70, for a concise summary of the textual controversy and interpretive options.

8　Some of this discussion is adapted from Hooley (1997), 225–9.

9　M. Griffin, *Nero, The End of a Dynasty* (New Haven, 1984), 162.

10　Does this perhaps offer some credence to Casaubon's long-discarded reading of line 49, "if you cautiously beat the *puteal* with many a whipping"? The *puteal* was a plinth surrounding a *bidental*, a spot made sacred by a lightning strike, like the one in the east corner of the Roman forum. The place was the site of much financial transaction, and most see here a reference to mad pursuit of profit. But Casaubon explains it with a passage from Tacitus that describes Nero's night-forays into Rome's streets, in disguise, along with a gang of thugs, beating and robbing passersby.

11　J. Henderson, "Learning Persius' Didactic Satire," in Henderson, *Writing Down Rome: Satire, Comedy, and Other Offences in Latin Poetry* (Oxford, 1999), 233.

Chapter 4　Juvenal

1　M. Coffey, *Roman Satire*, 2nd edn. (London, 1989), 119.

2　See R. Jenkyns, *Three Classical Poets: Sappho, Catullus, and Juvenal* (London, 1982) for a sensitive analysis of Vergilian presence in Juvenal.

3　S. Braund, *Juvenal: Satires Book I* (Cambridge, 1996), 236.

4　Crispinus appears at 1.26 as well, and though Juvenal promises to feature him often in his poems, he appears nowhere else.

5　Braund (1996), 306, where she makes several acute observations about the poem.

6　Braund (1996), 307.

7　Per litteras.

8 John Henderson, per litteras: "the reason the maxim is always cited out of context is that the lead-up to it cancels the sentiment out: 'if you really must wish for something after all I've written and you've now read, then reach for the perfect platitude, which *sounds* like the perfect placebo, all a wish can ever amount to – *in the end*.' "

9 E. Courtney, *A Commentary on the Satires of Juvenal* (London, 1980), 517.

10 Braund (1996), 39.

11 K. Freudenburg, *Satires of Rome* (Cambridge, 2001), 209–24, has full and challenging discussion of the poet's complex relationship to his Flavian past. The ghostly subtitling of this chapter derives from his "Ghost Assault in Juvenal 1," 234–42. S. Braund's commentary on Juvenal's first book (1996), 116–20, contains an illuminating comparative analysis of this and predecessors' treatments.

12 Courtney (1980), 80–2; quotation from 82.

Chapter 5   Menippeans and After

1 N. Frye, *Anatomy of Criticism: Four Essays* (Princeton, 1957); R. C. Elliott, *The Power of Satire* (Princeton, 1960).

2 See V. Rimell, "The Satiric Maze: Petronius, Satire, and the Novel," in K. Freudenburg, ed., *The Cambridge Companion to Roman Satire* (Cambridge, 2005), 160–76; also Henderson in the same volume, 316–17.

3 *Apoc.* 8.1.

4 P. T. Eden, *Seneca: Apocolocyntosis* (Cambridge, 1984), 115.

5 Eden (1984), 75.

6 *The Oxyrhynchus Papyri* vol. XLII no. 3010. For the fragments of the ancient novel see S. Stephens and J. Winkler, *Ancient Greek Novels* (Princeton, 1995).

7 See C. Connors, *Petronius the Poet: Verse and Literary Traditions in the Satyrica* (Cambridge, 1998), 1–19.

8 Review of J. Relihan's *Ancient Menippean Satire, Bryn Mawr Classical Review* 94.01.13. See S. Nimis' "The Prosaics of the Ancient Novel," *Arethusa* 27.3 (1994): 387–411.

9 J. Bodel, "The *Cena Trimalchionis*," in H. Hofmann, *Latin Fiction: The Latin Novel in Context* (London, 1999), 39.

10 See the nice summary in P. G. Walsh, tr., *Petronius: The Satyrica* (Oxford, 1997), xxx and references to §§ 28, 29, 34 in Martin S. Smith, *Petronius, Cena Trimalchionis* (Oxford, 1975).

11 Bodel (1999), 40.

12 See Walsh (1997), 171; Walsh's introduction to his translation too is helpful.

13 See on all these, and more, J. Relihan, *Ancient Menippean Satire* (Baltimore, 1993); also Relihan in Freudenburg (2005), 109–22.

14 See I. A. R. DeSmet, *Menippean Satire and the Republic of Letters, 1581–1655* (Geneva, 1996).

15 Frye (1957), 309.

16 *Problems in Dostoevsky's Poetics* (Minneapolis, 1984) and *Rabelais and His World* (Cambridge, MA, 1968).

17 Duncan Kennedy, for instance, cites Orwell, David Lodge, Flann O'Brien, John Barth, Thomas Pynchon and others as following within the categories established by Frye and/or Bakhtin: see "Modern Receptions and their Implications" in Freudenburg (2005), 299–308.

18 On Phaedrus and their satiric element, see now J. Henderson, *Telling Tales on Caesar: Roman Stories from Phaedrus* (Oxford, 2001) as well as his *Aesop's Human Zoo* (Chicago, 2004), 243–60.

19 See J. Ijsewijn, "Neo-Latin Satire: Sermo and Satyra Menippea," in R. R. Bolgar, ed., *Classical Influences on European Culture A.D. 1500–1700* (Cambridge, 1976); Ijsewijn's brief article lists a selection of some 40 neo-Latin writers of *sermo*.

20 Burrow in Freudenburg (2005), 243–60.

21 *English Bards and Scotch Reviewers*. Quoted by K. W. Gransden, *Tudor Verse Satire* (London, 1970), 24.

22 See D. Hooley, "Ben Jonson and Horatian Lyric," in L. Anderson and J. Lull, eds., *'A Certain Text': Close Readings and Textual Studies on Shakespeare and Others in Honor of Thomas Clayton* (Cranbury, NJ, 2002).

23 Though it should be noted that the production of satirical epigram remained strong throughout the period.

24 See D. Hooley, "Alluding to Satire: Rochester, Dryden, and Others," in Freudenburg (2005), 261–83.

25 A. B. Chambers and W. Frost, eds., *The Works of John Dryden*, vol. 4 (Berkeley, 1974), 65.

26 N. Rudd, *The Satires of Horace* (Cambridge, 1966), 273.

27 Chambers and Frost (1974), 70.

28 Chambers and Frost (1974), 71.

29 J. P. Sullivan, "Satire," in R. Jenkyns, ed., *The Legacy of Rome: A New Appraisal* (Oxford, 1992), 230.

30 Sullivan in Jenkyns (1992), 237.

Index